YVES CONGAR, O.P.

Diversity and Communion

TWENTY-THIRD PUBLICATIONS

Mystic, Connecticut

Translated by John Bowden from the French
Diversités et Communion.
Dossier historique et conclusion théologique,
published 1982 by Les Editions du Cerf, Paris.

© Editions du Cerf 1982

Translation © John Bowden 1984

North American Edition 1985
Twenty-Third Publications
P.O. Box 180, Mystic, CT 06355
(203) 536-2611

ISBN 0-89622-275-6
Library of Congress Catalog Card No. 85-51086

Cover design by George Herrick

First published in English in 1984
by SCM Press Ltd
26-30 Tottenham Road, London N1, England

To Cardinal Jan Willebrands and Fr Pierre Duprey,
in the service of unity,
in which the grace of the Holy Spirit
has worked so abundantly through them.

FOREWORD

When two eminent Jesuit theologians, Karl Rahner and Bernard Lonergan, died in 1984, many assumed that the age of the theological giants had finally been closed, at least for this century. Kark Barth, Rudolph Bultmann, Paul Tillich, Reinhold Neibuhr, Martin Buber — all are gone. It is sometimes remarked that those who remain — the Pannenbergs, the Moltmanns, the Schillebeeckxs, the Kungs — are not of the same stature. We shall not see such giants again in our lifetime.

The judgment may be substantially correct, but part of it is surely premature. The age of the giants may be in its final stage but at least one imposing figure remains. He is Yves Congar, OP.

By any reasonable standard of measurement, Father Congar is the most distinguished ecclesiologist of this century and probably since the close of the Council of Trent in the mid-16th century.

Diversity and Communion only strengthens his reputation as the Church's leading ecumenical theologian. Herein, he avoids no major issue or thorny problem. Whatever question he addresses, he does so with characteristic competence and balance. To read and ponder this book is to take a comprehensive course on ecumenism under the guidance of a master.

As of this writing, Yves Congar recently celebrated his 81st birthday. Bedridden, wracked by pain, completely debilitated by illness, Father Congar's pen is as immobile now as are his limbs. But for as long as the Lord delays calling him home, we shall have a precious, living link with one of the most creative eras in the entire history of the Church.

At Vatican II no theologian's influence was greater than Congar's. And, at the same time, no theologian had suffered more in giving birth to so vast a corpus of writings: first as a prisoner of war in the 1940s, then as the object of constant surveillance and vilification by reactionary forces in the Curia, and finally on the cross of inexorable illness.

Since he began teaching and writing in 1930 he has produced some 1,500 books and articles, among them: *Divided Christendom* (1937), a ground-breaking work in ecumenism; *The Mystery of the Church*

(1941); the magisterial article on "Theology" in the French-language *Dictionary of Catholic Theology* (1934); *True and False Reform in the Church* (1950), for which he was severely attacked by traditionalists; *Christ, Our Lady and the Church* (1952), which remains the major work on the subject; *The Mystery of the Temple* (1958); *Tradition and Traditions,* two volumes (1960, 1963) — all the way to his most recent, and undoubtedly his last major systematic effort, *I Believe in the Holy Spirit,* three volumes (1979, 1980). And now we also have the present volume, *Diversity and Communion.*

It is almost impossible to exagerate the impact that Father Yves Congar has had on the self-understanding of the Catholic Church, on the ecumenical movement, and on Catholic ecclesiology generally. He towers above all other figures.

In February 1954, he was forbidden to teach, and underwent an exile for several months in Jerusalem, Rome, and Cambridge before being given a fixed assignment at Strasbourg from 1956-58. Those dark years were a time of "active patience," as Congar has described it. He did not sulk. He did not withdraw. He did not give up.

But then the Council came. Vatican II was for Congar a time of spiritual and intellectual mobilization. At first, his role seemed modest, but he participated. Was it not "more true to be within and to work there than to criticize from without?" he asked. Little by little he became more involved in the preparation of important texts, especially the Dogmatic Constitution on the Church, as well as the documents on revelation, the Church in the modern world, ecumenism, religious liberty, missions, and priesthood.

Until his illness finally made all manner of scholarly work impossible, Father Congar had been laboring 12 to 13 hours a day.

In November 1984, he was given the Watson Prize for his valiant work in ecumenism. There was a celebration to mark the occasion at the Priory of St. James in Paris, where he has resided these past several years. His mood was characteristically honest and humble. He quoted Father Lacordaire: "What will remain in 200 years of what we have written? What is important is to have a life." He continued, "I think that my life is rather mediocre, but, too, it is not finished. I still have, at least in suffering, to unite myself to the chalice of Jesus (which is the unique chalice). ...For the rest, I really don't know."

He has come to understand that "whatever we have to ... say, as sublime as it is, it is really not worth much unless it is accompained by a praxis, by real action, by concrete service and love."

One hears much these days about how important it is for theologians to be saints and not just scholars. Yves Congar, OP, is both.

Richard P. McBrien
University of Notre Dame

CONTENTS

Part Three Looking towards the Reformation

Part Four Towards a Conclusion

Introduction

I announced my seminar course for the second semester at the Ecumenical Institute in Paris (February-June 1980) in the following terms:

> The theological basis of the contemporary problem of ecumenicity seems to be: can one find a foundation for a 'pluralist unity' or a 'reconciled diversity', which might be the form in which communion is re-established, in the idea of 'fundamental articles'? We shall have to trace the theme of fundamental articles through history, elucidate the values associated with them, assess them critically, and evaluate the prospects in the present situation (which includes facts like exegetical study and the conditions of proclaiming Jesus Christ in the present-day world).

That is the intention which led me to discuss this difficult theme historically on as large a scale as possible. At present the ecumenical situation seems to be at an impasse. We have achieved an understanding to the degree that today we do a great many things together. Doctrinal disputes have been largely removed, but some still remain.

I believe that the questions of the procession of the Holy Spirit and the eucharistic epiclesis will not be an obstacle between Orthodox and Catholics if we recognize the legitimate existence of two theological and even dogmatic traditions in the profession of the same faith. But that raises the question of diversity and communion which is discussed here. And, given that that is accepted and sorted out, we come up against the question of the papacy, the most obvious point of difference between the two ecclesiologies. Much remains to be done there. But sooner or later we will also come to recognize a difference in church government between the Christian East and a Latin church which corresponds to a Roman patriarchate extended throughout the world. Once again we come back to the problem of diversity and communion.

In connection with Protestantism, Roger Mehl could write:'At present, the differences between Catholicism and Protestantism, which in the sixteenth century related to the whole of the Christian message, concern only a single chapter of doctrine, ecclesiology.'[1] But what a chapter! Besides, one can ask whether the original differences, now thought to be outmoded, are not still reflected there. This is where we find the most difficult issues: the sacrament of order, the 'priesthood', apostolicity, and again the papacy! These are monumental questions. However, the questioning goes still further. In 1978 the French bishops, meeting at Lourdes, asked the observers from the other churches to say what they thought of the Catholic church today. Here is one of the Protestant responses: 'Since Vatican II, your church has put into practice everything possible in the perspective of unity which she has allowed herself. It seems that at present she cannot go any further. Might that not be a sign that your conception of unity is not broad enough, and that in particular it cannot recognize differences?'

The points of divergence have been discussed for centuries. To tell the truth, this has been done too often in a polemical climate of rivalry, defensiveness, mistrust and rejection of anything 'different'... Neither side has succeeded in convincing the other. Should they not accept that each is different? Perhaps, but to what extent and under what conditions? Again our problem arises.

Paradoxically, though one can see why, ecumenism has tended rather to revive and reinforce what could be called the confessional conscience of the various groups. That was inevitable, given that at meetings one side explained its position to the other. In one way that is a good thing. It is not the case that ecumenism is an easy way out, the approach of latitudinarianism and syncretism and ease.[2] 'The ecumenical movement has not been created by the half-hearted; one of its basic principles is in fact to note and express disagreements as clearly as agreements.'[3] On this basis each side has been given an account from the other. But have they really *listened*? The dialogue should have led to some changes. But have the churches changed anything after decades of dialogue? Has mine, which I love, perhaps done more than the others? If that is the case, it is because having dogmatized, fixed, condemned, hardened more than the others, it had further to go. In any case, where are we? Between us we have become aware of a good deal that is common to all Christians. From now on we can do a great many things together; we can become involved in exchanges. But each church keeps to itself, builds its own house. It visits the others on friendly terms, perhaps spends a week-end with them. We are in a situation of peaceful coexistence. However, ecumenism is ambitious to go further! But where, and how?

Dialogue and the exchanges which it involves have made us realize the relativity of more than one position, of an institution, of a form in which our Christianity is put into practice. For me, that has also followed from my knowledge of history. It particularly relates to those forms of the church which have proved to present obstacles after the route has been cleared of other difficulties which were in the way. Consequently, at a time when the future of unity could appear obstructed and ecumenism blocked, we have been made aware that obstructions and blockages do not perhaps have the absolute character which would make our differences irreconcilable. Everywhere to some degree the idea has been emerging of a unity which allows for quite widespread diversity.

Here we are only following a tradition to which, as we shall see in detail, history bears witness from the start.[4] However, we are reviving that tradition in new conditions, those of a Christianity gravely disunited and seeking reunion. This is so clearly indicated by the very nature and aims of the Ecumenical Movement, before and after the formation of the World Council of Churches, that there is no point in citing references. At Lausanne in 1927, Archbishop Nathan Söderblom spoke of 'unity in multiplicity'. From the Roman Catholic side, approaches on the same theme have been multiplied in recent years.[5] In a lecture given at Lambeth Palace on 4 October 1972, and at Cambridge, Cardinal Jan Willebrands suggested a very interesting view of *types of church*.[6] Others have described different models of unity, possible or already realized.[7] Whereas within the World Council the Faith and Order Commission has been pursuing the ideal of organic unity, the confessional families have sought to preserve their own confessional traditions in unity.

At Nairobi in December 1975, the World Council adopted the theme of 'conciliar community', which presupposes that the churches have realized unity of faith and eucharistic communion at a local level. Is not this to suppose that the problem has been resolved? However, it does avoid a kind of universal church – what the Germans call *Einheitskirche* as opposed to *Kircheneinheit*. If some put the emphasis on unity realized at the local level – as, for example, the Patriarchate of Moscow[8] – others put it on respect for diversity. Take, for example, the proposals by Pastor Roger Mehl:

> Conciliar unity presents itself as the unity of a diversity. It is not a monolithic unity, as the unity of ideological movements or the unity produced by an organizational centralization might be. Conciliar unity embraces and welcomes the diversity of traditions and liturgies, the diversity of ecclesiologies (as in the primitive church), the cultural diversity of forms of confessions of faith, the diversity of forms of ministry, the diversity of catechetical methods, and finally the diversity of the socio-historical forms of church government... Each church keeps its personality, its freedom in the order of organization and government, its liturgical and cultural traditions. The notion of conciliarity obliges us to give up one of the demands often formulated by certain churches, namely that one can only talk of unity when there is total agreement on all possible articles of faith and constitution.[9]

The interpretaton of a Catholic layman whose historical competence no one questions, Jean Delumeau, corresponds to this Protestant interpretation of the 'conciliar community':

> The future of Christianity goes by way of at least a partial success in ecumenism... However, the principal obstacles to the success of ecumenism seem from now on to be less doctrinal than administrative, since the structures have been ossified over the course of too long a divorce. It would seem a matter of urgency to 'decolonize the local churches'. This can only come about through the acceptance of a broad pluralism in the profession of the same fundamental creed.
>
> This lightening of structures and revitalization of the grass roots would ease the passage towards the 'conciliar unity' proposed by the World Council of Churches Assembly at Nairobi in 1975. In this new type of scheme which seeks unity in diversity, each church keeps its personality, its organization, its liturgies, but recognizes the catholicity and the ministries of the other Christian confessions and joins with them in conciliar meetings. Such a programme gives up the demand which is often made that we should speak of unity only when there is total agreement on the articles of faith and church organization.[10]

Obviously we shall have to make a critical evaluation of proposals in which realities that from both a Catholic and Orthodox perspective belong to the sacramental order are regarded as simple sociological facts. But that once again raises the problem: what diversity is possible (and desirable!) in unity?

The sixth plenary assembly of the World Lutheran Federation held in Dar-es-Salaam, Tanzania, in June 1977, favoured the expression 'reconciled diversity' put forward in 1974 by the Conference of Secretaries of World Confessional Alliances. Harding Meyer has explained it in the following way:[11]

> The defence of change and renewal implied in the concept of reconciled diversity relates rather to a process which one could describe as a redefinition of confessions by dialogue. This redefinition would have a twofold aspect. It would be a matter of eliminating the elements which have disfigured, narrowed and exaggerated the confessional traditions and which, superimposing themselves on the legitimate and authentic form of these traditions, have transformed the diversity of confessions into differences separating the churches. It is precisely by this process of change and renewal that the confessions must rediscover their authentic features in dialogue and can mutually recognize and affirm themselves as legitimate expressions of faith, witness and Christian life. That is the way in which reconciliation of differences will come about.

Is not this purification of confessional positions by reciprocal questioning and confrontation with them what is already happening in our encounters? Does it not come about on the basis of the 'agreements' to which they lead, whether through joint commissions or groups like the Dombes Group?

I am well aware of the seriousness of the questions which I am raising and of the conclusions which I shall try to formulate. But the questions are not mine: they are there on all sides, and have been for years. I am as aware as the next man of the principles one should hold. I recognize myself in these words of the French Episcopal Committee for Unity: 'Our destination will be a truth apprehended more fully in a form which is not *adequately* known to us at present but which, we believe, will be found to follow the basic line of the Catholic tradition understood in the most comprehensive sense of this term (and including the riches of Eastern Orthodoxy).'[12] However, we must take account, with humility, objectivity and realism, of the present state of thinking and of the approaches which have been attempted. On the whole, younger people feel that the problems that I still take seriously are already outmoded. This is an attitude which calls for both sympathetic and critical appreciation.

However, at a time when the disaffection of young people with the church of Christ is a matter of concern, we must be sure to be very attentive to their ways of feeling and seeing. If, in the words of Paul Valéry, 'youth prophesies by its very existence, being that which will be', we must not let a fear of the new put a bandage on our eyes. Let us open our eyes, strong in the faith, love and hope that the Spirit of God gives us. And let us begin a serious study, loyal and open to the past, the present and the future. This obligation justifies in advance any weightiness in the inquiry on which we are embarking.

This is in fact a documentary inquiry. You will not find here a developed theology of communion. I have sketched out aspects of that elsewhere, and perhaps at some time I shall offer a positive outline. Sufficient for the day...

PART ONE

Diversity in Time and Space

1

Diversity and Unity according to the New Testament

This question can be approached from different angles. Ernst Käsemann has kept raising it in a quite radical fashion from 1951 onwards, in 'The Canon of the New Testament and the Unity of the Church', ET in *Essays on New Testament Themes*, London 1964, 95-107, but above all in an account given at the Fourth Faith and Order Conference in Montreal on 6 July 1963, ET 'Unity and Multiplicity in the New Testament Doctrine of the Church', in *New Testament Questions of Today*, London 1969, 252-9, which I quote here.

Jesus, says Käsemann, did not found a church in our sense of the word, embracing both Jews and Gentiles. He simply announced a messianic renewal of the twelve tribes, with the addition of the proselytes. The first break came when pagans were admitted without being circumcised and without even having been proselytes. That made a new people of God. Different christologies correspond to these different views. In Corinth there was a community of enthusiasts. St Paul fought simultaneously against both the possible anarchy of the Corinthians and the legalism of the Judaizers. However, after St Paul came the Pastoral Epistles, where we find an early Catholicism with ordained ministers and a transmission of true doctrine as a 'deposit'; this is in contrast to St Paul, for whom common priesthood was a basis only for Christian service in the community and in the world. Acts, centred as it is on the church, is another instance of early Catholicism. After that we have the Fourth Gospel; it is full of Jesus, of his word and of his presence, but it does not have a theology of the ministry; it does not really have an ecclesiology; and it has only an implicit theology of the sacraments.

We cannot sacrifice these differences to a formal unity. There were evident tensions between Judaizers and Hellenists, between Paul and the enthusiasts of Corinth. The distance between John and 'early Catholicism' is no less than that which exists between Christian confessions today. They did not exclude the confession of the unity of the church. But that, says Käsemann, consisted in the sole Lordship of Christ and his kingdom. There is nothing but that in Ephesians 2. It exists through our eschatological orientation. It is perceived only in the faith which hears the call of the Shepherd to form a flock, the unity of which is beyond and in advance of our churches and our theologies.

'Faith and Order' envisages the organic and visible unity of the church here in the world. At Montreal, there was opposition to Käsemann's account; it was felt to be a contradiction. One phrase in particular was singled out: 'The New Testament canon as such is not the basis of the unity of the church. Rather, as such it is the basis of the multiplicity of confessions.'

The fact that the unity of the church in the time of the apostles was essentially oriented on the Lord Jesus is significant and of interest to us in our situation of disunity. It provides the basis for a real church community underlying our divisions. However, can we, without further ado, transfer the situation of the first Christians to that of a Christianity which has had to define its faith and organize structures of ministry and worship, following a process which begins after the end of the apostolic period (in the Pastoral Epistles)? Early Catholicism belongs to the apostolic age and the period of definitive inspiration. Many of the differences which Käsemann mentions have contexts in different historical periods. Each of the different writings of the New Testament corresponds to an intention on the part of the author. However, the fact remains that they all form part of the canon.

J.D.G.Dunn (*Unity and Diversity in the New Testament*, London 1977) also argues for a diversity in the New Testament on the basis of an integral understanding of the canon. This diversity should be taken into consideration in ecumenical matters. Unity is focussed on Jesus Christ and the identity between the historical Jesus and the glorified Lord. It determines the limits beyond which Christianity ceases to be Christianity. Those limits were reached with the Ebionites and with Gnosticism. (I know only the title of the book by J.Charlot, *New Testament Disunity. Its Significance for Christianity Today*, Leiden 1970.)

The greatest difference to be found at one specific time was that between Paul and the Judaizers or the 'people around James'. Galatians 2.1-10 indicates how the problem was solved. People met and explained themselves. On the one hand there was agreement over the content of preaching (v.6) and a recognition of the two zones in which Peter and Paul operated, both being settled by an appeal to the Lord; on the other hand, an effective bond of love was established with the apostolic centre in Jerusalem. So people were not content with a pure diversity. It is a pity that Käsemann does not make any reference to this significant episode.[1]

Obviously there is a unity in Christianity and in the New Testament. One could even say that there is a unity *of* Christianity. Everyone accepts this, and Käsemann is the first to admit it. For him, what is central and common throughout the New Testament is the reciprocity between a christology defined in terms of the justification of the sinner and justification defined in terms of christology.[2] We can recognize the Lutheran reading centred on the *pro me* of the satisfaction of Christ. This principle represents a kind of 'canon within the canon'. A 'Catholic' reading would see the unity of the witness of the faith more in the *reality* of the covenant of grace which makes Christians sons in the Son; the first verses of I John are an expression of it. For the ancient church (the Muratorian Canon and St Irenaeus), there was in fact a 'canon within the canon': the Johannine writings, the Gospel and I John.[3] This same ancient church, which knew and respected the plurality of witnesses – the 'tetramorphic' gospel of Irenaeus and Origen – saw in the unity of revelation and the church a demand and a reflection of the unity of God himself and of the Christ who has made him known to us. Unity is Christ. St Paul excludes from the church whatever would be incompatible with the truth of Christ, such as the denial of the resurrection (I Cor.15.12f.), a Gnosticism allowing of a metaphysical dualism and more or less divine intermediaries (I Tim.6.20; John), justification by works, or christological docetism: all that destroys the church![4]

The substance and truth of the unity of the church is made up in and by Jesus Christ. All the images by which the New Testament expresses it convey this. The New Testament speaks of the church as a building, a vine, a flock, a bride, a body, always in relationship to Jesus Christ. But the Christ is only the cornerstone of a single construction; he is only the stem of a single vine, the shepherd of a single flock, the husband of a single wife, the head of a single body which is organically one.[5] Of course there were different tendencies

and tensions in this church. There still are. They are possible
provided that together they serve to build up the church and do not
lead to the formation of *parties*, characterized by non-communica-
tion.[6] The church comprehended these tensions, to the exclusion of
anything that would have betrayed the truth of the Christian
mystery. It did not form itself in sectarian fashion into a single
school. That makes it illegitimate for us today to translate this New
Testament diversity into a plurality of totally separate or opposed
churches. On the contrary, the unity of living reference to Christ
forms the basis for the existence of a Christian communion between
the churches, encompassing them all, by virtue of which ecumenism
is possible and even necessary.

Jean Colson has discerned another diversity which is not uncon-
nected with those which Käsemann has denounced.[7] He sees a
difference between a Pauline line and a Johannine line, a difference
which recurs among the so-called Apostolic Fathers and continues
down to the middle of the second century. St Paul sees the church as
the body of Christ, a people dispersed in communities throughout
the world, of which Christ is the head. 'The Pauline tradition had a
perspective of universal redemption. Since one man had died for
all, it was necessary that the world should become aware of its unity
in the Christ, the sole head of ransomed humanity, and that all local
particularity should cease.' Hence on the one hand there were
'acephalous' communities with a college of presbyters, whose ultimate unity was assured by Paul in person; bearing 'the care of all the
churches', he exhorted and reprimanded, suffering so to speak the
pangs of childbirth until the Christ was formed among the faithful.
Hence, too, the essentially Pauline concern for liaison between all
the churches and, to ensure this in practice and to avoid closed
societies, the itinerant ministry of apostolic delegates (for these cf.
p.59).

   This Pauline line recurs in Clement of Rome and Hermas. Here,
at least, we also find the acephalous government of communities,
with their college of presbyters (Colson gives the references). 'This
college puts the stress on the community, represented as a body.
While its organs are indeed different, and hierarchical, they are a
function of this body with a view to its growth towards the complete
realization of the perfection of Christ.'

   Clement and Hermas are Romans. Colson goes so far as to write:
'We can understand how, when the apostle disappeared, it was the
Western churches which became most rapidly aware of the primacy

of the apostolic church of Rome, where Peter and Paul died; this
was the unifying factor and the control of unity'(123). Obviously
that raises a number of questions.

Colson takes up 'the Johannine tradition' in the letters to the
churches of the Apocalypse. In the earthly sphere these churches
are personified in their angel, who is their bishop. 'The community
is entirely summed up in him. He is the image of its living unity.
Underlying this there is an incarnational "mysticism" of the kind
dear to all the Johannine literature'(86). 'The Word of life has been
made flesh and men have been able to see him, hear him, touch
him... it is to this mystery of the incarnation that men must hold if
they are to be united among themselves and to the Father and his
Son Jesus Christ. And that is why in every city, the meeting together
in unity of the dispersed children of God is crystallized around a
responsible figure as around an image of this living unity...'(124).

The sequel to the Johannine tradition and its sovereign expression
is to be found in the letters of St Ignatius of Antioch.

Colson sees a fusion of the two lines especially in St Irenaeus. If
his analyses are correct, one could go so far as apply the two
traditions respectively to the East, with its ecclesiology of local and
episcopal churches, and to the West, with its sense of universal
mission and expansion. We could do so without making them in our
imagination into a church of John, a church of Peter, or a church of
Paul.[8]

I would add one further comment, on Christianity at the time of the
martyrs. We can note diversity among them, and even erroneous
formulas in their writings. For example, St Justin identifies the
Logos and the Spirit; Hermas is no more satisfactory. In the first and
second centuries people were less disturbed by statements which we
would find completely inadequate.[9] Of course there was a long
period of experimentation before precise concepts and terms were
found, particularly in trinitarian theology. However, it should be
noted that: 1. The first 'canon', the first rule, was the living church.
The church formulated its rule of faith and life before the end of the
second century, but first of all it had already lived it out.[10] 2. As
Möhler had already noted, and as Père Bouyer noted in his turn,
people like Justin and Origen unhesitatingly gave their life for a
christological or trinitarian faith which they could not formulate
adequately.[11] The faith of the church, its unity, was in the *life* of its
faithful. Progressively, what was felt to be contrary to this life was

rejected as heresy, and formulae of faith were imposed as rules for unity.

It is in the 'tradition' of the church, in the transmission of this life with all its diverse expressions, that diversities which might have proved discordant were harmonized. The danger then is of a certain levelling out, as it were the emasculation of differences which are also riches, riches by which the church lives. In his assessment of Käsemann's account Ebeling showed his understanding of this role of the tradition, but he saw tradition as being too dependent on an infallible *magisterium*.[12] What I have in mind is the society under grace which we find in the church of the Fathers and the first Councils, at the time when the liturgies were fixed. People sometimes talk about this period as the time of the undivided church, but that is a dubious notion: I shall devote a section to it later.

2

Diversity and Communion in the Early Church

(i) The question of Easter and the communion of the churches

This is a well-worn subject, but we need to return to it once again because its relevance to the monumental question with which we are concerned is so great. We shall consider it first at the two specific moments in history when it was raised, and then as an issue of lasting significance.[1]

1. For the second century, our essential information comes from Eusebius, HE V, 23-25. The issue emerged about 167 at Laodicea in Phrygia. The churches of Asia celebrated Easter, ending the fast which preceded the day when the Jews sacrificed the paschal lamb, on the fourteenth day of the month, 14 Nisan, hence the name 'Quartodecimans'. 14 Nisan could fall on any day of the week, even a Wednesday or a Thursday. It is not, as some scholars have thought, that they were celebrating the death of Christ and not his resurrection: they were celebrating the two inseparably.[2] A number of local councils, the first councils for which we have historical evidence, met to consider the question and decided that Easter should be celebrated on the Sunday. A large number of bishops wrote to the same effect. About 190 or 191, Victor, Bishop of Rome, threatened to excommunicate the Quartodeciman Christians of Asia for being heterodox, despite the defence of their custom made by Polycrates, who argued for its apostolic origin. It was then that a number of bishops intervened with Victor to restrain him from proceeding with excommunication. Eusebius summarizes and to a large extent even quotes the letter which St Irenaeus wrote to him. It is of enormous interest to us. It contains the phrase, 'The difference in the fast

confirms the agreement in faith', a theme which we shall find abundantly orchestrated all through history. Irenaeus points out to Victor that his predecessors respected the diversity of customs: under Anicetus (154-165 according to Funk), Polycarp had come to Rome, and the pope, as a sign of communion, had allowed him to preside at the eucharist. The peace was kept along with the difference in practices. However, Irenaeus stresses above all what Polycarp had already pointed out to Victor, namely the apostolic origin of the Quartodeciman practice. Irenaeus does not say in so many words that the Roman custom, which was also that of Gaul,[3] was itself apostolic, but what he says elsewhere about this church is sufficient indication of its apostolicity. However, in 255 Firmilian of Caesarea rejected the claim to apostolicity of the Roman paschal custom and defended the right to differ without any detriment to unity.[4]

Although it was not a matter involving belief, a difference in the celebration of the most important Christian festival marred the expression of unity. The first council summoned by the Emperor Constantine, at Arles in 314, to resolve the Donatist question, was disturbed about it (*primo loco de observatione paschae dominici, ut uno die et uno tempore per omnem orbem a nobis observetur*) and charged Pope Sylvester to communicate the date of the celebration by letter to all the churches.[5] Unity called for uniformity. Rome, the centre of the empire and of Catholicity, was designated to ensure this uniformity of observance.

Rome took the charge very much to heart and saw it as an expression of concern for the unity of the church; we can note this in the letter from Innocent I to Aurelius of Carthage exactly a century after the Council of Arles,[6] and then, fifty years later, in the numerous pressing letters from St Leo.[7] According to St Cyril of Alexandria (died 444), the technical information about the phases of the moon was given to Rome by the church of Egypt, which was an authority in this kind of knowledge.

Constantine was concerned to establish a unity which was at the same time both that of the church and that of the empire. Furthermore, before raising the question yet again in connection with those who still followed Jewish calculations, the council summoned by the emperor at Nicaea in 325 returned to the matter. The synodal letter to the Egyptians announces that the Quartodecimans have come round to the Roman and Egyptian custom.[8] It was on the occasion of this decree of Nicaea that Athanasius explained the difference that he saw between the church's simple affirmation of its faith (*sic credit Ecclesia*) and the promulgation of a disciplinary decree (*decretum est*).[9]

2. Three English bishops participated in the Council of Arles in 314, so they took back to England the Roman method of calculating Easter. However, Rome changed the system and Augustine, sent by St Gregory, followed the new way. Under St Leo, Rome had adopted the new *cursus paschalis* of Victor of Aquitaine, favouring the cycle accepted at Alexandria, and Dionysius Exiguus drew up a list of dates for Easter from 532 to 626 on the basis of the Alexandrine rules. The cycle accepted by Columbanus and the Celts did not agree, and the Irish and the Bretons followed their own usage.[10] Augustine had tried, vainly, to bring them round to the Roman observance of Easter, baptism and confirmation (at his meeting with the Bretons in 602 or 603). Although St Columbanus was summoned from Luxeuil to explain himself to a council at Chalon-sur-Sâone, he would not give way over his calculation of Easter.[11] As he wrote to the Pope, he wanted to observe the paschal rite which he had received from his ancestors. In 629, Pope Honorius required the Irish to fall in with the Roman calculations. Only the south of the island obeyed. It was not until the Synod of Whitby (Streaneshalch), in 664, that a decision was made, and even that did not put an end to Irish particularism. Wilfrid, a lawyer from Rome, had a confrontation with the abbot-bishop St Colman, a Celtic monk from Iona, in the presence of King Oswin.[12] Was it not necessary to put the universal church before the corner of a distant island and the apostle Peter before Columbanus? asked Wilfrid. Had not Christ promised to Peter the keys of the kingdom of heaven? 'Is that true?', the king asked Colman. 'Yes,' he replied. 'Then in that case,' the king concluded, 'he is the gatekeeper and I cannot go against him. As far as I am able, I will obey his rules for fear that on arrival at the gates of the kingdom of heaven I should be helpless before the one who holds the keys and he turns his back on me!'

So it was to conform to Rome and to fall in with the universal church that the decision was taken to abandon the peculiarly Celtic observance. However, Iona and a number of other monasteries prolonged their resistance. The matter seemed so serious that Irish ordinations were put in question. Wilfrid, nominated Archbishop of York, went to Compiègne in Gaul to be consecrated, because he regarded the Bretons and the Scots as 'Quartodecimans' and schismatics.[13] Theodore of Tarsus, sent by the Pope as Archbishop of Canterbury, had Chad reordained when he was transferred from

Northumbria to be Bishop of Lichfield. Theodore's *Penitential* includes a number of very strict canons against those who, in contempt of the Council of Nicaea, celebrated Easter according to Jewish dating. A little later, Wynfrith, who subsequently was known as Boniface, had to combat Irish monks in Bavaria, who had introduced the usage of their country there; he regarded them as 'false priests', heretics and schismatics. The calculation of Easter was not the only matter involved, but it was part of the discipline that had to be observed in the cause of Catholic unity. Unanimity in the celebration of the feast of feasts is a major sign of unity.

3. The question is still very much alive today. It is now bound up with the desire expressed by the civil authorities of many countries to see a fixed date for Easter; numerous studies have been made of the question and there is more than one plan.[14] Pius X would have happily fixed Easter on the second Sunday in April. The fact that 'the heterodox' would not allow it, since it was not a primitive tradition of the church, did not seem to disturb him. By contrast, on 4 December 1963, Vatican II published a declaration to the effect that it was 'not opposed to the feast of Easter being fixed on a particular Sunday in the Gregorian calendar, with the assent of those for whom this question was of importance, *above all "brethren separated from communion with the apostolic see"'*. Better, in the decree *Orientalium Ecclesiarum* of 21 November 1964, no.20, the Council pronounced:

> Until all Christians agree, as is hoped, on one day for the celebration of Easter by all, in the meantime as a means of fostering unity among Christians who live in the same area or country, it is left to the patriarchs or to the supreme ecclesiastical authorities of the place to consult all parties involved and so come to an unanimous agreement to celebrate the feast of Easter on the same Sunday.

That has happened in Egypt, in Syria and in Greece, where the Catholics of the Eastern rite and the Latin rite, who are minorities, have followed the Orthodox observance of Easter. The question of finding a date for celebrating Easter common to all Christians is a preoccupation of the Orthodox sister churches. Responding to a call by Patriarch Athenagoras, the Orthodox held a European ecumenical symposium on the question in Athens, during June 1969.[15] They took part in the colloquium organized at Chambésy in March 1970 by the Faith and Order Commission.[16] Finally, the question is part of the agenda for the Pan-Orthodox Council that is in preparation. The preliminary report of the commission on the matter is brief, positive and cautious.[17] All these texts say firmly that, since Easter is the centre of Christianity, unanimity in its celebration is a powerful sign of unity and division is an cause for offence. Without advocating the reordinations once performed among the Celts, we can understand the importance that the Catholic church attached to this question.

Still, we do need to go back to the appeal that Polycrates and St Irenaeus made to the legitimacy of the two equally apostolic traditions, not as a return to the diversity that they justified in this way, but because of the importance of the appeal in an ecumenical context. On the subject of the Eastern churches, the decree *Unitatis redintegratio* says: 'However, the heritage handed down by the apostles was received differently and in different forms, so that from the very beginnings of the Church its development varied from region to region and also because of differing mentalities and ways of life' (no.14,3). This point is very important. We know that there is every difference between East and West, even in what seems to be held in common or to be identical in substance. The differences need to be noted point by point. However, it is very important to recognize that some of them are not just the result of Catholicity and a variety of spiritual gifts, but go back to apostolic origins. That is of profound importance for the very notion of 'sister churches'.

(ii) Is the idea of the 'undivided church' a valid one?

Protestant theologians have denounced the idea of an original unity, subsequently lost, which needs to be rediscovered; they believe this to be a fiction.[18] To suppose that there was once a unified church, they claim, is to project on to local churches, the diversity of which is indicated by the letters of Paul, the transcendent ideal of the Epistle to the Ephesians. Celsus, in the middle of the third century, simply found himself confronted with a diversity of Christianities.

In 1934, W.Bauer showed that in the context of earliest Christianity we cannot talk in terms of the prior recognition of an orthodoxy in relation to which one position or another will have been judged 'heretical'.[19] At Edessa, Bauer says, the first Christians were Marcionites; in Egypt, before the episcopacy of Demetrius (178-231), a syncretistic Gnosticism prevailed. As Catholics, Christians have often held views which were later judged to be unorthodox. Bauer argued that the Roman Church borrowed the idea of a norm of orthodoxy from the Old Testament, as can be seen from its famous letter to the church in Corinth; Rome then represented and extended this orthodoxy. In the fourth century, other elements than the confession of faith, i.e. juridical and political factors, contributed towards the realization of an unity.

Leaving aside Bauer's personal position, without discussing either the cases which he cites or those which he fails to consider (cf. C.R. de Simonin), we can accept that there is no reason to be surprised that the distillation of an 'orthodoxy', at the level not only of ideas but also of dogmatic terms, should have been slow and difficult. The history of christological and trinitarian dogma is an illustration of this. One has only to think of the difficulties encountered over the terms *hypostasis*, *physis* and *ousia*. That did not prevent people from living, as a church, by *the reality* of Christ and his spirit, any more than it did in the apostolic age: they lived by faith and by the continuity of the apostolic confession of this faith. About 180, that led St Irenaeus to say: 'The belief and tradition of the churches in Germany is in no way different from the belief and tradition of the churches of the Iberians and the Celts, those in Egypt, in Libya and at the centre of the world.'[20] So at that time people were well aware that Marcionitism and Gnosticism were alien to the apostolic faith – heresies! At the time of St Irenaeus – as he himself bears witness – certain criteria of orthodoxy were recognized: the apostolic tradition attested in the episcopal succession, the canon of the New Testament and the *regula fidei*.

The apostolic succession *alone* was not an adequate criterion. W.Elert illustrates the impossibility of taking too naively the ideal of union in the bishop, as in Christ, by the following facts, presented by St Ignatius of Antioch.[21] It was necessary to beware of any errors that might be around and to remain united to the bishop. However, about a hundred and fifty years after Ignatius, Paul of Samosata, the arch-heretic, was actually bishop of Antioch; moreover, a century later, schism at Antioch lasted for several decades and produced three, and even four, rival bishops on the same cathedra. With which of these was communion to be maintained?

As to schism, Mgr Duchesne counted five great breaks in communion between Constantinople and Rome between 323 and 787, totalling 203 years.[22] There were squabbles among clergy and bishops, but much more serious was a progressive 'estrangement' between the two parts of the church: there was a difference in languages, concepts and canonical structures, and in the way of understanding the respective roles of emperor and pope in the councils; there was a diversity of customs, each party absolutizing its own and judging the other's from its point of view; and finally, there were different theologies, which under the pressure of polemic became different forms of dogma.

Attempts at establishing dogma led to breaks which have still not been healed. Ephesus (431) led to Nestorianism, Chalcedon (451) to 'monophysitism', and so on. Do we have to follow C.Journet in holding that the church only achieves greater dogmatic precision at the expense of divisions which finally prove necessary? At least, to this view of the past must be added Karl Rahner's view of the present and the future: these are and will be marked by a concentration on fundamentals. That is my view also, and it is a source of joy; it is also very much in line with the development outlined in the present book. It is also a possible way of avoiding the simplistic idea of 'rediscovering' a unity which is supposed to have been 'lost'. And that allows us to look for a unity which allows of diversity, a unity which has existed despite the fact of divisions which I have already touched on.

This unity does not consist only in the fundamental dogmas of the *regula fidei* and the baptismal confession of faith. That kind of unity has certainly been a very real one, but I mean something more: the unity to which I am referring also consists in what may be termed the sacramental nature of the church. It is the common foundation of the ecclesiologies of East and West. In the East, they even talk of divine humanity or theandrism, a concept which Thomists tend to handle with caution. I understand this to be essentially a union of supernatural and eschatological reality, with the tangible forms of the specific church that we know. When we speak of the undivided church, we are well aware that it had its diversities and tensions, not to mention differences, but we recognize this organic, sacramental or mystical unity of the body of Christ. That is something that can be misunderstood to some extent when critics talk of a 'romanticization' of the concept of the church.[23] I would see this common basis as existing at the time of the fathers, of the creation of the liturgy, of monasticism, and of the period of the seven ecumenical councils. As far as we are concerned, this is the point of reference for the changes to which the churches are called, second only to Holy Scripture. We need not so much to return to it *materially*, as to give life to the principles which inspired the existence of the church during these centuries of wretchedness and of grace. In this sense we can speak of the undivided church. Opening the theological dialogue between Orthodox and Roman Catholics at Patmos on 29 May 1980, Metropolitan Melito of Chalcedon, envoy extraordinary of the Ecumenical Patriarch, said: 'We have come to Patmos, the place of apostolic theology *par excellence*, in the first place to listen and not to speak; to rediscover the theology of the apostles and the fathers of the undivided church and, in so doing, again to submit everything to "the word of God and the witness of Jesus".'

That is certainly what we need.

3

Diversity has always been Accepted in the Unity of Faith

The firmest tradition is that, given the unity of faith, a diversity of customs and opinions is quite legitimate.

We have evidence of this from the period of the persecutions. St Justin, in about 150, declared that he did not want to follow the faithful who refused to have anything to do with those who, while putting their trust in Christ, wanted to observe as far as possible the prescriptions of the law of Moses.[1] Justin was extremely tolerant of approaches which he neither shared nor approved.

We have seen how St Irenaeus intervened to dissuade Pope Victor from excommunicating the churches of Asia which celebrated Easter and broke the fast on 14 Nisan, whether or not it was a Sunday. He wrote 'in the name of the brothers whom he governed in Gaul':

> Such a diversity of observances has not just arisen now, in our time, but dates from long ago, from our forebears... They all nevertheless kept the peace, as do we, one with another; the difference in the fast confirms the agreement in the faith.[2]

Firmilian of Caesarea cited the precedent of the paschal question when Stephen, the bishop of Rome (254-7), approved those bishops who recognized the baptism of heretics and threatened to excommunicate those who did not: this was a question which involved doctrine and not just a mode of practice.

> One sees among them (the people of Rome) differences over the days of Easter, and on many other points of religion, and one does not observe among them exactly what one observes in Jerusalem, just as in most of the other provinces many things vary along with the differences in places and peoples, but despite this

one never feels removed from the peace and the unity of the Catholic church. However, Stephen has just dared to do precisely that, to disturb the peace which his predecessors have always kept with us.[3]

Firmilian wrote those words to Cyprian. The latter opposed the Bishop of Rome on the rebaptism of heretics, but for all that he did not break communion with him.[4] Opening the Council of Carthage in 256, where this question was to be discussed, St Cyprian declared: *Superest ut de hac ipsa re singuli quid sentiamus proferamus, neminem iudicantes aut a iure communicationis aliquem si diversum senserit amoventes* ('Each one of us must say what he feels on this question, without judging anyone nor removing his right to communion if he thinks otherwise').[5] This is a remarkably forceful and concise formula, though St Augustine summed it up even more tersely: *Censuit Cyprianus licet, salvo iure communionis, diversum sentire* ('Cyprian thought that he was allowed to think differently, while keeping the right to communion').[6] Charles Gore, as an Anglican participant in the Malines conversations, invoked this text and even used it as the title of a memorandum in which he argued that it was possible for the Anglican church to be in communion with the Roman Catholic church without accepting all its doctrines.[7]

St Augustine discussed on a number of occasions the question how far diversity in practice was legitimate and how far the local churches were free in this respect. These discussions occur in his letters to Januarius, which became the classical authority on this point through the Middle Ages and even down to the Council of Trent. Augustine conjured up the memory of his mother and a comment made by St Ambrose on the fact that in Rome people fasted on Saturday, but not in Milan. 'There are things which vary according to places and regions... There is freedom of observance in connection with them. There is no better way for a wise and prudent Christian to behave than to conform to the usages of the church in which he is. For anything that is neither against the faith nor against good morals must be a matter of indifference and observed with due regard for those in whose society one lives.'[8] The only absolute unity to be observed is that of the faith, interiorized in every believer. At the same time, that was also the position of St Jerome,[9] a position shared in the East in the fifth century by the historians Socrates and Sozomen, the former of whom attempted to collect examples of different practices observed by the different churches.[10]

That brings us to Gregory the Great (590-604), whose declarations are well known. Gregory wrote to Leander, Bishop of Seville, in April 591, about baptism by one immersion rather than by three, a matter of practice which had implications for the essentials of belief. Gregory declared: 'If there is unity of faith, a difference of custom does no damage to the holy church: *In una fide nihil officit sancta Ecclesiae consuetudo diversa.*'[11] Gregory's comment to Augustine in July 601 has also been quoted frequently. Although at one time the authenticity of the text was challenged, in essentials it has again been accepted. Augustine, used to Roman liturgical customs, had encountered others in his travels across Gaul, and asked which were to be introduced into England: 'The faith being one, how is it,' he asked Gregory, 'that the customs of the church are so different and that the ceremonies of the mass in the church of Rome are so unlike those in the churches of Gaul?' Gregory replied:

> My brother, you are familiar with the custom of the church of Rome, in which you know you were nurtured. But this is my decision: you should choose with care, whether from the church of Rome or from that of the Gauls, or perhaps from some other, whatever you have found most fitting for the better service of Almighty God, and you should introduce into the church of the Angles, which is still new in the faith, whatever you have found from the customs of many churches, by a careful process of education. Practices are not to be assessed on the basis of locality, but localities on the basis of what one finds valuable there. So choose, from each of the different churches, whatever is pious, religious, just, draw them together and use them to establish a custom in the spirit of the Angles.[12]

One could easily note many other declarations along the lines of St Gregory's reply to Leander of Seville. There was John the Deacon (John I?), about 520, who spoke of a unity of apostolic faith fixed by the holy fathers, but a variety of rites and customs, as part of the beauty of the church.[13] We know how forgetfulness of these principles in a climate of rivalry and polemic poisoned relations between Rome and Byzantium. It is all the more welcome to note, in sombre moments, the declarations made by the patriarch Photius, as when he wrote to Pope Nicholas I that a difference in customs is of itself unimportant and should not lead to schism,[14] or his statement at the council of 879-880 which re-established him:

> Each see observes certain ancient customs which have been

handed down by tradition, and it is wrong to enter into dispute
and litigation on this subject. The Roman church conforms to its
particular usages, and that is fitting. For its part, the church of
Constantinople also observes its customs, which it has from an
ancient tradition. The Eastern sees do the same thing.[15]

This is the point, at the moment when things began to evolve
differently, to recall the conditions in which the early church lived
and the régime under which unity and diversity were realized.

Mgr P.Batiffol has developed a fruitful approach by speaking of
three zones of papal *potestas* in connection with the church of the
first centuries. In Italy, and then, when the north of the country was
under the influence of Milan and Ravenna, in the southern part,
from Tuscany down to the boot, and in the islands (Corsica, Sicily,
Sardinia), there was just one ecclesiastical province of which the
bishop of Rome was the metropolitan and in which he ordained
bishops and intervened to judge or bring about judgments in difficult
cases.

Elsewhere in the West the bishops were grouped in ecclesiastical
provinces, each one with its metropolitan and its provincial council.
These provinces formed larger entities which could be said to be
national, a fact which led to their usually leading an autonomous
existence.[16] Rome exercised a moral authority and its faith was an
example; it did not intervene much on the disciplinary level, but
kept itself for *causae maiores* (where a bishop was involved). It had
a role in maintaining communion between the churches, in unifying
discipline by communicating the decisions of the councils (e.g. of
Arles or of Sardica). The pope had the role of arbiter (cf. Batiffol,
summary, p.54). Africa maintained a shadowy independence, going
so far as to excommunicate those who appealed to Rome.[17] However, it was felt that a judgment made by the Roman see settled a
question (*causa finita est*).

The East never accepted the regular jurisdiction of Rome, nor
did it submit to the judgment of Western bishops. Its appeals to
Rome for help were not connected with a recognition of the principle
of Roman jurisdiction but were based on the view that Rome had
the same truth, the same good. The East jealously protected its
autonomous way of life. Rome intervened to safeguard the observation of legal rules, to maintain the orthodoxy of faith and to ensure
communion between the two parts of the church, the Roman see
representing and personifying the West (cf. Batiffol, p.75). In
according Rome a 'primacy of honour', the East avoided basing this

primacy on the succession and the still living presence of the apostle Peter. A *modus vivendi* was achieved which lasted, albeit with crises, down to the middle of the eleventh century: L.Bréhier has given a clear and optimistic account of it, reacting against a history which puts particular stress on these crises. But Bréhier has not paid sufficient attention to the existence of *two* universes where even what is basically held in common proves to be different.

From the perspective of an ecclesiology which is not only theoretical but is also put into practice, we are confronted by two logics. The East remained oriented on the logic of local or particular churches in communion with one another in the unity of faith, love and eucharist; this unity was realized by means of exchanges and communications and then, when the need made itself felt, by the holding of a council. It was a unity of communion. The West, which Islam had cut off from North Africa, accepted the authority of the Roman see, and over the course of history Rome occupied an increasingly prominent place. It is a fact that the two gravest crises between Byzantium and Rome arose in times when papal authority was affirmed most strongly: with Photius under Nicholas I and John VIII, and with Cerularius at the time of the so-called Gregorian Reform (Nicholas II, Leo IX, Humbert, Gregory VII).

Declarations about the varieties of customs in the unity of the faith continued. In 1006, Fulbert of Chartres remarked: 'However, we have heard that it is in other areas that the churches differ one from another in worship and observances... This diversity of custom is not always such as to offend us, since the unity of the faith is not involved. Now in numerous areas the church of Greece differs from that of Spain, and the Roman church differs from both the former and the latter, and the same is true of the Gallican church. But that need not scandalize us in any way at all if we consider that diversity of observances has always existed in the church of Christ, but not diversity of faith...'[18] Between 1018 and 1050 the great spiritual teacher John of Fécamp followed St Augustine in writing: 'This mother church, which we call Catholic, spread all through the world in the unity of the same faith, recognized three rules of existence: the authority of scripture, a universal tradition, or a distinct and particular form. As to the private constitutions and the particular forms, each (community) exists and governs itself either in accordance with the variety of places or in accordance with what it finds beneficial. The customs are different, but there is only one single and identical integrity of orthodox faith in the church.'[19]

In the East, at the very time when the patriarch Cerularius and his

followers were engaged in polemic against the Latins over a whole
host of customs on which they differed, Theophylact, Archbishop
of Bulgaria, reaffirmed that, since dogma was not involved, the
diversity of usages could not justify a schism.[20] A message to this
effect arrived at Rome. Leo IX wrote to Cerularius: 'The holy
Roman church knows that customs differing according to times and
places are not injurious to the salvation of believers when a same
faith, active in love, commends them all to the one God.'[21] This text
was reproduced more or less faithfully in the canonical collections
of the twelfth century.[22]

Affirmations to this effect appear regularly in the West after the
schism of 1054. St Anselm, a fervent supporter of the views of
Gregory VII, writes: 'We have received from the holy fathers that,
if one keeps the unity of love in the catholic faith, a different custom
does no wrong.'[23] Speaking specifically of the Greeks, Anselm
affirms, following Gregory VII himself, that one can celebrate the
holy eucharist just as well with leavened bread as with unleavened
bread.[24] Anselm similarly recognizes the real equivalence of two
different vocabularies in the matter of trinitarian theology.[25] One
could cite a large number of similar declarations.[26] At the beginning
of the twelfth century the principle was also applied to a situation
which caused problems for some people, namely the multiplication
of religious orders, each with its own customs and observances.[27]

One could go on gleaning references. St Thomas Aquinas cites
the text of St Gregory to Augustine of Canterbury, and comments:
'Different liturgical customs in the Church do not imply a disrespect
for truth. They should be observed, and to disregard them is
unlawful'; he takes up St Cyprian's axiom almost word for word.[28]
In his memorandum addressed to the pope for the Council of Lyons
in 1274, which was intended to bring about union with the Greeks,
Thomas's contemporary Humbert de Romanis wrote:

> Remedy for the second point of discord: that in all the rites
> (procedures) where the church can give dispensation, one accepts
> their procedures, provided that they are in accord with the
> substance of faith and that they do not condemn our procedures.
> Remedy for the third point of discord: that we do not expect from
> them the perfection of obedience (full obedience), provided that
> their patriarch is confirmed by the pope and that they receive the
> Roman legates with honour.[29]

In the climate of the great schism, of conciliarism, and of new
prospects of union with the Greeks, Jean Gerson[30] and above all

Nicolas of Cusa[31] were favourably inclined to the recognition of diversity in unity.

Melanchthon maintained the traditional line when he wrote: 'It is not necessary for the true unity of the Christian church that ceremonies, instituted by men, should be observed uniformly in all places...'(*Augsburg Confession*, 1530, art.VII). I say that without endorsing the famous *satis est* of the same article, if taken in a restrictive and exclusive sense.

This principle of variety in unity, affirmed so many times by the popes and still to be found today, has been misunderstood by popes themselves. In my view, the beginnings of the assertion by the Bishop of Rome of his authority to regulate the life of the churches are to be found with Damasus (366-384), Siricius (384-399) and Innocent I (401-417). These popes begin to identify unity of discipline with unity of faith and then to interpret unity in terms of uniformity.[32] Damasus, to whom, according to E.C.Babut, we owe the first 'decretal', writes: *Si ergo una fides est, manere debet et una traditio. Si una traditio est, una debet disciplina per omnes ecclesias custodiri.*[33] Unity of faith calls for (or demands?) unity of discipline.

Damasus' successor Siricius, to whom some scholars (e.g. H.Getzeny) attribute the 'first decretal', mentioned above, and the beginnings of the legalistic and quasi-military style of Roman documents, wrote this to the bishops on the question of ordinations: 'I say that having the same faith we should also have the same feeling in the tradition, showing ourselves of one mind and in accord, at peace in Christ, and with charity in apostolic observances'.[34] There is no doubt that the major preoccupation of the Roman see is the unity of faith. That is part of its mission. However, it already identified the expression or the formulation of this faith with its content or its aim, leaving no room for questioning today.[35]

In replying to the Bishop of Carthage, Innocent I did not stop at commending accord and unity on the date of the celebration of Easter.[36] In his famous letter to Decentius of Gubbio, Innocent makes such important requests that I must quote them in the original. A translation follows:[37]

Si instituta ecclesiastica ut sunt a beatis apostolis tradita, integra vellent servare Domini sacerdotes, nulla diversitas, nulla varietas, in ipsis ordinibus et consecrationibus haberetur, sed dum unusquisque non quod traditum est, sed quod sibi visum fuerit hoc aestimat esse tenendum, inde diversa in diversis locis vel ecclesiis aut teneri aut celebrari videntur; ac fit scandalum populis qui dum nesciunt traditiones antiquas humana praesumptione corruptas, putant sibi aut ecclesias non convenire, aut ab apostolis vel apostolicis viris contrarietatem inductam.

 Quis autem nesciat aut non advertat id quod a principe apostolorum Petro Romanae ecclesiae traditum est ac nunc usque custoditur, ab omnibus debere servari nec superduci aut introduci aliquid, quod auctoritatem non habeat aut aliunde accipere videatur exemplum? Praesertim cum sit manifestum in omnem Italiam, Gallias, Hispanias, Africam atque Siciliam et insulas interiacentes nullum instituisse ecclesias nisi eos quos venerabilis apostolus Petrus aut eius successores constituerint sacerdotes. Aut legant, si in his provinciis alius apostolorum invenitur aut legitur docuisse. Qui si non legunt, quia nusquam inveniunt, oportet eos hoc sequi, quod ecclesia Romana custodit, a qua eos principium accepisse non dubium est, ne dum peregrinis assertionibus student, caput institutionum videantur omittere..., ut maiore auctoritate vel tuos institutos, vel si qui a Romanae ecclesiae institutionibus errant, aut commoneas aut iudicare non differas, ut scire valeamus qui sint, qui aut novitates inducunt, aut alterius quam Romanae existimant consuetudinem esse servandam.

If the priests of the Lord wanted to maintain in purity the rules of the church as they come down to us from the blessed apostles, there would be no diversity, no variation in orders and consecrations; but it is when each person thinks that he should hold, not what has been handed down to him but what pleases him, that we can see different things believed or celebrated in different places. And that causes offence: not knowing that the ancient traditions have been corrupted by presumptuous men, people think either that the churches do not agree or that contrary things have been introduced by the apostles or by apostolic men.

 But who does not know or fails to consider that what has been handed down by the prince of the apostles, Peter, to the Roman church, and which it has kept down to the present, must be observed by all, and that one may not add nor introduce anything which has no authority, or which has its precedent elsewhere? Above all when it is well known that no one has founded churches throughout Italy, the Gauls, the Spains, Africa and Sicily and the intermediate isles, other than those whom the venerable apostle Peter or his successors established as bishops. Or let them investigate whether there was another apostle in these provinces or if he taught there. And if they do not read it, because it does not appear anywhere, they must follow what is observed by the Roman church, from which they took their origin, taking care lest, in following alien statements, they forget the head of their institutions.

This important document deals with what Batiffol regards as the second area of papal *potestas*, not just like the first (the dioceses round Rome), but as a pure extension of the church of Rome. St Leo the Great (440-461) wrote to Dioscurus, Bishop of Alexandria, that he could not allow (*non ergo patimus*) the disciple to do other than his master, Mark other than Peter: the questions at issue were on which day ordinations should be performed – Sunday – as in Rome, and the multiplication of eucharistic celebrations.[38] Moving on three centuries, we know the union, the submission to Rome, which was a mark of the apostolate of St Boniface in Germany. But he introduced a custom which came from Gaul, a formula of blessing before the communion. Pope Zacharias, in 751, reproved him for this in terms of incredible harshness:

> As to the blessings which the Gauls practise, you know, brother, that they are tainted in various ways. For they do not do this by virtue of an apostolic tradition, but by vain glory, thus incurring condemnation, for it is written: 'If anyone proclaim to you another gospel from that which has been proclaimed, let him be anathema.' You have received, dearest brother, the rule of the apostolic tradition: preach to all and teach what you have received from the holy Roman church, of which, thanks be to God, we have received the charge.[39]

Gregory VII not only prohibited the celebration of the divine office in Slavonic in Bohemia,[40] since he mistrusted the translations of scripture made there, but he ordered the kings of Castile and Aragon to abandon the Hispano-Visigothic liturgy and adopt that of Rome. Spain, he said, had been carried away by Priscillianism and Arianism; it had been invaded by the Goths and the Saracens, and was separated *a Romano ritu*. It was to return to the fold, and it too was to observe the *ordinem et officium* of this church founded by Peter and Paul, against which error could never prevail.[41] As Père Gy has commented, whereas the principle in tradition is that diversity in liturgy does not hinder the unity of faith, Gregory VII – and he is not the first, Père Gy also cites the *Libri Carolini* – says that if one holds the faith of the Roman church, one must practise its liturgy![42]

The modern popes have produced countless declarations promising the East that its rites would be respected and retained, excluding only whatever might be contrary to dogmatic truth.[43] That has not always signified a positive taste for diversity: there has still been confusion between unity and uniformity, loyalty and conformity.[44] However, Pius IX said: 'If the Roman pontiffs have taken care that uniformity of discipline should correspond to the unity of the church, at least in the most important matters, they have also respected rites when they have not departed from either true faith or honesty.'[45] And again: 'Our predecessors knew that the spotless bride of Christ is characterized by an admirable variety, of a kind that does not damage unity.'[46] 'The diversity of rites and usages,' wrote Leo XII, 'manifests the catholicity of the church.'[47]

With a degree of optimism Benedict XV, in the Consistory of 10 March 1919, said: '(Our predecessors) took care not only to keep the customs and institutions of the East distinct from those of the Latins (*seorsum a Latinis*), but also to preserve unaltered and intact their rites, which are both noble and splendid, so that in them the bride of Christ, "in golden vestments and clothed in variety", may better show her beauty.'[48]

Pius XI insisted that rites should be respected equally:[49] he made this fine declaration: 'The Roman pontiffs think that liturgical variety, which expresses the genius and the particular character of the peoples, is not only not repugnant to the unity of the holy faith and divine worship, but is rather a beauty worthy of praise.'[50]

Pius XII developed this theme in his encyclical *Orientalis Ecclesiae decus* of 9 April 1944 for the centenary of St Cyril of Alexandria.[51] From then on it has become classic, as with John XXIII[52] and widely at Vatican II, which extended legitimate variety to the approach to and theological expression of the mysteries.[53] However, in conclusion one cannot fail to mention the words of Paul VI to the patriarch Athenagoras:

> To rediscover unity in diversity and faithfulness can only be the work of the Spirit of love. If unity of faith is required for full community, diversity of usage is not an obstacle. On the contrary, did not St Irenaeus, 'who bore his name well because he was a peacemaker both in his name and in his conduct' (Eusebius, HE V, 24, 18), say that 'the difference of customs confirms the

agreement of faith'(ibid., 13)? As for Augustine, the great doctor of the African church, he saw the diversity of customs as one of the reasons for the beauty of the church.[54]

Very recently, John-Paul II has again made variety a quality of unity itself.

It is fundamental for this dialogue to recognize that the richness of this unity in faith and spiritual life must be expressed in the diversity of forms. Unity – whether on the universal level or at the local level – does not signify uniformity or the absorption of one group by the other. It is rather at the service of all groups, to help each one to give better expression to the gifts which it has received from the Spirit of God.[55]

4

Pluralism in Ethnic and Cultural Areas

This is an immense problem, one of the most urgent which Christians have to tackle. I am very well aware of my limitations in discussing it and even in raising it. My specific experiences of cultural pluralism are very limited, and my knowledge is little more than elementary; however, I do think that it is authentic, and that is the most important thing. In approaching the problem *theologically* it is enough for us to recognize it, to see its dimensions and finally to attempt a theological appreciation.

The problem is only relatively a new one. The church has been aware of it since the apostolic age, since the time when its mission took it beyond the religious sphere of Judaism into the Graeco-Roman world. It was symbolized or prophesied in the miracle of the tongues at Pentecost: 'We hear them proclaim in our language the marvels of God' (Acts 2.11). The tangible sign of it was the shift from 'Saul' to 'Paul' as the apostle's name. That happened in Cyprus, between 45 and 49 (cf. Acts 13.9). Then came the growth of the churches in the cultural and political world: first Graeco-Roman, then Persian, Coptic, Punic, and so on.

However, the problem is relatively new, even in a missionary context, where it has been of major significance (e.g. in the sixteenth and nineteenth centuries). It is new in the degree to which people are aware of it and in the urgency, extent and depth of their recognition of it. That is evident from the development of the vocabulary connected with it. There has been talk of indigenization and adaptation, but that presupposes that there is a model to transplant and that the only question is how to apply it. There has been talk of 'acculturation' (P.Charles), or rather, as people would tend to say these days, 'inculturation'. Again, rather than speaking of 'planting the church', which would also suggest the transplantation of a model, even if its elements were indigenous, the terms used nowadays suggest the birth of the church in a country, in a people, from this people.

What is relatively new is the recognition of the *other* as such. For centuries people have attempted to make others conform to them. The other person has been loved, esteemed, as a step towards his or her taking the same direction as ourselves. The new development is marked by an interest in the other precisely where he or she differs. That is what makes the climate in which Orthodox and Protestant observers were invited to the Second Vatican Council so different from that of the First. However, while recognizing the fact that this question goes beyond the visible limits of the Catholic church, I shall restrict the discussion to the situation within that church and the framework of its life.

There are countless declarations of principle: by the Propaganda, in 1659,[1] by modern popes,[2] and by Vatican II.[3] Quite recently, at Kampala in Uganda, on 31 July 1969, Paul VI declared: 'Your church must be above all Catholic... But, given this first response, we must pass to the second... In this sense you can and must have an African Christianity.'[4] John Paul II repeated this declaration at Kinshasha in Zaire on 3 May 1980:

> One aspect of this evangelization is the *inculturation* of the gospel, the *Africanization* of the church. A number of people have confided to me that this is very close to your heart, and that is a good thing. It is one of the indispensable efforts to incarnate the message of Christ. Granted, the gospel cannot be identified with cultures, and transcends them all. But the kingdom which the gospel proclaims is lived out by people who are deeply involved in a culture; the building of the kingdom cannot be done without using elements from human culture (cf. *Evangelii nuntiani*, no.20). Indeed, evangelization must help people to bring out from their own living tradition original expressions of Christian life, celebration and thought (cf. the exhortation *Catechesi tradendae*, no.53). You seek to be both fully Christian and fully African. The Holy Spirit asks us to believe that the leaven of the authentic gospel has the power to raise up Christians in the various cultures, with all the riches of their heritage, in a purified and transfigured form.

Africanization involves broad and deep areas which have yet to be fully explored, whether this is the question of the language needed to present the Christian message in a way which attracts the spirit and heart of the people of Zaire, or the catechism, or theological reflection, or the most suitable expression of the common forms of Christian life in the liturgy or sacred art.[5]

A programme put in these terms raises many questions. We must thank God that serious work has begun: among books available, there are general discussions of the problem of culture,[6] colloquia or volumes raising the whole range of relevant questions,[7] and monographs based on the best methodology. Here I shall mention only those that I know; my references are those of a 'fool'! However, here are some major parts of the programme.

Liturgy. There is an overall problem here.[8] Welcoming the Holy Father to Kinshasa, in plain terms Cardinal Malula expressed his regrets that he could not offer him an African (eucharistic) liturgy. Rome had in fact forbidden it. However, it could be asked whether local products corresponding to unleavened bread and wine, which are not cultivated locally, might not be used in the celebration of the eucharist. At the 1974 Synod, Mgr Zoa, Archbishop of Yaoundé, had asked for manioc bread to be authorized.[9] The question was raised at the colloquium in Abidyan in 1977.[10] Some theologians would be in favour.[11] Two principles are involved here, pulling in different directions. On the one hand there is the positive and singular fact of Christ who, though a specific figure, takes on a normative value. On the other hand there is the principle of sacramental symbolism in the consecration of 'the fruit of the earth and the labours of men' which are used for our nourishment. Hitherto the Roman authorities have been absolutely opposed to any departure from unleavened bread and wine or from anything that would in reality alter their nature.[12] I recognize the importance of a theme which is bound up with the sovereign fact that all our consecrations operate by the virtue of words pronounced *once* by Jesus at the Last Supper, a virtue communicated by the Holy Spirit. However, the argument from sacramental symbolism, supported by the words of the Lord about the significance of the nourishment it gives, also carries great weight. Only an integrally ecumenical council (involving both East and West) could settle the question.

Ancestor cult and initiation. The African is never separated from his ancestral roots. This is a decisive feature of his anthropology and his social, or rather communal, involvement. This value can be accepted into Christianity. The Old Testament explains a man's condition by his genealogy. The problem is to purify, to evangelize so profound an element from the awareness of what one is. As to initiation, bound up as it is with the same values, what does the purity of faith at baptism and confirmation demand? What is acceptable? Only the faithful, with their pastors, can judge that. What can be accepted is not contrary but rather proportionate to the intensity of the purest faith in the sacrament of Christian initiation.

Marriage and the practice of the sacraments. The missionaries began by transplanting to black Africa the Western model of marriage: a monogamous union, brought about by love, creating an independent family the children of which are promised a Christian education. This conception is obviously linked with a theology and with canonical rules of sacramental marriage which issue in a unique ceremony, entered into by free mutual consent, and establishing an indissoluble union. However, this discipline clashes with the reality of traditional African marriage,[13] which is the union of two larger families, even two clans, essentially finalized by the continuation of life, hence by fertility. It comes about progressively and involves a whole series of presents, a dowry, and is only thought to be consummated when the wife has proved not only her good qualities but also her fertility by bringing children – in some ethnic groups these have to be male – into the world. In default of that she can be sent back, or a second wife can be introduced to assure descendants, though this would raise a great many questions.

How does one reconcile Christian marriage as determined by doctrine and law with a structure which is so closely bound up with those of a whole society whose tradition makes it strong and stable? The proposals made so far have been said to be ineffective or unacceptable. The result is that only a small number of marriages of baptized Christians are celebrated in church and that a large number of the faithful are deprived of the sacraments over long periods. The same thing goes for those whose marriage is polygamous; it is immoral for them to send away all their wives but one, and they can only 'regularize' their situation at the end of their lives.[14] Of course these countries have developed or received the present discipline of marriage only progressively. Time has been needed for customs to grow. This must be accepted, and while we wait, we need to consider to what degree and on what conditions black Africa could be given a canonical statute which was specifically adapted to these different facts.

An African theology? Since 1960, Mgr Tshishitu Tshibangu, now in charge of Superior Instruction in Zaire, has been a champion of an

African theology. He is not alone: my colleague on the Theological Commission, Vincent Mulago, and others, including Westerners, have spoken along the same lines. At the 1974 synod in Rome, the African bishops affirmed: 'Our churches must further African theological research by every possible means. An African theology open to the basic aspiration of the peoples of Africa will lead to the effective incarnation of Christianity in the life of the people of the continent.'[15] The Holy Father Paul VI then said: 'Our task is that of the sentinel who watches at the gateway... We cannot allow people to take false directions', and he gave a warning against the danger of a particularism which would imperil the unity of the faith.[16] He returned to the theme on 26 September 1975, when he addressed the fourth Symposium of Episcopal Conferences of Africa and Madagascar. He commended 'a thorough investigation of the cultural traditions of the various populations and their underlying philosophical positions so as to discover there those elements which are not in conflict with Christian religion and those contributions which are capable of enriching theological reflection', but gave a strong warning against the peril of introducing in the name of African authenticity elements which might encourage ideologies harmful to the purity of the faith.[17] These principles are clearly indisputable. To apply them is no easy matter... The unity of reason and its well-tried methods of working come between the Catholic unity of the faith and specific cultural values. However, even at this level there could be an authentic pluralism, for example, between East and West. We should note that the journal founded at Kinshasa in April 1977 is not called *Revue de théologie africaine* but *Revue africaine de théologie*. The nuance is important. Our brotherly hope is that the Africans will move on from a general establishment of the principle to an effective way of putting it into practice. Their place is ready; they have only to occupy it.

I have spoken of Africa, which is close to us. However, analogous yet different comments must be made on Asia, Japan, the Pacific religions, and even Latin America. The questions of principle are the same, the actual conditions are new and varied. I cannot even hint at them.

Since Origen in the East and St Augustine in the West, classical theology has held that the unity of the *ecclesia* derives from the reality to which it adheres by faith, but that faith arrives at this reality by means of various signs. St Augustine's reflections have their starting point in a text of St Paul: 'Our fathers ate the same spiritual food and all drank the same spiritual drink. For they drank from the spiritual rock which accompanied them, and that rock was Christ.'[18] The Jews ate and drank Christ by the signs of the exodus; we eat and drink him by the eucharistic bread and wine; but for them, as for us, communion with his reality is by faith. Since this is the same, it makes both them and us a single church.[19]

These ideas are the basis for the conclusion that the same principle of unity can perhaps be respected by different signs. However, it must be added that under the new dispensation, that of Jesus Christ, the reality which he constitutes has been revealed, and then expressed in dogma, and that what the Council of Trent calls the unchangeable 'substance' of the sacraments of the faith has been fixed.[20] That imposes a limit and norms on theological and sacramental pluralism, which continues to be confined within the framework of these limits and these norms. How it is to be put into practice is then left to the discernment of pastors and Christian communities. The sign must give form to what is signified and cannot betray it.

5

'Pluralism', Intrinsic Value of Unity

Compared with 'unity', 'unitarism' would have a pejorative sense, but the word 'pluralism' has acquired a positive value and a new connotation as over against 'plurality'. Pluralism connotes diversity in unity.[1] It is an intrinsic value of unity. In expressing a diversity, 'pluralism' also refers to something held in common. It is not cacophony, it is not sheer dispersion, but rather the differentiation of something held in common.

That pluralism existed in the ancient church and that it exists in the church today is a fact on which there is no point in dwelling: there were rites and cultic expressions, theologies, schools of spirituality, traditions and customs, organizations peculiar to a country or socio-cultural area.

These pluralisms hold fast to two great truths: 1. The transcendence of Reality has to be translated into history, whether it is taken at its source, the Alpha, or at its goal, the Omega. The great doctors had an acute awareness of this transcendence. St Hilary complained that heresy forces us to *illicita agere, ardua transcendere, ineffabilia loqui*[2] and, when he had recognized the *homoousios*, he said of it: 'The infinite and immense God cannot be understood or expressed by the brief terms of human language.'[3] Thomas Aquinas defined the article of faith (dogma) as *perceptio divinae veritatis tendens in ipsam*, a perception of divine truth moving towards the truth itself.[4] Since no expression is ever totally adequate to what it expresses or its final outcome, a number of expressions are possible and even desirable. 2. Faith, sacraments, various Christian realities are received and set in motion by living subjects, who have their own already existing views, their culture, and their problems. Faith is necessarily formulated first and then interpreted.[5] That is already the case with the biblical witnesses. Christianity is subject to geography and history. The individual or collective subjects who live it out make it their own. Inevitably they express it in different ways.

That has two consequences which are important for us:

1. First, that tensions and conflicts are inevitable; and if they are accepted, brought out into the open and worked through, they are beneficial. That has been demonstrated by psychologists and sociologists, not to mention those who have made studies of community life.[6] For a Catholic it is an effort to accept that demand freely, for we have been brought up to consider all disagreement a consequence of sin, and we have a uniform and hierarchical conception of unity, of a military kind. We spontaneously see unity in terms of identity. I have already quoted these lines by R. de Montvalon elsewhere:

> *What everyone called unity was perhaps a desperate attempt to absorb the other*, to make him like us or dependent on us, to obliterate our differences. One can understand why the present time disturbs us: it confronts us with the following alternative: we must either agree to recognize our solidarity with different people, that is to say, to agree to being changed by them – or we must push away these people without being able to get rid of them because the world has grown smaller; in other words, we must live with rejection, polemic, tension, isolation, the devouring and impotent desire not to owe anything to anyone.[7]

A *community* allows and even demands differences, which it resolves by a principle which transcends them. Obviously the unity of faith must be safeguarded.

2. The spirit is ordered and open to the totality of truth, but it is limited in each person and even in each group of people. Each spirit, each group has only a certain number of experiences and realizes only a part or certain aspects of the truth. That is why the spirit is structurally in need of giving and taking. It is structurally directed towards dialogue, towards welcoming the other, towards what is *different*. If ecumenism is a quest for the purity and the fullness of the truth about God and the mysteries of salvation, it must be specifically and supremely a welcoming of differences on the basis of a common point of reference and a common destiny.[8]

These facts and principles apply to ecumenism. On 22 June 1979, John Paul II declared to a Coptic delegation: 'It is vital for this dialogue that we should recognize that the richness of this unity in the faith and spiritual life should be expressed in a diversity of forms. Unity – whether universally or on a local level – does not signify uniformity or the absorption of one group by the other. It is rather at the service of all groups to help one another to give better expression to the gifts which have been received from the spirit of God.[9]

It is clear that ecumenism presupposes a particular ecclesiology. The one which was predominant between the Council of Trent and Vatican II did not allow a real ecumenism, but at most an eirenic apologetic. One of the most important failings of this view of the church was the absence of the eschatological dimension.[10] The church presented itself in the legalistic categories of *societas, societas inaequalis, hierarchica, societas perfecta*. Even the encyclical *Mystici Corporis* of 1943, which went beyond these categories, taught a strict identity between the mystical body of Christ on earth and the Roman Catholic church. Other Christians were said to be 'ordained to the mystical body'; there was no question of other churches as such. More dominant, above all after the Gregorian Reform and the appearance of the mendicant orders, was what has been called the ecclesiology of the universal church.[11] That is taken to be a view in which the church is seen as a homogenous whole of which the dioceses are considered to be quantitative parts. In the end, the universal church would be only an extension of the Church of Rome, with the Pope as bishop.[12]

Vatican II did not in any way lessen the prerogatives of the Bishop of Rome. However, 1. it saw the church as a *mystery* dependent on the mystery of God the Trinity: the church is primarily communion with the divine missions of God the Trinity; 2. it accepted the eschatological reference: ch.VII of *Lumen Gentium* affirms that eschatology is part of the very nature of the church; cf. also *Ad Gentes divinitus* no.9; 3. it rediscovered an ecclesiology of local or particular churches and then saw the universal church as a communion of these churches: 'They are constituted after the model of the universal Church; it is in these and formed out of them that the one and unique Catholic Church exists.'[13] In a number of its documents the Council defines the local church as realizing through the Holy Spirit the gospel, the eucharist, the episcopate; realizing, we should say, the one, holy, Catholic and apostolic church of Christ.[14]

To what degree, and on what conditions, can one apply this theology of local and particular churches to the disunited churches which are not in full communion with the Church of Rome? Some ecumenists have tended to do this, and as a result have incurred the criticism of two of my ecumenical theologian friends.[15] Do the ecumenists criticized in this way take sufficiently into account what is required by communion on the level of faith, professed by the church and at the level of the ordained ministry? There are demands which we cannot surrender. However, as we shall see abundantly, great diversity is possible within this framework, and we must not confuse the faith with one of its historical formulations.

PART TWO
Looking towards the East

6

Some Relevant Eastern Concepts

(i) Adiaphora

This is a category used in philosophy to qualify things which, from a moral point of view, are in themselves indifferent. The Fathers made use of it, but without applying it to doctrinal questions. This is what is said of it in *A Patristic Greek Lexicon*, ed. G.W.H.Lampe, Oxford 1961, 35:

Adiaphoria

A. Indifference. 1. In philosophy, as the end of life (Justin, Clement). 2. Concerning food (Eusebius, Chrysostom). 3. Culpable indifference about conduct.
B. Carelessness.
C. Promiscuity.

Adiaphoros

A. Not different (the divine hypostases).
B. Indifferent, neither good nor bad, of food (Chrysostom), celibacy and marriage (Origen).
C. Unimportant (Origen, Chrysostom)
D. Unrestricted. 1. In general; of communion (Socrates). 2. In a bad sense: of use of words (Gregory of Nyssa); of persons in relation to sexual intercourse (Athenagoras, Epiphanius).
E. Undifferentiated.
F. Not making a difference or distinction.

Adiaphoros

Without making a distinction, indifferently. 1. In general. 2. Morally (Clement, Basil). 3. Referring to sexual intercourse, promiscuously (Athenagoras, Clement).

There is no difficulty in the sphere which Peter of Antioch touched

on when he wrote to Michael Cerularius: 'If the Latins would agree
to suppress the addition to the creed, I would not ask any more of
them, including among the number of indifferent things, along with
all the rest, even the question of unleavened bread.'[1] However, we
shall see something rather different.

This category of *adiaphora*, things indifferent, as opposed to
anagkaia, necessities, was applied to doctrine by Barlaam of Cala-
bria in a plan for union between the Eastern church and the Roman
church.[2] Having come to Constantinople out of a love for letters and
Greek philosophy, Barlaam acquired such a reputation there that in
1333-34 he was entrusted with discussing the procession of the Holy
Spirit with two Dominicans. In 1339 he was allowed to present to
the Synod of Constantinople a plan for the union of the churches
which he was even commissioned to present to Pope Benedict XII
at Avignon. There he made two speeches which C.Giannelli has
edited. In the first he makes further points about the procession of
the Holy Spirit: 'indifferent' doctrines, as reason is powerless to
make it more precise. This issue is not necessary for the union of the
churches. The Greeks could renounce *a Patre solo* and the Latins
the addition of the *Filioque* (p.192,25 to 123,12). However, the
Pope replied that the question of the procession of the Holy Spirit
is not at all secondary. It is part of the faith![3]

Here is the passage which interests us, following the translation
made by my colleague H.D.Saffrey of pages 191,23 to 192,12 in
Giannelli's edition based on MS Vatican Cod.gr.1110:

> Then those things the addition of which was not judged necessary
> by the venerable Fathers (= the Fathers of Nicaea): would you
> not think that their suppression was necessary? For it is not
> necessary that we should be in agreement with one another on all
> subjects; indeed, I would say that this is not even possible. And in
> fact I think that the Fathers saw that, nor did it escape them that
> it is impossible that all men should have the same opinions on all
> subjects. In fact, since one cannot always think the same things on
> the same subjects, how can one not be in disagreement with
> someone on some matter since one is dealing with another soul
> who is using another body? Thus, since opposite opinions arise on
> many subjects, a division should be introduced in each of them if
> it is not possible to determine by reason on what subjects one
> must part company with those who think the opposite, and on
> what subjects such a course is not necessary. What is needed,
> then, is a division which separates all subjects into two areas,

those which provide necessary agreement between Christians and the others which do not, in such a way that on the basis of this distinction we know quite definitely which issues determine whether or not parties in a dispute are Christians, whether or not they are Orthodox, and which issues do not, so that we do not part company over everything, and do not judge heretical anyone who shows the slightest difference. The Fathers, then, were well aware of this, because they saw that there is an infinite number of subjects which are irrelevant to unity, and a limited number of relevant subjects; and in noting these necessary subjects and collecting them together, they have handed down to us what we have called the symbol of faith. This symbol is in fact a summary of all the dogmas which are sufficient for those who may differ on other matters but are not in disagreement over these dogmas, so that they are not excluded from that name which comes from Christ, but may call themselves one thing or another in an appropriate way. In fact the creed mentions some of the necessary dogmas directly, while others are deduced from the content of the creed. For example, the creed does not say in so many words that the Holy Spirit is God, but it can be inferred from the fact that the Holy Spirit is called Lord, Giver of Life, and so on. And the same holds for the other dogmas.

(ii) Theologoumenon

This is an interesting category, but it is rather vague. Very few writers have made its meaning specific. This is what I have found:

B.Bolotov: After their break with the Church of Rome in 1871, the Old Catholics sought to establish relationships, and if possible to enter into communion, with the other churches with a 'catholic' structure. This led in 1875 to the Bonn conference, with twenty-two representatives of Orthodoxy. In 1892, the Holy Synod of Russia nominated a commission to follow this up and establish a specific relationship with the Old Catholics. Two historians were asked to edit a report on the question of the procession of the Holy Spirit, A.L.Katanski and B.Bolotov (who died in 1900). The report, published in German, without the name of the author, in the *Revue internationale de Théologie* 6, 1898, 681-712, has recently been translated into French and is published in *Istina* 17, 1972, 261-89. Bolotov distinguished three levels in doctrinal statements: dogma formulated in the creeds and by the ecumenical councils; specific theologies and, between the two, theologoumena. He explained:

You might ask what I understand by theologoumenon. In essence, it is a theological opinion, but an opinion which makes more sense for a 'catholic' theologian than for any other: the theologoumena are the theological opinions of the fathers of the *one and undivided church*; they are the opinions of men who include those who are rightly called *didaskaloi tes oikoumenes*... The content of dogma is the *truth*; the theologoumenon conveys *probability*. The sphere of dogma is that of the *necessaria*, the sphere of the theologoumenon that of the *dubia*: *in necessariis unitas, in dubiis libertas*.

No expert has the right to prevent me from expressing a theologoumenon (as being my private opinion), even if this theologoumenon has been formulated by no more than a single Father of the Church, provided of course that it has not been proved that a competent authority of the church has declared it to be an erroneous position.

Conversely, no expert can require of me that I receive as my private theological opinion a theologumenon which, though affirmed by some Fathers of the church, nevertheless neither attracts me by its great theological beauty nor convinces me by a sovereign authority accessible to my reason. In such a case, one thing is clear to me: while I myself may not accept the theologoumenon mentioned, I have no right to condemn theologians who do accept it; and if I was compelled to discuss this theologoumenon, I would deal with it faithfully, and with the respect due to the authority of the Fathers of the church (262).

Bolotov then applies the distinctions of his theological criteriology to three formulas expressing, beyond dogma, a doctrine of the procession of the Holy Spirit:

Thesis 1: The Russian Orthodox Church regards as a dogma (*credendum de fide*) only this truth, that the Holy Spirit proceeds from the Father and is consubstantial with the Father and the Son... As dogma, it (the doctrine of the procession of the Holy Spirit) cannot be supplemented either by the addition of an explanation 'by the Son' or by the addition of a restriction 'only from the Father'. But if the Fathers like John of Damascus (*De fide orth.*, ch.12) say that the Holy Spirit is a power of the Father, making known his hidden divinity which proceeds from the Father by the Son... in such a way that the Holy Spirit is also the Spirit of the Son... they certainly do not say that just to change the fullness of being of the Holy Spirit but to bring it nearer to our understanding, to illuminate it. They say that because they recognize this illumination as a possible and exact theologoumenon (281f.).

Thesis 2: The idea that the Holy Spirit proceeds, comes, shines out from the Father through the Son occurs so frequently among the Fathers, and the great significance, the importance that they attach to it... is so evident and so great that theologians cannot simply regard this *dia tou huiou* as no more than a private opinion of a Father of the Church; it is as it were an ecumenical theologoumenon, with authority everywhere in the Orthodox East (282).

Thesis 7: The Holy Spirit proceeds from the Father *alone*, in the strict sense of the term *ekporeutos*. But this proposition is only a theologoumenon and not a dogma (285).

It is amazing that Bolotov did not, in the same way, regard the *Filioque* as a theologoumenon.

Thesis 14: We cannot accord the Western *Filioque* equal rights with the Eastern *di'Huiou*, even as a private opinion, for the following reasons.

Thesis 15a: The Western *Filioque* has received no recognition analogous to that of the *di'Huiou*, which Tarasius recorded in his synodical.

Thesis 16b: Even in the West the *Filioque* seems not to have any other support (despite its diffusion) than the authority of St Augustine (287).

There we must leave Bolotov. These last two theses are historically inaccurate.[4] However, that is not my concern. See the accounts by Swete and Jugie, and indeed my own (*I Believe in the Holy Spirit* III, ET London 1983, 194f.). In conclusion, however, having given his historical reasons, Bolotov writes:

Thesis 27. As a private theological opinion, then, the *Filioque* cannot be considered an *impedimentum dirimens* to the re-establishment of communion between the Eastern Orthodox Church and the Old Catholic Church.

In the theological discussion on *Koinonia* held in Vienna on 1-7 April 1974 under the auspices of the *Pro Oriente* Foundation, Evangelos Theodorou took up Bolotov's idea again:

We should begin to consider certain questions giving rise to controversy between the two churches as theologoumena, that is to say, as free theological opinions and not as absolute pronouncements which might lead to hostility and even divisions. That is true in particular of the mystery of the Trinity, for every formulation resorts to categories and to human notions which seek to express the transcendence of the mystery 'without achieving it in terms of the recognition that theological notions participate in the reality under consideration without being identical with it. There are true statements, but they only look on the mystery from afar.'[5]

This extensive application of the idea of theologoumenon was criticized in the course of the discussion.[6]

Christos Androutsos, *Dogmatike tes Orthodoxou Anatolikes Ekklesias*, Athens 1907, [2]1956 (cf.*Irénikon* 32, 1959, 260, which I quote) 'comments on the particularly important role played by the theologian in Orthodoxy. Whereas the Catholic theologian already has the dogmatic formulae of the Council of Trent, the Vatican Council and the papal definitions, the Orthodox theologian has to formulate and refine the theologoumena and to investigate the dogmatic content in scripture and especially in holy Tradition, and its homogeneous evolution from the time of Christ and the apostles down to the present day.'

Panagiotis N.Trembelas (*Dogmatique de l'Église orthodoxe catholique*, Chevetogne and DDB, I, 1966, 30) defines the theologoumenon along the same lines, as a theological opinion which, within the limits laid down by dogma, is expressed on subjects on which the church has never pronounced, like 'the fall of the angels, the refreshment enjoyed by souls after death by reason of the celebration of the divine eucharist on their behalf'.

From the Latin Catholic side, M.J.Scheeben certainly gave the most precise definition of the status of the theologoumena. He distinguishes between truths of various kinds in the content of revelation:

> The fourth difference, finally, arises from the fact that one part of revealed truth is pronounced immediately, formally and actually in revelation and is illuminated by its light, whereas other truths are enunciated and illuminated only indirectly and in essence (*in radice*); we can instruct ourselves in them by reflection, using revelation as a basis and acting in the light of it. The former are termed *res fidei simplicitur*, the latter, in so far as they can be inferred with complete certainty from the truths of faith, are called *consectaria* or *corollaria fidei*, or theological truths (theologoumena) in the broad sense of this word, because they are

drawn from the source of the Word of God by the word or human reason (*Dogmatik*, 40).

We can also sense a difference in the Orthodox and Catholic-Latin ways of seeing the theologoumenon. The two are in agreement that the theologoumenon differs from dogma. But the Orthodox characterize it with relation to the person of the theologian and the reception by the church of his conception or formulation; the Latins in connection with the way in which the truth is contained in the object revealed.

That is again clear in the following passage from C.Journet (*Esquisse du développement du dogme marial*, Paris 1954, 48f.) inspired by the analyses of Fr Marin-Sola (*L'Évolution homogène du dogme catholique*, Fribourg 1924).

Before the infallible definition of the magisterium, all that was contained in the deposit revealed only in implicit fashion was already, by virtue of this fact, revealed *essentially* (*quoad se*), but not yet *manifestly* (*quoad nos*). It is after the infallible definition of the magisterium that what was already revealed essentially (*quoad se*) is also revealed manifestly and for us (*quoad nos*). Before the infallible definition of the magisterium, with divine aid, the whole implicit revelation can only be the object of human consent, on a theological level; it remains a theologoumenon.

I think that this notion of a revelation *quoad se* and not *quoad nos* is very much open to discussion. For on the one hand by definition revelation consists in a manifestation to our minds; on the other, there is confusion between an 'implicit revelation' and the objective reality of the mystery. What is of interest to us here is the application of the category of theologoumenon to a theological truth when it is taken, not from the periphery or the final conclusions of a series of arguments, but from the heart or the substance of the mystery revealed.

As far as I know, the *Lexikon für Theologie und Kirche* is the only dictionary of religion which has an article on theologoumenon (Vol.10, Freiburg 1965, cols. 80-2). K. Rahner gives the following definition, related less to an analysis of the object than to the activity of the believing theologian:

The theologoumenon is a proposition constituting a theological statement which cannot be directly considered to be an official doctrine of the church, as a proposition relevant to dogma and demanding a commitment of faith. It is primarily the result and the expression of the effort made to understand the faith by clarifying the relationship between binding propositions of faith and comparing the teachings of dogma with the general experience (of life in the world) and the academic achievement of an individual (or a particular era). It is not necessary for such a proposition to be materially distinct from a statement of faith in the strict sense of the term. It can also be contained implicitly in this statement of faith within the horizon of understanding which it indicates, in the historic origin of the conceptual instrumentation...

After this Rahner shows why such theologoumena are necessary in the life of faith and in the intellectual activity which it promotes.

The notion of the theologoumenon does not seem to occur in Protestant theology. I have found just this one reference in K.Gründer, *Figur und Geschichte, Johann Georg Hamann 'Biblische Betrachtungen' als Ansatz einer Geschichtsphilosophie* (symposium), Freiburg and Munich 1968, 83 n.1: 'The expression "theologoumenon" is most often employed to designate a theological and speculative statement without a biblical foundation, in which case it has a derogatory sense. By contrast here it signifies a purely theological statement which is not philosophical but is based solely on the biblical faith.'

(iii) Kat'oikonomian

The word 'economy' has several meanings, or at least has had several applications. Its biblical and patristic usages have been abundantly studied.[7] If we had to determine its semantic values and nuances precisely, we would obviously have to examine authors and texts one by one, but there can be no question of that here. In *A Patristic Greek Lexicon*, Oxford 1961, 940f., G.W.H.Lampe distinguishes four senses or groups of senses:

A. Ministration, charge, office.
B. Disposition, organization, constitution.[8]
C. Dispensation, ordering: the ordered succesion of acts by which God provides for human salvation. The history of salvation, saving revelation. Its main element is redemption in the incarnation. Furthermore, in the second half of the fourth century, a distinction was made between *theologia* (the Trinity) and *oikonomia* (Incarnation, sacraments).
D. Adaptation of means to ends, assessing certain means by

the end they produce to see whether this end justifies compromises or special pleading.

Senses C. and D. are the most interesting: the former because it denotes the theological richness of God's saving plan, his revelation and its realization, the latter because it brings us near to the reality that we are studying here. I shall ignore sense C., because while it is of considerable significance it is not our specific concern. Sense D. had antecedents or roots in paganism: Xenophon, the Stoics, the rhetoricians.[9] In practical life it was a matter of doing everything possible to achieve an end: the art of rhetoric justified a training in adaptation and even dissimulation to instil the lesson that it wanted to teach. The Fathers used this 'economy', sometimes under that very term and sometimes under that of 'condescension', *synkatabasis*.[10] There are innumerable examples. Here are some of them. You can find others in Lampe's *Lexicon*.

A canonical law must permit by 'good economy, necessary by reason of circumstances and profitable to the church'; this is how St Basil justifies the transfer of Euphrone to the see of Nicopolis (*Epist.* 227; PG 32, 852).

Certain expressions in scripture were explained by a pedagogical view of accommodation: e.g. where it is said that God repents of having made man (Gen.6.6) or that he hardens Pharaoh's heart (Ex.4.21): Origen, (*De Princ.*III 1,14; PG 11, 276f.) speaks of an 'economic' delay in order to bring about penitence; or when scripture speaks of the wrath of God, this is an 'economic' pedagogy with the conversion of men in view (Origen, *Hom.in Jer.* 18.6; PG 13, 476f.). Cf. also the articles cited in n.10.

The Fathers often noted acts of condescension on the part of the apostles: St John Chrysostom interpreted the episode at Antioch between Peter and Paul as a scene devised by 'economy' for the instruction of the faithful (*Hom. in Gal.* 2 and *Hom.in illud 'In faciem ei resisti'*:PG 61,641 and 51,371f.). Paul made himself all things to all men, a Jew to the Jews and a Greek to the Greeks, by 'saving economy but preserving the essential doctrines' (Clement of Alexandria, *Strom.* VI, 15, 124: Stählin II, 494; Chrysostom, *Hom.22.2 in I Cor.* and *Hom 6 in Ephes.*: PG 61, 184 and 62, 46D). So it was that he had Timothy circumcised (Origen, *Comm. Joan.* I, 9; XIII 18; PG 14, 37 and 429) and a large number of people afterwards; there are references in K.Duchatelez, *NRT* 92, 1970, 288 n.63 and 291 n.71; or again where he had yielded to James and took upon himself the expenses of a legal rite of purification (John Chrysostom, *Hom. 46 in Act.*:PG 60, 323).

But the most interesting examples are without doubt the very numerous ones in which the Fathers who fought hardest for the truth of doctrine proclaimed that once the essentials had been preserved they did not want to press things further. That is why St Basil held back from calling the Holy Spirit God or saying that it was consubstantial with the Father and the Son. Basil had even made a pact with Gregory Nazianzen that, taking account of local conditions, the latter would speak more cautiously.[10a] Moreover the aged Athanasius had approved this 'economy'.[11] He had made use of it himself. St Cyril of Alexandria had applied the same principle more ardently. He explained it often. It was by economy, he said, that the Council of Ephesus, having condemned error, had avoided designating Theodore of Mopsuestia (*Ep.* 72: PG 77, 345) by name. Peace was not to be sought too easily. However, 'the economy sometimes demands that one should abandon a little to gain by it, like sailors who in a storm throw part of the cargo into the sea to save the vessel' (*Epist.* 56: PG 77, 319; cf. *Ep.* 76, col.353). Thus it is enough for ordinary people to anathematize the heresy of the Messalians without asking too precise a declaration from them, for in such cases economy is better and wiser, whereas exactitude causes trouble (*Epist.* 82: PG 77, 376). Cyril was able to make peace with John of Antioch without demanding that he adopt his formulae, by reason of economy (*Epist.* 57: PG 77,321).

The West knew similar practices. St Cyprian criticized the Novatians for their severity over the *lapsi* and advised them to practise *temperamentum salubri moderatione*, 'a temperate and healthily moderate position' (*Epist.* 55.6: Hartel, 627). St Thomas Aquinas accepts that clergy who are converted from heresy can be re-instated *dispensative*, 'using the dispensation', to the ecclesiastical positions which they held beforehand, *et hoc pro bono pacis frequenter legitur esse factum*, 'they tell us that this happened often for the good of the peace' (II^a II^{ae} q.11 a.4).

At the time of the Fathers and in the ancient Eastern church, the notion of economy came to be connected with the reception of heretics or schismatics, first in the recognition of their baptism and then, more generally, in the question of the validity of their sacraments. The norms of the Council of Nicaea (canons 8 and 19) were clarified by St Basil, who in this sphere introduced the expression *oikonomias heneka ton pollon*: the baptism of the Cathari is accepted by some in Asia 'as a matter of accommodation with the many'. Similarly, Basil rejects the baptism of the Encratites, 'but if that should harm the Catholic church (some texts have "the general accommodation", *te kathodou oikonomia*) it would be better to follow custom and the accommodation of the fathers'. However, if they practise our baptism, they should observe the rigour of the canons, *douleuein akribeia kanonon*.[12] In Canon 47, St Basil says that he rebaptizes the Encratites, even if by accommodation ('economy') his correspondents, like the Romans, do not rebaptize them.[13] Although, as F.J.Thomson points out (408f.), St Basil did not develop a precise theory of economy, his first canon is a good expression of the basis of the Eastern position (cf. n.12). There is something sacramental about a celebration outside the church, but if the sacrament is to have the efficacy of grace which can exist only in the one church, it must be received in accordance with the 'economy', the conditions laid down by this church. J.Lebon sums up the position of the Fathers very precisely in a note on economy and *akribia*: 'The question of the validity of the sacraments conferred by the heretics was raised by the Fathers when they were determining the different conditions to impose on converts who entered the church. Where there was no provision for their repetition, these sacraments were essentially valid, but their full efficacy in the collation of grace could only be exercised in the true church, by the pronouncement of the bishop after the fulfilment of the conditions laid down for reconciliation.'[14]

Granted, in the course of history the idea of 'economy' has tended to take on a broader meaning and to denote the possibility for the church to look kindly, in mercy, on matters which did not conform to its rules. Thus for example the Basileus called on the Byzantine church to use 'economy' in accepting the Council of Lyons in 1274 at which he had subscribed to union with the Roman church.[15] One can and one should recognize the fact that the theory of economy has remained imprecise and fluctuating among theologians and Orthodox canon lawyers. It has served to justify practices which have differed in the course of time and between one church and another, like the recognition of the baptism of non-Orthodox Christians.[16] Even those who do not read the Eastern languages fluently now have a wide range of Orthodox studies on economy and on the various theologies proposed on this subject by the theologians and canon lawyers.[17] But these have operated in the framework of an ecclesiology which can claim descent from Cyprian and Firmilian[18] and which affirms that the grace of the Holy Spirit, communicated by the sacraments, can be found only in the one true church, which is the Orthodox church.

We may also note that an affirmation of this kind has a very formal place in the ecclesiology of St Augustine. Here the circumstances are very different and governed by his criticism of Donatism, in which he took up St Cyprian's theology in a very rigid way. 1. Augustine did not so much dissociate the ministerial action *of the church* from the sovereign act *of Christ*; he saw them as being completely different: Christ is the one who baptizes and consecrates. Augustine would not have said, as do the Orthodox theologians, that the church is mistress of the grace of the sacraments. 2. Augustine distinguished between a first element or effect of the sacrament, which it acquires by being celebrated in accordance with the rite of its instituion, and a second element, that of its spiritual fruits, sanctifying and bringing salvation; this presupposes in the recipient certain moral characteristics and union in the community of grace which is the church, the body of Christ indwelt and given life by his Spirit. I have argued that these two elements can be connected respectively with institution by Christ and the action of the Holy Spirit at work in the *unitas, caritas*, and thus the communion of the church.[19] However, the Orthodox theologians, with the exception of some who come near to these positions, reject this theology: they misunderstand or reject the analysis which expresses it, and insist on a firm affirmation that there are true sacraments only in the one church.

The Orthodox theologians make one serious objection to the Augustinian theory: in a way, it would make the church exist outside itself. The Augustinian synthesis has a reply to this difficulty, but in fact the difficulty itself can be turned to advantage. It can be the basis for a theology of the *vestigia ecclesiae* (or whatever else one cares to call it) which is called for by the fact of ecumenism; all Christian communions recognize this reality, to some degree, in one way or another.

One cannot but agree with F.J.Thomson when at the end of a well-documented study he writes: 'The extreme Orthodox theories of economy seem to have arisen in an attempt to explain how the Church could accept or reject the validity of the same sacraments at different times, or at the same time by different autocephalous churches' (418). In 1850 the baptism of William Palmer was considered invalid in Greece but recognized in Russia; there, however, his baptism had been considered invalid in 1620 (by the

Synod of Moscow). There is no point in going over the history of similar variations: they can be found in the studies I have cited. The question of the validity of Anglican orders has been examined many times since the beginning of the century, by theologians, by commissions or by official synodical authorities. The verdict has been generally favourable, whether on the nature of the orders themselves, though the Anglican Church is asked to give a better official declaration of its belief,[20] or in connection with the orders of an Anglican minister who asks to be received into the Orthodox church.[21] However, these decisions have been contested, and the churches who have made them have themselves said that they are provisional, arguing that only a Pan-Orthodox council could pronounce a firm and normative decision.[22] In fact since the Congress of Orthodox Theology held at Athens in 1935, the question has been deferred to a possible or future Pan-Orthodox synod. It figured in the schema approved by the 1961 Conference of Rhodes (ch. VII). At present it stands as the sixth theme in the preparatory plans for the Holy and Great Council. Study of it has been entrusted to the church of Roumania.[23]

The work will be very necessary. While Orthodox theologians and canon lawyers agree on a certain number of fixed positions, in particular on the need for agreement in the faith, they have developed very divergent theories on the practice of economy and even on the extent of the privileges on which it is based. F.J.Thomson sums up the positions of the Greek theologians in the following way (384: he goes on to examine those of the Russians, which are different):

1. Economy can invalidate what is valid and validate what is invalid (Androutsos, Dyovouniotis).
2. Economy can invalidate what is valid, but it cannot validate what is invalid (patriarch Meletios).
3. Economy cannot invalidate what is valid but it can validate what is invalid (Georgiadis).
4. Economy cannot either invalidate what is valid or validate what is invalid (Amvrasis, Alivisatos).

The most extreme formulation is that of Constantine Dyovouniotis, in 1913 and in 1931: 'The church, as treasurer of grace and guardian of the sacraments, has the power to change the validity of the sacraments, validating what is invalid and invalidating what is valid.'[24] This position has often been criticized, in particular by Mgr Meletios, Patriarch of Alexandria, in his discussions with Anglican bishops.[25] Generally speaking, the Orthodox theologians accept, at least in certain circumstances, the first part of Dyovouniotis' formula but not the second (invalidating what is valid). Many would support the thesis of Archimandrite D. Georgiadis: a baptism which is invalid in itself – as is the case with all heretical baptisms, even when celebrated in the name of the Holy Trinity and according to canonical forms, since otherwise the transmission of grace would be possible outside the church! – can be miraculously validated by economy. By contrast, the church cannot invalidate a valid baptism. In the first case, baptism effects 'pseudo-commencement of the kingdom of God, but grace is missing'.[26] This position, to which that of Fr Trembelas and others comes very close, seems to approximate to a common standpoint and to represent a basic element in Orthodox thought. Hamilcar Alivisatos (1940 and 1949), if I understand him rightly, differs from this only by his refusal to call sacraments thus received and validated by the church 'invalid in themselves'. Although he rejects the category of 'indelible character' and speaks in terms of 'charisma', Alivisatos seems to me to come very close to an Augustinian Catholic position.[27] In fact he criticizes an excessive view of the church's power in the realm of grace: the church is only an instrument of the administration of grace, and has no control over it. Others have made similar comments, in particular Russian theologians with ecumenical experience: Nicolas Zernov (in *Put*, February 1939) and George Florovsky. The charism (grace) does not stop at the canonical or legal frontiers of the church. If the sacraments and grace are properties of the church, we must accept that the church exists in some way outside the canonical limits of the Orthodox Church.[28] This overcomes the objection made against Augustinian theology, that it dilutes the unity of the church. The fact of ecumenism requires this development. Once one abandons the idea, which in any case is difficult to sustain, that the economy could validate invalid sacraments, one accepts in the sacraments celebrated outside the canonical frontiers of Orthodoxy a primary reality which is simply the fullness of grace that is to be found in the communion of the true church. St Basil made a good comment on this.[29] That brings us very close to what for Catholics is the theology of the *Sacramentum tantum*, the *sacramentum et res* and of 'revivis-cence'. Of course these realities must be expressed in categories acceptable to the Eastern tradition.

Clearly we cannot be satisfied with studies or declarations by canon lawyers or theologians. We would like to be given an authorized, official doctrine. However, while we wait to hear what the forthcoming pan-Orthodox Council might have to say on this question, it is worth recalling three important pointers which to some degree represent the view of the hierarchy:

1. The conference of autocephalous Orthodox churches held at Moscow in July 1948 studied the question of the recognition of Anglican orders.[30] The declaration which resulted first noted the inadequacy of the teaching of the Thirty-Nine Articles on the sacraments, and that of ordination in particular, and went on to affirm that a recognition of the validity of the Anglican hierarchy presupposed unity of faith and confession with the Orthodox Church. It then added: 'Our ruling is that the contemporary Anglican hierarchy could have the validity of its priesthood recognized by the Orthodox church provided that unity of faith and confession had first been established and explicitly formulated (as was said above) between the Orthodox and Anglican Churches. Given the establishment of this unity, which we so desire, recognition of the validity of Anglican ordinations could come about in accordance with the principle of *economy* by the decision of a Council of all the Holy Orthodox church; only such a decision can be authoritative for us.' It is not clear whether in this case the economy would create a validity which did not exist beforehand (the majority of the members of the conference believed that Anglican orders were invalid; the exception being the Roumanians, on the matter of Archbishop Parker's ordination) or whether it presupposes a sacramental rite which is valid in itself but which needs to be 'received' by the only true church by economy to obtain all the grace it conveys: that seems to be the position of Patriarch Sergius of Moscow.[31]

2. As a historian and canon lawyer, Mgr Jerome Kotsonis published an important study on this question (cf. n.17). This study is authoritative not only because the author subsequently became Archbishop of Athens and of All Greece but because it is based on documents which have an authority or legal relevance. However, one must recognize that some of the examples or even the canons invoked envisage historical situations which have now disappeared, or heresies of which only the name remains: if, in the context of tradition, this study were to do full justice to contemporary *realities* it would need to be brought up to date. However, it is his knowledge of past cases, texts and history which allows Mgr Kotsonis to achieve greater precision and firmness than his predecessors. He defines economy.[32] He specifies its aim, conditions, extension and duration, and he specifies the limits of its competence. It does not authorize any concession in the sphere of piety (= true relationship with God,

true praise) and faith (dogmas, 153-60). In dealing with the sacraments of the heterodox it is important to make a distinction
depending on whether or not those involved return to Orthodoxy
(166-75); despite texts to the contrary, it is possible to recognize
baptism, chrismation, priesthood and marriage, whether by *akribia*
or by economy; where those involved remain heterodox, their
sacraments have never been recognized as valid in themselves
(175-80). Mgr Kotsonis is anxious to note that economy and condescension cannot be identified *tout court* (94f.): of course, some
texts take this course because the use of economy is motivated by
indulgence.[33] Condescension applies to a broader sphere than
economy; it is a general and inward inspiration, whereas the
economy is a precise and relatively well-defined institution. Finally,
Mgr Kotsonis affirms that the Orthodox economy is a very different
matter from the Latin *dispensatio* (92f.). The two were identical
during the first millennium, but, from the time of Gratian, the
dispensatio came to be used in specific legal contexts, homologous
and governed by a strict law: it 'ceased to be a spontaneous activity
of the church, governed on each occasion by a tender concern for
man, and it has become a legal institution with the result that it often
loses the freshness and flexibility which it previously had' (93).

This brings us to that genius of Orthodoxy, which not only has no
need to make definitions, but even has a need not to make definitions, while at the same time demonstrating the *theological* aspect
of the economy. Mgr Kotsonis shows that economy imitates the
'philanthropy' of God; his comments are to the point, interesting
and profound. However, to oppose the Latin West at this point,
even if support could be found in the literal sense of many of the
canonical texts and treatises, would reveal a failure to take into
account the legal realities, the question of authority and how to
exercise it; of legal procedures, their justification and application,
though a number of studies have clearly brought this out at a certain
level: one need only cite those by C.Lefebvre, L.Buisson, P.Fedele
and W.Bertrams. However, that is a question we cannot discuss
here. In fact the Eastern use of economy as explained by Mgr
Kotsonis seems to be identical with the canonical or pastoral power
of the church.[34]

3. In a very brief but substantial report, Mgr Pierre L'Huillier,
Bishop of the Chersonese, sought to give a very precise definition of
the *official* positions of Orthodoxy, which are betrayed rather than
explained by the comments of some canon lawyers.[35] In fact this
report is directed towards only one question: the validity of the

sacraments celebrated outside Orthodoxy. That simplifies matters a great deal. The point he seeks to make is to establish that *'the economy has no specifically creative power:* it can compensate for deficiencies but could not make good a defect either in a constitutive element of the sacramental rite or in the capacity of the minister' (the continuity of the apostolic succession and a correct doctrine of the priesthood and the sacraments). The author distinguishes 'three categories: 1. what is authentic; 2. existing practices which are defective but can be made good; 3. the taints of an intrinsic defect which results in absolute nullity. The economy could only apply to individual cases in the second category'.

As a further help to reflection on the possible use of the idea of economy in doctrinal matters, at this point I want to quote at length M.J.Marx, *Filioque und Verbot eines anderen Glaubens auf dem Florentinum. Zum Pluralismus in dogmatischen Formeln*, 1977, 333-40.

The indeterminacy of the concept of economy corresponds with the genius of a theology which cannot and will not make definitions. Interpretation, too, must be content with describing the various situations in which this concept has been used: thus by noting the differing weight placed on its semantic value we can identify what the Greeks at Florence understood by economy.

In the middle of 1437, against the background of a conciliar discussion with the Latins, Demetrios Palaeologos Cantacuzenos, the imperial minister, proposed 'that the orator designated to address the Latins should maintain a tone of gentleness and friendship, with a bearing, deference and economy which make it clear that the reason for the schism is the addition to the creed'.[36] We can see that 'economy' here has no theological connotations. It is the equivalent of sweetness and friendship.

Three years earlier the question had been raised as to who was to preside over the council of union to be called at Constantinople. Christophoros Garatoni argued that the papal legate should preside, as an expression of his rights of primacy. The patriarch and his entourage were against this. Taking their stand on the acts of the ancient synods, they showed that the representatives of another patriarchate had never presided over a synod during the lifetime of the person who held title to the see under whose jurisdiction the synod was to be held. They could cite the Second Council of Constantinople, which Pope Vigilius had attended in person without being president. That role had fallen to the emperor. However, the emperor supported Garatoni. Syropoulos reports: 'And he praised the economy highly, adding that as far as he was concerned, if it would do some good he would go so far as to surrender one of his imperial prerogatives' (*synkatabainein*).[37] Here, *oikonomia* is synonymous with *synkatabasis* and signifies a magnanimous renunciation of personal privileges; more generally, it signifies being easygoing in the application of canonical prescriptions.

From that point the concept is open to a pejorative sense. Thus Scholarios argued, before the Council, for a union which would be dogmatic and not just economic. In concluding his two memoranda he sums up:

> My advice has been that we should not think of the economy as some would like to do: rather, we should form a union on the basis of truth and common dogmas. Such a union is brought about by accepting a single proposition on the point at issue and promulgating it in a symbol of faith: perhaps accepting an addition or perhaps rejecting it, depending on what the grace of God may prescribe.[38]

Here 'economy' denotes a bad compromise over a matter of faith, which is what happened at the Council of Lyons for purely pragmatic reasons. A contrast is made between economy of this kind and honesty in dogma, which seeks to define a common formulation as a basis for union. In this case the alternatives are: either the Latins remove the *Filioque* from the creed or the Greeks introduce it.[39]

As will emerge in due course, from this point on Scholarios envisaged a solution along the lines of the compromise at Florence. After the Council, he hesitated for a while between that and the rigorist position of Mark Eugenikos. It was then that Mark wrote to him: 'We have been filled with great sorrow on learning that you have gone over to the position of our adversaries and that with the worst "economists" you peer from the side of the *middle ways* and the *economies*.'[40]

The economies (in the plural) fought against here denote the same thing as the *mesotetai*, the bad compromises, which are similarly condemned. Elsewhere Mark Eugenikos leaves no doubt that he is thinking of the definition of Florence.[41] The 'economists' are the Latin-speaking opportunists who have embarked on a bad compromise.

The response of Scholarios is interesting here. First he insists on the fact that his pleas for union were misunderstood and falsified by those 'who did not know how to distinguish between economy and *akribia* or their *kairoi*'.[42] From that point on he also wants to keep silent, but in conclusion he affirms:

> Certainly, as you say, there is no middle term between truth and lie. But this problem is full of difficulties and questions, as is known by anyone versed in the subject. When the truth has to be established, antithetical statements are pure lies, while the true doctrine is to be defined as a *mean* and yet as the truth.[43]

This is what Scholarios means. Confronted with the alternatives of the Latin *filioque* and the Photian *ek monou tou patros*, *akribia* leads him to decide for one or the other, a choice which has to find its expression in the creed. But in that case *akribia* comes out wrongly, as the question is too complex to be settled by a pure 'either-or'. It would end up contrary to the truth, which in this case can only be found in a *via media*: recognition of the *filioque* on the level of doctrine and the *status quo* in the case of the creed.[44]

We find the same position in Gregory Mamus who, like Scholarios, appeals to Gregory of Nazianzus over against Mark Eugenikos.[45] According to him, the true faith is a mean between Jewish monotheism and pagan polytheism.[46] Anyone who takes an extreme position is thus, according to Gregory Mamus, hyperbolic, since *he mesotes esti kai aletheia*.[47]

These ideas were less completely strange to MarkEugenikos than his polemic at the Council might suggest. He has no difficulty in coming to terms with the fact that the Fathers can depart from *akribia* in matters of faith depending on the various *kairoi* and take a middle course. At Ferrara he affirmed this quite explicitly when the Latins argued that the purifying fire after death was material and limited in duration, following Gregory of Nyssa and Augustine: that was to go beyond the requirements of the time and human needs. However, they did this only to avoid the contradiction of an opposition to the Origenist thesis of a universal remission of sins, which would have involved the equally false antithesis that there was no remission of sins.[48] Mark Eugenikos himself also made a proposal for union:

> We ought rather to understand this purifying fire that your doctors have affirmed for the time immediately after death in allegorical terms, and not materially, as they have done by economy... In this way we live united, and with the truth.[49]

Here we can see clearly the ultimate significance of the economy for Mark Eugenikos: it is a concession of love, which, considering the philanthropy of God, takes the specific situation into account and can make even dogmatic rigour subordinate to it when it is a matter of leading men to God. With this 'economy' even Mark Eugenikos can excuse new and unusual doctrines, not to mention the *filioque* of the Latins.

Filioque *and economy*

Before the Council, the Greeks were already open to the idea that the *filioque* had been introduced into the creed on the basis of economy. We can see this from Scholarios, who led the Latins to think that they would not disgrace their saints if they suppressed the addition. In fact, the saints decided well, because they only put the *filioque* in the creed 'of necessity and for clear reasons'.[50] Mark Eugenikos echoed Scholarios when, at the beginning of the discussion, at Ferrara, he said:

> I have heard from one of your philosophers that this addition was made on the basis of the economy and to correct certain people who did not believe correctly. In that case, act now as well with economy and suppress it, so as to win over the brothers whose separation must cause you a good deal of pain, unless you are inhuman.[51]

Mark Eugenikos concedes nicely that the addition to the creed may have had its *kairos*. But that is no reason for keeping it in a commmon creed. He gives his reasons in another context: one should not impose on the whole church as a binding truth of faith what several Fathers have said by economy.[52] That would be the case if the *filioque* remained in the creed. That is why the Latins should magnanimously renounce any right they might have had in a particular situation to insert the *filioque*, and for the good of the church and its unity, restore the creed to its ancient integrity.

Of course the compromise at Florence called for quite a different economy. It was the Greeks who were to be generous enough to renounce the right given to them by their interpretation of the conciliar decree forbidding any change, and to recognize the historical legitimacy which the *Latin* form of the creed had acquired. The majority of the Greeks showed themselves ready for this economy when, at Florence, they became convinced that the Latin pneumatology really came from the Fathers. Scholarios had already foreseen this before the council as a 'third way', if the alternatives which he had first envisaged, the reception or the suppression of the *filioque*, proved impracticable.[53] In that case, the two sides ought at least to unite over a common opinion (*gnome*) and leave the creed as each had recited it hitherto, with or without the *filioque*. In this connection Scholarios said: 'That does not agree totally with the *akribia* of the faith, but at least it respects the agreement of the fathers and our correct understanding of the faith.'[54]

After the interruption to the public sessions, the Greek majority began to move together in the direction indicated by Scholarios. An intervention by Dorotheos of Mytilene on 11 April is typical:

> Why do you still discuss and torment yourselves over insoluble problems? Recognize that our dogma is pious, but also that what the Latins have put in the creed by way of explanation and explicitation comes from the Fathers and is pious. Finally, the sacred creed has been composed from the writings of the saints, and it is from them that the Latins have taken the *filioque*. Our creed, too, is certainly pious, but theirs is by no means without value. We are both governed by one faith, one piety and one God, triune and one.'[55]

At this moment the Latins seem finally to have made it plain that in the question of the addition to the creed they would be content with the *status quo*. That emerges from the sources, even if they did not say it in so many words. Indeed, on the very day that Dorotheus made the comments quoted above, the Emperor sent a message to the Pope.

> We have received the creed of the Seven Holy Councils. We have added nothing to it and taken nothing away. Rather, we are content with what the Fathers have expounded to us. You have shown that what what you have inserted in the holy creed comes from the saints. You want to retain it. We are not in a position simply to receive the addition. You cannot remove it from the creed. What is the point of discussions, confrontations, proofs and oaths? But your Holiness can reflect, and, if there is another way of union, we shall take it; otherwise, we shall go home in peace.[56]

There was another way. Three days afterwards, Scholarios was able to communicate to the Greek synod that union was possible without the Greeks accepting the addition or the Latins having to suppress it:

> There is no longer anything to hinder us from doing that for which we have come. For the dogma of the Latins has the support of

numerous witnesses, of which each is worthy of faith. And we can ally ourselves with them without any innovations in the creed.[57]

From that moment, according to Mark Eugenikos, there began to be talk in favour of the economy and condescension (*oikonomia kai synkatabasis*) and references to the agreement of the Fathers.[58] Syropoulos gives a detailed account of this disussion.[59] Particularly at this point, we need to read his account with care, since his bad conscience after the council led him to attach an exclusively pejorative sense to the terms *oikonomia* and *synkatabasis*,[60] which completely disguises the agreement indicated above.

According to Syropoulos it was above all the Patriarch who argued for the compromise on the basis of the possibility of economy and condescension and the urgency of political considerations. Thus, against Syropoulos, he argued:

> The union and the peace of the churches are very necessary and useful to us. We should also make use of some economy to achieve them, for if we agree on some partial concession and as a result obtain an advantage which proves of great benefit both for us and for the preservation and increase of our land, our enemies, seized by fright, discouragement and dismay as a result of this, will energetically treat with us and negotiate our friendship. We should in no way be prejudiced against making some small concession.[61]

The Patriarch tried to convince Mark Eugenikos with the same arguments,[62] but the latter and his circle objected that in matters of faith it is impermissible to make accomodations.[63] When the Patriarch pointed out that it was not as if the concession was a great one, Mark replied that the same proposal had been made to St Theodore Graptos.[64]

Theodore Graptos had come from Palestine to Byzantium under the first iconoclast Emperor, Leo III, and there, with his brother, he had preached against iconoclasm. Both were put in prison and tortured. One day – this is what the brothers wrote to Bishop John of Cyzicus – the prefect came again to their cell and in exchange for their freedom asked nothing more than that they should receive communion together. Mark Eugenikos used Theodore's response in his reply to the Patriarch: 'What you have just said is like someone making the following request: All I ask is to cut off your head once, and after that you can go where you like!'[65]

In the Memoirs of Syropoulos there are other discussions of economy in passages which Marx does not quote: p.450, 22, the Patriarch's comment that 'dissidents must be treated with economy'; p.400, 5f., Philanthropenos urging Syropoulos himself to sign: 'You too should make some economy and concession.'

7

A Structure of Duality in Unity?
East and West, 'Complementarity'

The problem of the one and the many is one of the most basic questions to have preoccupied philosophers in their thinking. There is a certain unity of being among entities. That is our problem, too. V. Soloviev saw uniplurality as the ideal of Christianity.[1]

In this universal problem, human experience has discovered something like a structure of duality in unity. It seems that things are distributed in pairs, or between two bounds which contain and embrace reality: heaven and earth, two poles, high and low, rising and setting. And again, day and night, sun and moon, man and woman, father and mother, right and left, two sides of the body. Granted there is only one heart, but there are two legs, two arms or two hands, two eyes.

Biblical thought also adopted this dual structure. Hebrew expresses a totality by linking two categories, coupling two terms which are relatively opposed: land and sea, man and woman, young and old, bone and flesh, day and night, and so on.[2] One has only to reread, for example, the Benedicite in Dan.3.57-88. Biblical language, Hebrew, is fond of expressing the same idea twice, in equivalent terms: 'What is man that thou art mindful of him, or the son of man that thou rememberest him?'[3] This is the famous parallelism of the Psalms.

In both Old and New Testaments, testimony has to come from two witnesses.[4] That is more than a judicial procedure; it is a plenary structure. That is why I have also argued that one can appeal to this law over the duality of scripture and tradition.[5]. Beyond question the gospel commandment to send out messengers two by two is connected with this twofold testimony.[6] It is certainly legitimate to recall in the same context the figures of Moses and Elijah (the law and the prophets), Peter and Paul, the two witnesses of the Apocalypse (11.3f.).

I have done no more than touch on what seems to be a structure of creation and the revealed divine economy, in order to explain the mediaeval vision of the two powers, a vision which is also presented in the monuments.[7] Duality in unity. Dual unity. Might that not have a hidden but profound relationship with the one who was the climax and the model of all creatures, the incarnate Word: two natures in hypostatic union?

My question now is whether north and south, east and west might not represent a typical distinction and division of the people who together are called to form the church. I think they do. In my view this is a significant fact for unity and catholicity, above all the duality between east and west.[8] That between north and south is important, but it is to be found in the same Western cultural world.

There can be no question of giving a detailed and documented account.[9] Here is a very basic outline:

(i) The East

General character. Mode of theologizing

The East takes its stand on the Fathers and the Ecumenical Councils, which have stated the essentials. Philosophy and reasoning serve for training theologians and for discussion; not, as in Latin Scholasticism, to extend doctrine by new conclusions. Furthermore, there is little or no reference to a central *magisterium*; there is no Denziger. The manuals of theology are comparable to those of Roman Catholics, and moreover make wide use of Western publications, but theologians express their views of things in a climate independent of magisterial interventions.

Given the link with the Fathers, the Councils, the liturgy, this is a theology much suffused by 'theology' (Trinity) and 'economy' (christological dogma).

The Orthodox tradition is marked by a very lively sense of the impossibility of knowing 'God'. Hence its apophatic character. We can find in the West a large number of extremely strong statements about the transcendence of God, the reality of which surpasses every creaturely conception or expression, but the use made of concepts and reasoning as a means of knowledge is much more active than in the East. Western scholasticism strikes Easterners as being rationalism.

Eastern thought is happier with synthesis than with analysis. Symbolism plays a great role here: think, for example, of what is said about the eucharist, leavened bread and the zeon rite (the addition of boiling water to the chalice). The West theologized in an analogous fashion down to the last third of the eleventh century (the so-called Gregorian reform; the first scholasticism; that was the great turning point).

General ethos. The root of the differences

I think that this lies in different ways of seeing the relationships between nature and grace. But while one may talk of 'grace', in the East there is no developed theology of 'created grace' (this expression appeared in the West in 1245); here the concern is with the gift (and gifts, charisms?) of the Holy Spirit. Nature and grace are like image and likeness. Grace perfects nature, turns the image into the likeness and finally leads to *teleiosis* or *teleiotes*, which is properly speaking 'divinization', by communicating that aspect of the divinity in which human beings can share. Similarly, the true and living knowledge which produces other things than concepts is fulfilled in a *gnosis*-faith.

That produces an optimistic and joyful note. By the exercise of virtue (asceticism), human freedom cooperates (synergy) with the gift of God, which is particularly communicated in the sacraments. Everything is illuminated by Easter. Hence, too, there is a *cosmic* optimism. The world is called to be transfigured.

There is intense experience of this in the holy liturgy, penetrated throughout by the mystery of the Trinity, by Easter, by the presence of the Mother of God and the saints. This is the *mysterious* character felt by the Protestants F.Kattenbusch and A.Harnack.[10] One could almost establish an equivalence between church, tradition and liturgy. The liturgy is utterly penetrated by the tradition, handing it on in a vivid way and making it live. A number of Greek accounts of the church are commentaries on the liturgy or explanations of the church building. The liturgy is the communication of the mystery of the Trinity, it is 'heaven on earth'. At the same time, it communicates the reality of the church. The priest celebrating behind the iconostasis signifies the hidden mystery of God. The deacon establishes, as did Christ, communication between the priest and the faithful. Those in whom the Spirit distributes the variety of his gifts, bring about the mystery. St John Chrysostom speaks in this connection of the 'priestly *pleroma* of the bishop'.[11]

Some specific topics

The church is felt to be a mystery. It is understood in very sacerdotal terms. But the whole body is living and active; there is a theology of sobornost, reception. Roman ecclesiology gives the Orthodox the impression of being legalistic, external. To tell the truth, they are all too ready to label everything Western in this way: the West is the place of darkness; they spit in that direction as against the devil. This feeling shows a good deal both of clear-sightedness and of ignorance, of a lack of interest in whatever is not Orthodox.

Sacraments. The way in which the liturgy is expressed demonstrates that it is God who is at work there. Not 'I baptize you', but 'X is baptized...' and so on. The mediaeval West put the accent more on the priest. That is right and proper for the eucharist; consecration comes about through the recital of the institution or the epiclesis. However, the revision of rites since Vatican II has brought them much nearer to the rites and the spirit of the East.[12]

Church Government. In the East, the patriarchates are like nations, with a Holy Synod around the Patriarch; the decisions are taken by councils and there is a steady refusal of what Vatican I made a dogma. The breaking points have corresponded to the times when papal authority was at its greatest.

Monasticism. In the East, there are no orders or congregations (in the plural) created in response to the needs of the church militant, but one, eschatological *monastic* state, dedicated to the other world. The monks have played a major role down history, embodying and expressing the conscience of Orthodoxy, sometimes with quite stubborn violence.

Piety. One of the characteristic features of Orthodoxy is the significance and the cult of icons. While we share the dogma of Nicaea II (787), the role played by images and the significance attached to them are very different in each case. However, it must be recognized that we Westerners are at ease in the prayer and among the mysteries of Orthodoxy. This is truly the same church on the spiritual level.

(ii) Complementarity?

More than fifty years of careful study, numerous contacts and a good deal of reading have led me to the firm conclusion that at the sacramental level, i.e. where the supernatural mystery is expressed in our world, East and West are the same church. Let me anticipate here what will be one of my final conclusions. The bull of union *Laetentur coeli* proclaimed at Florence on 6 July 1439 speaks of the *mater ecclesia* who rejoices at the union of the Latin church and the Greek church. In our present situation, with communion still imperfect, Paul VI has spoken of a 'universal and holy church of Christ' which always embraces the two sister churches.[13] Here are two ways of expressing this unity, even identity, which exists in two different ways of living out this same identity. Even what is held in common differs on the level of tangible and historic expression.

I think that Christian humanity is made up of two types, with some secondary inward variations. It would be difficult for me to *prove* that my conclusion is correct. My conviction has grown out of fifty years of study of the present as well as the past. Others may not agree and offer their criticisms, but that is how I feel. It is on that basis that I touch on the notion of 'complementarity', though an examination of this notion could and even should be undertaken, even if my convictions about East and West are rejected. In fact this notion is of concern to the problem of 'diversity in unity' as such.

The idea of complementarity was introduced by Niels Bohr at the International Congress of Physics at Como in 1927.[14] As a scientist Bohr made a most important contribution towards developing our knowledge of the atom. The basic elements of matter had been classified under two distinct categories, waves and particles. However, in 1905 Einstein questioned whether light should be interpreted solely in terms of waves. In 1924, L. de Broglie showed that a wave is associated with every particle, and vice versa: electrons, classic types of particles, displayed the characteristics of waves. Particle and wave are concepts which cannot be reduced to each other. 'The concept of a particle is bound up with the idea of localization, while by contrast the idea of a wave supposes a certain diffusion in space. The concept of frequency is essential to the idea of the wave and is completely foreign to the concept of the particle. Nevertheless, one was led to associate the two representations in the same entity' (Morren, 138).

> The electron, like the other basic elements of physics, thus has two irreconcilable aspects which it is necessary to invoke in turn to explain all its properties. These are like the faces of an object that one cannot contemplate all at once in its entirety but which have to be envisaged in turn if the object is to be described completely. Bohr calls these two aspects 'complementary aspects',

understanding by this that these aspects are on the one hand contradictory and on the other complementary.[15]

Bohr himself generalized from his idea of complementarity, making it a kind of epistemological principle. He applied it to science and religion, to cultures, to justice and mercy, to the antimony of will and intelligence in God. Others have extended the applications further, e.g. Pascual Jordan to psychiatry, to express a presence of the non-dominant 'mes' in the actual 'me'. G. Howe connects the Barthian concepts of *Enthüllung* and *Verhüllung* repectively with the notions of mercy and justice (no.13).[16] M.H.Schrey (cf. n.13) recalls the pairs *Glauben-Verstehen*, history and kergyma, institution and event, not to mention analysis and synthesis.

One can see that because of its vagueness, there is a risk that the idea of complementarity will be employed too easily. That the same reality should be seen in two different ways is insufficient justification for describing these views as complementary, except in this broad sense which proclaims the limitation of all intellectual human constructions and hence the possibility, the need and the advantage of another construction enriching the treasure of our cultural heritage. The quest for truth calls for relationship and dialogue between minds.[17] Speaking of the syntheses achieved by St Thomas and by St Bonaventure, Etienne Gilson wrote:

> It is clear that if these two doctrines are organized in accordance with two different initial preoccupations, they will never see the same problems in the same perspective, and that consequently one will never respond to the precise question that the other raises. The philosophy of St Thomas and that of St Bonaventure complement each other as the two most universal interpretations of Christianity, and it is because they complement each other that they cannot either exclude each other or coincide.[18]

That is not quite the same as Bohr's complementarity. In the case of Bonaventure and Thomas, the same individual mind cannot appropriate both visions at the same time. Would that not be the case for the trinitarian theology of Orthodoxy on the one hand and Roman Catholicism on the other? It is in this sense that the decree *Unitatis redintegratio* declares:

> What has already been said about legitimate variety we are pleased to apply to differences in theological expressions of doctrine. In the study of revealed truth East and West have used

different methods and approaches in understanding and confessing divine things. It is hardly surprising, then, if sometimes one tradition has come nearer to a full appreciation of some aspects of a mystery of revelation than the other, or has expressed them better. In such cases, these various theological formulations are often to be considered complementary rather than conflicting, *potius inter se compleri dicendae sint quam opponi* (no.17).

My study of the procession of the Holy Spirit in the Greek Fathers on the one hand and in the Latin tradition on the other has led me to recognize that there are two constructions of the mystery, each of which is coherent and complete – although each is unsatisfactory on some point – and which cannot be superimposed. It is a case for applying Bohr's saying, 'The opposite of a true statement is a false statement, but the opposite of a profound truth can be another profound truth.' The equivalence affirmed by the Council of Florence between *dia tou huiou* and *Filioque* is not really adequate. More than theology is at stake here. As Fr Dejaifve has noted, it is at the level of dogma that the two constructions are to be found.[19] However, these are two constructions of the mystery experienced by the same faith. The *Mater Ecclesia* of Florence, the 'universal and holy church of Christ' of Paul VI (above, n.12) embraces the two. She breathes through her two lungs!

8

What is a Rite?

There is an argument over the origin of the word, cf. A.Joubeir. Its primary meaning is very general. It signifies:

A habitual mode of action

Erat ei vivendum latronum ritu, 'he had to live as a brigand' (Cicero, *Philippics*, 2,25,62); *Graeco ritu, non Romano, facere*, 'to act in a Greek, not in a Roman way' (Varro, *De lingua latina* VII, 88); *ritu animalium*, 'like animals' (Pelagius and numerous mediaeval authors, cf. S.Alszeghy, *Nova Creatura*, Rome 1956, 188); *secundum ritum paganorum*, 'as the pagans do' (*Leges Saxonum*, 775-99, in Mirbt, *Quellen zur Geschichte des Päpstums*, 237, VII; *secundum ritum sacri palatii*, 'according to the manner, the custom, of the palace' (Leidrad, Archbishop of Lyons, to Charlemagne, MGH, *Epp.* IV, 543); *licet consuetudines pro ritu et proprietate gentium sunt discretae, uno spiritu omnes consecrantur*, 'although the customs vary depending on the modes of action peculiar to each people' (Rathier of Verona, c.940, *Praeloquiorum libri* VI, lib. III, tit.V. n.9, PL 136, 224); one could add examples indefinitely, e.g. Ordericus Vitalis, *...qui novas traditiones praeferunt Patrum ritibus*, 'those who prefer new traditions to the customs of the Fathers' (*HE* III, lib.VII chs.25f., PL 188, 644).

The totality of religious observances or practices

In the *Passio Sanctorum Scilitanorum*, in 180, of which we have the proconsular acts (no.22), the proconsul Saturninus pronounces the death penalty on Speratus and others who profess *ritu Christiano vivere* and refuse to return *ad morem Romanorum* (Kirch, no.73). However, in the *Acta proconsularia* of the martyrdom of St Cyprian it is the noun *caerimoniae* and the verb *caerimoniari* which are employed by the proconsuls Paternus and Valerius. Cyprian refuses

Romanas caerimonias recognoscere, 'to honour Roman rites'. Cf. nos.301, 303/4, 304 in C.Kirch, *Enchiridion Fontium*.

In the Theodosian Code, *ritus* = all religion, including faith (XVI, 5,52: in 412). *Cultus* there has the same sense: XVI, 5,12 *catholicae communionis cultus*. St Augustine: *Schisma, ni fallor, est eadem opinantem atque eodem ritu colentem quo coeteri, solo congregationis delectari dissidio*, 'Unless I am mistaken, schism consists in agreeing to depart from the community while keeping the same ideas and practising the same ceremonies' (*Contra Faustum* XX,3; PL 42, 369).[1] Cf. St Isidore, *De fide catholica* II, 27, 1 (PL 83, 535 C); Fourth Council of Toledo, 633, canon 59 (Martin-Martinez, *Concilios Visigoticos*, Barcelona-Madrid 1963, 211).

The pope promised *disciplinam et ritum ecclesiae, sicut inveni... custodire* , 'to keep the discipline and the ceremonies of the church as I have received them' (*Liber diurnus*, form.83, ed. Sickel, 92). Gregory VII reproaches the kings of Leon and Navarre that Spain has become separated *a Romano ritu: Reg.*I, 64, ed. Caspar, 93, which is explained in these terms: *Romanae ecclesiae ordinem et officium, in ordine ecclesiastico divinum officium*, 'the ritual and liturgy of the Roman Church', 'the divine office in the celebration of the church'.

In the twelfth century, the word sometimes has the global sense of 'a way of doing (*consuetudo*)', thus in Anselm of Havelberg (*Dial.* III,2, PL 188, 1211, numerous instances in cols.1140f.) and in St Bernard (*Vita Malachiae* 4, n.8; PL 182, 1079), but sometimes the more precise sense in which we are interested, thus in the famous *Epist.* 174, 1 to the canons of Lyons who introduced a feast of the Immaculate Conception: *novam inducendo celebritatem, quam ritus Ecclesiae nescit...*, 'introducing a new celebration of which the custom of the church is unaware' (*PL* 183, 333); ibid., no.9 : *alioquin nulla ei ratione placebit contra Ecclesiae ritum praesumpta novitas*, 'otherwise there would be no reason for him to agree to introduce an innovation against the custom of the church' (col.336).

This extensive sense of *ritus* can extend as far as to signify the statutes or the laws which govern the social order of a particular people. That seems to me to be the sense of this text of Simon of Tournai (died after 1219): *Numquam princeps habet excommunicationis gladium nisi aliquo foedere religionis subiecti ei essent astricti ad parendum iureiurando vel alio secundum consuetudinem diversorum rituum. In omni enim ritu coniuncta sunt ista duo: regnum et sacerdotium*. 'The prince only has the sword of excommunication by virtue of some bond of religion; his subjects would be obliged to obey him by an oath or otherwise according to the custom of the diverse established rites. For these two things are conjoined in every established rite: the royal and the priestly power.'[2]

Frequently, however, *ritus* is used in connection with a particular act of worship: in connection with Gregorian chant, *ritum nostrum sequamini*, 'follow our way of doing things'.[3] Leo IX to Michael Cerularius and Leo of Ochris on the subject of unleavened bread: Christ did not hide from Peter *cultum sive ritum visibilis sacrificii*, 'the celebration or the rite' (Jaffé 4302, PL 143, 748). With the extraordinary 'Anonymous Norman', about 1100, the word goes back to denoting the way of practising an act of worship.[4]

Gerhoh of Reichersberg, about 1130: *baptismus, ritu ecclesiastico celebratus, ullo modo sit iterandus*, 'baptism, celebrated according to the rite of the church, must never be performed a second time'.[5] Innocent IV (died 1254): *ritus seu consuetudo ungendi, in baptizando, per totum corpus* (no.2), *ritus secundum quem patriarcha una cum... simul Chrisma conficit* (no.5). 'The rite or practice of anointing all the body at baptism', 'the rite according to which the patriarch, with ..., consecrates the chrism'.[6] Albertus Magnus, on the subject of the way in which the Orthodox baptize, *baptizatur N...* (*IV Sent. d 3 a.2*), Borgnet XXIX, 65. At the Council of Trent, in the discussion whether communion should be in two kinds or in one kind, the word *ritus, ritus Catholicus*, is used.[7]

It seems to have been when the Latins encountered the Greeks in southern Italy, and from the time of the Fourth Crusade, that *ritus* in the singular came close to having the sense which we give the word when we say, for example, 'the oriental rite'. Hergenröther thought that this began with Celestine III (1191-1198).[8] The question concerned the proper time for ordinations, and also the ordination of a Latin by a Greek bishop. The Pope pronounced the general principle of the *non commixtio rituum*, the principle of the non-mixing of rites, *Decretals* 1,11, 9 (Friedberg II, 120).[9] Innocent III, who succeeded Celestine III, said that everyone has to be ordained and to celebrate in accordance with his rite:[10] the word has a specific meaning, 'what is done regularly', and not yet the modern sense of '*the* rite'. In 1254, Innocent IV published his letter *circa ritus Graecorum* (DS 449-57). In 1273 the Franciscan Jerome of Ascoli sent Gregory X the report that the pope had asked for in connection with the Council of Lyons. Its title is *Littera ad concilium transmissa de errore Graecorum et ritu, quem tenebant*, 'Letter sent to the Council on the error of the Greeks and the customs that they observe'; this says *quid si quis Latinus ad ritum eorum transeat, vel baptizant eum, vel reconciliant suo modo*, 'what (is to be done or thought) if a Latin goes over to their rites or they baptize him or reconcile him in accordance with their way of doing things'.[11] *Ritus* tends to take on its modern sense. St Thomas Aquinas always makes his concepts precise. Evidently he uses the word *ritus*, in the plural, in the sense of ceremonies (e.g. IV *Sent.* d.13, q.1 a.2 qa 6; *ST* Iª IIae q.102 a.6 ad 11; IIa 2ae q.10 a.11); perhaps also the *novo cedat ritui* of the *Pange lingua* does not denote the substitution of the whole of rule of the gospel for the rule of law, but only the substitution of the bread and wine for sacrificial animals (cf. *Comm.in Heb.* c.5.lect.1). But in more formal passages Thomas gives *ritus* (in the singular) the precise sense of the conditioned expression of a religion. There is *cultus, religio*.[12] The *ritus* is a precise form of this, it is the form, because *cultus = quaedam fidei protestatio per exteriora signa*, 'a certain expression of the faith by outward signs' (IIIª q.63 a.4 ad 3). There is the *cultus sacerdotii Christi* (IIIª q.63 a. 6 ad 1), but *duo dixerat (apostolus) de sacerdotio Christi, scilicet virtutem ritus eius, quia per proprium sanguinem*, 'the apostle has made two pronouncements on the priesthood of Christ, namely the efficacy of his way of working, because it is by his own blood' (*in Hebr.* ch.10 lect.2). There are *quae pertinent ad cultum Dei secundum ritum christianae vitae*, 'that which appertains to the worship of God according to the practices of the Christian life' (q.63 a.1): that would necessarily include outward signs, and thus signs in the sense of liturgical or ceremonial forms.[13] So *ritus*, used in the singular, signifies ordinances, the whole of the expressions of a religion; cf. again IV *Sent.* d.1.q.1. a.5; d.24 q.3 a. 2 qa 3 obj.2; *ST* Iª IIae q. 103 a.4 ad I; IIª IIae q.96 a. 2 ad 3; IIIª q. 75a 2 c. end. This is throughout a religious ordering as seen from the outside. The notion is *theological*.

We then find, sometimes alternating in the same writing, the global sense of *ritus*, the way peoples, the church, behave.[14] Following an identification which we find earlier in Gregory IX (1233) and Urban IV (1263), the Council of Florence uses *consuetudo* in connection with the eucharistic rite, whether speaking of the Greeks and leavened bread, or of the Latins and unleavened bread, which are said to be of equal worth.[15]

In 1521, in *De abroganda missa privata*, Luther wrote: 'I was reprimanded for speaking against this practice of the church: *clamaturi quod contra ritum Ecclesiae*.'[16] Quite habitually, he uses the term in the sense of a way of acting which is a ceremony and a usage.[17] There are passages in the Augsburg Confession, art. VII, which speak of *traditiones humanas seu ritus aut ceremonias* and of the visible existence of the church as *societas externarum rerum et rituum*. Calvin has the same identification of rites and ceremonies.[18] As to the Thirty-Nine Articles of the Anglican Church, they affirm on the one hand that the Roman Church has erred *non solum quoad agenda et caeremoniarum ritus, verum in his etiam quae credenda sunt* (art. 19), and on the other hand that *habet Ecclesia ritus statuendi ius* (art. 10).

The popes have always been concerned for unity with the Greeks. They have thought of this in terms of a return, more precisely of a return to offering obedience to the Roman Church, or to the Roman pontiff.[19] The Roman church is *mater et magistra*; at the Council of Florence the pope is called *omnium christianorum pater et doctor*. It is accepted that the Greeks, the other Orientals and then the Ruthenes (Union of Brest-Litovsk, 1595) have their rite, but they must correct their doctrines in order to make them agree with those of the Roman Church.

It was above all after the Council of Trent – a new organization of Roman centralization – that the popes and the canon lawyers came to be preoccupied with rites. The thirty years which followed the Council ended with the *Perbrevis instructio* of Clement VIII (1596), which marks a stage in the development with which we are concerned. It was necessary to prevent the Greek clergy of Italy going off to be ordained by the Greek Orthodox bishops. The Latin bishop of the local church was paired with a bishop of the Greek *rite*.[20] Thus the rite becomes an institution which takes place in its normal church sphere. It becomes an independent entity. With Pius V, who was charged by Trent to unify the Latin liturgies, the rite is seen above all from a liturgical perspective. Under Pius IV and Pius V the rite had already taken on a kind of distinct personality and ultimately came to denote a tradition in its entirety, considered as a system of laws with a life of its own, which in theory one could discuss independently of the people who made use of it; in this way Pius IV spoke of the *ritus germanicus*, Pius V of the *ritus graecus*. Paragraph 5 of the Clementine Instruction (1595) said: *Maritus latinus uxoris graecae ritum non sequatur. Latina uxor non sequatur ritum mariti graeci. Greca vero uxor sequatur ritum mariti latini. Quod si id fieri non possit, quisque conjugum in suo ritu, Catholico tamen, manere permittatur. Proles sequatur patris ritum, nisi praevaluerit mater latina*:[21] 'Let the Latin husband not follow the rite of a Greek spouse. Let the Latin spouse not follow the rite of a Greek husband. But let the Greek spouse follow the rite of her Latin husband. If that cannot

be done, let each of the spouses remain in their rite, provided that
it is catholic. The children will follow the rite of the father, provided
that the mother is not Latin.'

We should note two things from this text. 1. One can see the
glimmerings of what would be formulated explicitly by Benedict
XIV in 1742, the *praestantia ritus latini*.[22] 2. Pius IV, Pius V and
Clement VIII speak of *the* rite. These are not rites or customs, but
an entity which has its own consistency: the Greek Rite. This way of
using the word is relatively rare in the pontifical documents. One
might cite Pius IX and his decree *Romani Pontifices* of 1862, creating
the *Sancta Congregatio pro negotiis rituum Orientalium*, where he
speaks of the *ritus orientalis gentes*,[23] and Pius XII's encyclical
Orientalis Ecclesiae of 9 April 1944: 'It is necessary that each and
every one of the peoples of the Eastern rite should enjoy a legitimate
freedom over everything connected with their particular history,
and their own genius and character, provided that it does not go
against the true and integral doctrine of Jesus Christ.'[24]

There are numerous papal texts which promise the Orthodox
churches that their rites will be respected in any union.[25] It is easy to
understand matters from the Roman point of view. Putting oneself
in the place of the Easterners one might ask, 'By what right?' The
Eastern rites belong to the Oriental churches and have no need to
be guaranteed or protected outside the sphere in which they are a
living custom. The sovereign pontiffs have reserved for themselves
rights over all liturgies, Latin and Eastern. The Roman church is
mater et magistra of all churches (above, n.3). In fact this is
represented by the introduction into Eastern communities of pious
Latin practices like the rosary, stations of the cross, exposition and
worship of the Blessed Sacrament, and devotion to the Sacred
Heart, practices which had long been commended and favoured.[26]

The notion of the rite has evolved from the time of Pius IX so that
it is now identified with the liturgy in so far as there are laws for its
celebration. Since Vatican II, the *Annuario Pontificio* has had three
pages of historical notes on the Rites. There we find: 'Rite properly
signifies the organization of official prayer or the norm of liturgical
action fixed by authority, which has its public and specific expression
in the liturgy.'[27] This gave a status to the 'uniate' churches which
claimed to be authentically Eastern although they had grown up in
the Catholic Roman Latin world, taking shape in the midst of
Orthodox churches which preserved the richness and vitality of their
tradition, a tradition which Leo IX, writing to Michael Cerularius,
had called *paterna traditio sive consuetudo*.[28] In fact, as E.Lanne

shows (n.10), this was to sever the rite from its roots in the church (cf. p.23), monasticism (cf.p.31) and even dogma.[29] Hence – and I am not making this up! – purely Latin and Western priests thought that they could 'go over to the Eastern rite' simply by growing a beard and celebrating in Greek and Slavonic: better, sometimes, with 'indult', the Byzantine rite could be borrowed for a particular day or occasion! But the rite is more than just a collection of rubrics! The Orthodox were quite right to criticize such practices. Sometimes they did so with excessive aggression, suspecting the Catholics of a sinister Machiavellianism: Rome simply wanted to draw them into its net, without believing in the validity of the rite or recognizing the profundity of what it represented. We should recognize that some facts and some texts could have justified this suspicion![30]

Pius XII had already gone beyond the legalistic and liturgical concept of a rite: cf. the text quoted in n.7 above. That is what Vatican II did, since on the one hand it listened to the voice of the East, thanks particularly to the Melchite bishops and their patriarch Maximus IV. The decree *Orientalium Ecclesiarum* of 21 November 1964 began with a section *De Ecclesiis particularibus seu ritibus*.[31] This title sought to link the notion of the rite with the reality of a particular church, in short, to define the rite by the church and not the church by the rite. Paragraph 2 reads as follows:

> The holy Catholic Church, which is the Mystical Body of Christ, is made up of the faithful who are organically united in the Holy Spirit by the same faith, the same sacraments and the same government. They combine into differnt groups, which are held together by their hierarchy, and so form particular churches or rites.

Vatican II also put forward an *ecclesiological* view of the rite, not purely a liturgical one, far less one which did not go beyond rubrics: cf. *Lumen Gentium* no.23, 4; *Unitatis redintegratio* nos. 15-17; the rite is then taken as the multiple and coherent expression of the faith which a church has and continues to experience. It includes above all the liturgy, steeped in dogmatic truth, the images, the style of monastic life, the disposition of the churches, the presiding genius in the ordering of church life. I would like to illustrate the significance of this from the *Historia ecclesiastica et mystica contemplatio* attributed to St Germanus of Constantinople (PG 98, 9-454). It seems to me to meet up with authentic Orthodox accounts.[32] In this I have the agreement of Catholic friends. For example:

Those (the liturgical usages) constitute the highest, most sacred expression of the faith and life of a particular church, that is to say the church of Christ as it takes the form of a human community with its own culture and legitimate traditions.

...to take the diversity of rites as the hieratic expression of an entire conception of Christian life forged in the agelong experience of a community conscious of keeping and transmitting the apostolic tradition and the fullness of the message of Christ, refracted through its own genius.[33]

9

The Orthodox Church and the
Roman Catholic Church

(i) 'Sister churches'

The relations between the Orthodox Church and the Roman Catholic Church, which have been so difficult for more than a thousand years, have entered into a really new phase. This has come about discreetly and without haste, thanks to a prophet and a saint, Patriarch Athenagoras I and Pope Paul VI, in the happy climate of Vatican II.

The two men had embraced in Jerusalem on 6 January 1964; they had read together, from the same copy of the New Testament, one in Greek and the other in Latin, the peerless prayer of Jesus in John 17. On 21 November of the same year the Council had promulgated the very fine decree on ecumenism, *Unitatis redintegratio*, which states, among other things:

> For many centuries the Churches of the East and of the West went their own ways, though a brotherly communion of faith and sacramental life bound them together. If disagreements in faith and discipline arose among them, the Roman See acted by common consent as moderator. The Council gladly reminds everyone of one highly significant fact among others: in the East there flourish many particular local Churches; among them the Patriarchal Churches hold first place, and of them many glory in taking their origins from the apostles themselves. Hence, of primary concern and care among the Orientals has been, and still is, the preservation in a communion of faith and charity of those family ties which ought to exist between local Churches, as between sisters.

This extremely concentrated text discreetly recognized and described a form of church life different from that which has prevailed
in the West with the dominance of the development of the papacy
and in the framework of that kind of ecclesiology of the universal
church on which I have commented above (p.42).

On the last day of the Council, 7 December 1965, at one and the
same moment, in Istanbul and in the assembly in Rome, the mutual
excommunications of 1054 were consigned to oblivion, expunged
from memory. This was a liberation, a clearing of conscience: now
it was possible to start all over again. The bad memories and the
mistrust were replaced by feelings of brotherly love; the creed of
separation was replaced by the creed of love.[1] The dialogue in
charity had begun. However, from that time on it has been ballasted
with a theology of extreme importance, that of sister churches.
Before I discuss the way in which this admirable term has been used
since the Council, I shall indicate the modest information that I have
collected on its use over the course of earlier history, in connection
with the Roman church and the Eastern church.

I shall leave on one side the remoter theological foundations for
the title of sister churches which Fr E.Lanne has noted, i.e. the deep
mutual brotherly feelings in the churches of antiquity (cf. art.cit.,
n.13). I am looking for actual verbal occurrences of the expression.

In 415, Pope Innocent I called the church of Antioch 'sister of the
Roman church' (PL 20,546), That was because they both had the
same father, the apostle Peter. This is not, then, the profound
sense that we shall find with Paul VI. It is the same when, in 429,
Nestorius wrote to Pope Celestine I, 'We owe each other fraternal
and reciprocal information' (Mansi 4, 203).

When the patriarch John II (518-520) writes twice to Pope
Hormisdas that the church of Constantinople and that of Rome
make one church, he seems to be thinking in terms of the unity of
the empire and of Rome, old and new Rome.[2] There is no longer
any question of that today. To arrive at the meaning we know,
was it perhaps necessary to experience the Byzantine protest
against a degree of papal imperialism, reinforced by the ecclesiology of the Gregorian Reform?

It was Nicetas of Nicomedia who, in 1136, said to Anselm of
Havelberg, *Ita, frater charissime, in antiquis historiis nostrorum
scriptum invenitur. Verum Romana Ecclesia, cui nos quidem inter
has sorores primatum non negamus, et cui in concilio generali*

praesidenti primum honoris locum recognoscimus: 'So, ᴅᴄarest brother, that is written in our ancient chronicles. It is true that the Roman church, to which we do not refuse the primacy among its sisters, and to which we accord the place of honour as president over the general council...'[3] The whole text needs to be read! I copied it and sent it to Paul VI.

It was on another occasion, in the face of a supreme affirmation of papal authority, that Patriarch John X Camateros (1198-1206) wrote to Innocent III: 'Where do you find in the holy Gospels that Christ said that the Church of the Romans is the head and universal mother and the most catholic of all the churches at the four points of the compass; or by what ecumenical council was what you say about your church decided?... It is not, then, for these reasons that Rome is the mother of the other churches, but, as there are five great churches adorned with patriarchal dignity, that of Rome is the first among equal sisters... So the church of the Romans has the first rank, it is the first of the other churches which, as sisters (*adelphon*) equal in honour (*time*) are born of the same heavenly Father from whom, according to scripture, all fatherhood in heaven and earth derives.'[4]

We come to the modern period. At the First Vatican Council, which was hardly open to ecumenism, Mgr Papp-Szilégyi, who was opposed to the declaration of infallibility, recalled that 'the Church of the East has been our sister' (Mansi 52, 601). In 1853, N.A.Muraviev called the Western Church the sister of the Eastern Church.[5] In 1884, the metropolitan of Kiev, Plato (died 1891), did the same thing.[6]

In 1927-1928, Mgr Georges Calavassy, Bishop in Athens of the Greeks faithful to Rome, whom I knew well, carried on a theological correspondence with Mgr Chrysostom Papadopoulos, the Orthodox Archbishop of Athens. In his first letter he called Mgr Papadopoulos 'head of a sister church'.[7] We are coming close! In July 1948, in Moscow, Patriarch Alexis called the Roman church 'sister church'.[8] And so we arrive at our 'acceptable time'.

It is indeed a time of grace, with an ecumenical climate as a general background. On the Catholic side, neither John XXIII nor Paul VI nor Vatican II diminished the prerogatives of the Roman see, but they no longer acted in the imperialist manner of the Gregorian Reform and Innocent III; theirs was an attitude of openness, of service and humility, which was to lead Paul VI to fall to his knees before Metropolitan Melito and to kiss his feet, and which would make him say to Patriarch Demetrius I: 'Paul VI has made the papacy out of date.'

It was Paul VI, always an ecumenist, the creativeness of whose thoughtful and profound ventures will be appreciated by history, who took the initiative, first by announcing his election to the heads of the Eastern churches (25 June 1963) and then by writing a letter in his own hand to Patriarch Athenagoras, on 20 September 1963. This letter opened up the way to a new future; it already made the essential points.[9] Patriarch Athenagoras understood this: he had the Greek version published in the bulletin of the Patriarchate, *Apostolos Andreas*, 6 November 1963, under the title 'The Two Sister Churches'. The patriarch had already used this term in a letter to Cardinal Bea on 12 April 1962. These were the first uses of this term in the new climate of mutual openness.[10]

From that time on the use of the phrase 'sister churches' has multiplied. It was used by Patriarch Athenagoras in a telegram of 27 March 1964 to Pope Paul VI (*Tomos Agapis*, no. 58, 130f.), in a letter to the Pope on 19 May 1964 (no.65, 140f.), in the allocution made by Metropolitan Melito of Hilioupolis to Pope Paul VI on 16 February 1965 (no.87, 174f.). It was taken up again by Cardinal Willebrands at the meeting of the joint commission charged with preparing the declaration that would consign the anathemas of 1054 to oblivion, at Istanbul, on 22 November 1965 (*Tomos*, no.123, 266f.). However, by far the most profound and important text is that of the bull *Anno ineunte*, sent personally by Pope Paul VI to Patriarch Athenagoras on 25 July 1967, after Mgr Willebrands had read it out. This is the passage which is of immediate interest to us:

> In each local church this mystery of divine love is at work. Is this not the reason for that fine traditional expression, 'sister churches', which local churches love to use of one another? (cf. the decree *Unitatis redintegratio* III, 17). We have lived this life of sister churches for centuries, celebrating together the ecumenical councils which defended the deposit of faith against any alteration. Now, after a long period of division and mutual incomprehension, the Lord has allowed us to rediscover ourselves as sister churches, despite the obstacles with which we had been confronted. In the light of Christ, we see how urgent is the need to transcend these obstacles, so that we can bring to its fullness and perfection the communion existing between us, which is already so rich.[11]

This very fine text, and others like it,[12] have been worked out very carefully. Fr Emmanuel Lanne has made a thorough commentary on it, showing how it is based on the communion and brotherhood of the churches of the first three centuries and their agreement with what the decree *Unitatis redintegratio* says of the Eastern church.[13] This character of sister churches is based on the reality of a common quality as children of the same Father, in Jesus Christ, which makes the relationship fraternal; however, this quality is made specific at the sacramental level of the church not only by common baptism – which the Roman church shares with the Protestant communions – but also by a common priesthood, the apostolic succession, and the eucharist. These are realities which ensure that there is truly a church, indeed a true church.[14] Let me add three major comments from my own perspective.

1. *It is the same church.* That is presupposed by a number of historical facts, or is implied by canonical theological positions. For example, it can be found in the idea, which is quite common in the East, that it would be impossible to hold an *ecumenical* council without the patriarchate of Rome. In Florence, both sides were aware that only the participation of the two parties made the council ecumenical. According to the vocabulary used at the Council of Florence, it was a question of restoring *unio* or *unitas* between two churches, the schismatic situation between which had not affected their profound substantial community.[15] There was not a church on the one side and a group which was not the church on the other. The church was split in two.

Many of us would hold that on the level of the ancient conception of the church as a unity of faith, a sacramental reality and spiritual organism, which the Orthodox retain, it is the same church. I have often suggested this[16] and more than once have wished that the church would begin to breathe through its two lungs,[17] an image which His Holiness John Paul II has also used several times.[18] Fr Christophe Dumont, for a long time a specialist in Orthodoxy and ecumenism, has often expressed his basic conviction of the real unity between the two churches. But it is Fr Louis Bouyer who, in the framework of a positive doctrine, and by virtue of his excellent knowledge of Eastern theology, has most explicitly affirmed 'that the Orthodox Church and the Catholic church, although both sorely tempted by the spirit of division, remain a single church, and do so as of right, despite appearances which are so contrary'.[19] Do the Orthodox accept that?[20] Certainly not all do. But when he received members of the joint Orthodox-Roman Catholic commission at Rhodes on 30 May 1980, Metropolitan Spyridion twice called them 'brothers of the Eastern and Western sections of the one, holy, catholic and apostolic church'.

2. *According to two different traditions.* I have already spoken of this above (p.71) and in various publications (*L'Ecclésiologie du Haut Moyen Age*, 1968; *I Believe in the Holy Spirit*, III. *The River of Life flows in the East and in the West*, ET 1983). Between East and Catholic West, everything is similar and yet it is all different, even what is essentially the same thing!

3. The substance of faith and sacramental reality which is common to the Orthodox Church and the Roman Catholic Church does not come from the Roman church, as is the case with the Protestant communions of the Reformation. *Unitas redintegratio* links it with apostolicity. So it is that the churches are sisters, not daughters. Paul VI went so far as to speak of a 'universal and holy church of Christ' embracing the two sister churches. All these texts seem to me to raise a serious question when we think not only of all the quarrels that can now be relegated to the past but basically of the age-old ecclesiological opposition between the East and Rome. It was in fact a basic criticism of the Byzantines that the Roman church put herself in the position of *mater et magistra*, mother and mistress, and then went on to treat the other churches, particularly those of the East, not as sisters but as daughters and infants. One need only recall the protest of Nicetas of Nicomedia in dialogue with Anselm of Havelberg in 1136: *quae fraternitas, seu etiam quae paternitas haec esse poterit? ... sola Ecclesia Romana (...) jam non pia mater filiorum, sed dura et imperiosa domina servorum videretur esse ... non contemnat fratres suos, quos veritas Christi non in servitutem sed in libertatem in utero matris Ecclesiae generavit*: 'What brotherhood, or even fatherhood could there be?... only the Roman church... would not be a tender mother of her sons, but an authoritarian and harsh mistress of slaves... let her not scorn her brothers whom the truth of Christ has engendered, in the bosom of the church, not for servitude but for liberty'.[21] The comments of John X Camateros were more precise still, since they were in response to equally precise affirmations by Pope Innocent III. Writing to the emperor and the patriarch, the pope had spoken of the Roman church as *Cunctorum fidelium mater et magistra*, and of the return of the daughter to her mother.[22] After a first reply and a new letter from Innocent, amounting to a treatise on the view that Rome had of its primacy at this time, John X Camateros replied again. He said in particular: 'It is not because of the martyrdom of Peter at Rome that this Rome seeks to be the mother of the other churches. There are

five great patriarchal churches: the Roman church is the first among sisters of the same dignity (*proten hos en adelphais homotimois tynkanein auten...*). The church of the Romans is the first in order (*te taxei*); it has only this prerogative of being the first of the other churches which are, like sisters, of the same dignity and the same father, he of whom it is said that all fatherhood in heaven and on earth comes from him... But we have never learnt that she is mistress and head.'[23]

After that, we can see that to speak of sister churches raises a serious question. What do we mean by this expression? The idea of John X Camateros, taken up a hundred times by the Greeks? Athenagoras I once called the church of Constantinople 'younger sister', *neotera adelphe*.[24] Has Rome revised, adjusted, sharpened up the conception of what she is to the other churches, particularly to the Eastern churches? How can she, why should she, continue to be mother, mistress and head? Replying on 30 November 1969 to Patriarch Athenagoras, Cardinal Willebrands spoke of the ministry of Peter, coryphaeus of the college of apostles, being transmitted to his successors, and he said: 'This service of authority for unity must be looked at again in the light of the gospel and the authentic apostolic tradition, in a dialogue of love and truth between our churches, as being all churches and ecclesial communities of Christianity.'[25]

This new study is taking place. It presupposes patient and profound historical and ecclesiological rethinking.

Could one extend the character and title of sister churches, for example, to the Anglican church and the Lutheran churches? Paul VI took a step in this direction, towards the Anglican church, in the speech which he gave on 25 October 1970 for the canonization of the forty Catholic English Martyrs:

> May the blood of these martyrs cure the great wound inflicted on the church of God by reason of the separation of the Anglican church from the Catholic church... Their faithfulness to their nation assures us that on the day when – God willing – the unity of faith and Christian life is restored, there will be no prejudice to the honour and the sovereignty of a great country like England. We would not seek to diminish the legitimate prestige and the worthy patrimony of piety and usage proper to the Anglican church if the Roman Catholic church – this humble 'servant of the servants of God' – could embrace its ever-beloved sister in the one authentic commmunion of the family of Christ: with common

origins and faith, a common priesthood and discipline, a communion of saints in the freedom and love of the spirit of Jesus.[26]

The expression does not have the same content here as it does in the case of the churches of the East. There is no apostolicity here independent of that of Rome. Furthermore, the two sisters are not 'sisters' at present: the passage is about the future that is hoped for. In their reunion, which obviously presupposes agreement over the essentials of faith, they recognize each other, embrace, and behave as sisters. That signifies that each will have her own personality, that one, the younger, will not be absorbed by the other to the point of being no more than an extension of the other at the level of customs and spiritual heritage. That, then, is the theme of the 'Anglican church united, not absorbed'.

That last phrase was the title of a paper produced by Dom Lambert Beauduin which Cardinal Mercier read in his own name during the Fourth Malines Conversation in 1925.[27] There were several doubtful points, above all in the historical argumentation, in favour of an Angl.can patriarchate of Canterbury, but the basic idea is worth keeping. Mgr B.Butler has taken it up,[28] and Paul VI went so far as to echo the expression at his reception of Archbishop Donald Coggan on 28 April 1977.[29] The idea would produce the status of a uniate church. In fact, one ecumenical Anglican theologian has argued for such a status.[30] But it raises many questions.

The idea of 'types of churches', which is more general and less definite than 'the Anglican church united, not absorbed', was ventured by Cardinal Willebrands in a lecture given at Cambridge on 8 January 1970.[31] It recurred at the end of a conference given at Lambeth on 4 October 1972,[32] and then at Toronto on 8 June 1979.[33] This is the idea on which my own research has all been oriented: given that the axis of Christian faith is assured, one can accept various expressions of it. The formula seems ideal; the problems arise when it is put into practice.

(ii) 'Ecumenical' councils

Government by council occupies a very important place in Orthodox ecclesiology. Furthermore, it has always been thought that union with the Catholic church could be achieved only in a joint council.[34] That would certainly have to be the case in the future developments I would hope for and that it is our task to prepare. However, some questions arise now. Both the Roman Catholic church and the

Orthodox church have held councils separately, and call some of them 'ecumenical'. For Roman Catholics there are ecumenical councils, and John XXIII designated Vatican II the twenty-first of them. So: 1. What is it that makes a council ecumenical? 2. How valid is the list of twenty-one? 3. You cannot ask a church to do more than 'receive' a council which has been celebrated by another church. What would be the status of Roman Catholic (and Orthodox) 'ecumenical' councils held since the break in full communion? These questions have received a reply which I shall try to summarize here.

1. Various criteria of ecumenicity have been proposed and even employed, without any of them suddenly becoming valid:[35] imperial summons, the number of participants, the involvement of the five patriarchates. The approval of the bishop of Rome, at least in receiving the council, is an easy criterion to apply. It has validity, even from the point of view of Orthodox theology. This reception at least is a necessary condition. However, the best criterion is ultimately reception by the church, when the church recognizes its faith and its well-being. Still, one cannot ignore the fact that one part of the church has frequently refused to accept a particular council. The most notable case is without doubt that of the non-Chalcedonians, the self-styled Monophysites, whose christological faith is now recognized as authentic.

2. Vittorio Peri has brought into the open the question of the Roman list of ecumenical councils.[36] This list has no official status. It was made by Bellarmine, adopted on 21 October 1595 by the commission charged with specifying which Councils should go into the edition of ecumenical councils prepared by the Vatican printers. History, the touchstone of authenticity, allows us to question again the designation of the eighth council which follows the seven recognized by both Roman Catholics and Orthodox. In Bellarmine's list, this is the council of 869-870 which condemned Photius. However, Pope John VIII scrapped and abolished it.[37] It must be deleted from the list. Numerous Orthodox and Roman Catholic theologians have proposed that the eighth ecumenical council should be that of 879-880, which reinstated the patriarch Photius and communion between the two churches. I would agree with them.

3. When in 1974 I considered the question of Roman Catholic councils held during the second millennium, when full communion with the Orthodox East was broken, I proposed distinctions which had been formulated by the Anglo-Catholic theologian Darwell Stone or the Byzantine scholar Venantius Grumel, an Assumption-

ist, and indicated my agreement with this very succinct text from Fr Louis Bouyer:[38]

> The position that I have adopted in this book, according to which the Catholic Church of the West and the Orthodox Church of the East have never ceased to be one church, inevitably raises one question; can the general councils which have met in the West since the ninth century be considered ecumenical in the full sense of the word? In fact, all that I have done here is to take over a position held by the Latin Middle Ages, at least in practice, and to seek to draw all the consequences. The Latin Middle Ages never in fact put these general councils of the West on the same footing as the seven ecumenical councils of antiquity. It is only since Bellarmine, and following him, that a different position has come about. This has been established in what may be called a definitive way by Vittorio Peri in his book *Concilii e Chiese*, Rome 1965.
>
> It does not follow that the dogmatic decisions of the general councils held subsequent to the separation should not have a very high authority. In fact I have established that the church has always accepted that partial councils, in certain cases, could give definitive expression to the *mens ecclesiae*. That should be the case, up to a certain point, with all the councils summoned by the Pope and confirmed by him provided that there was substantial episcopal representation.
>
> It is no less true that because their decisions have been taken in the absence of a considerable part of the episcopacy, which would have represented a theological tradition of great antiquity, these could call for later additions which would not have been needed in the case of an ecumenical council in the earliest and fullest sense of the word, even when they can be considered infallible and therefore irrevocable.
>
> Besides, even councils of this last kind (one might think of Chalcedon after Ephesus, and then the Council of the Three Chapters) could only have dealt with one aspect of a complex question, so that their definitions would have to have been illuminated by later definitions, perhaps without the process having been finished (cf. T.Sagi Bunic, *Problemata christologiae chalcedonensis*, Rome 1969). *A fortiori*, one should admit that this could be so in the case with which we are concerned. That amounts to the fact that an acceptance, pure and simple, of the general councils of the West and their definitions without the

oppportunity for discussion cannot constitute a prelude to the reunion betwen East and West. All that the West can and should ask of the East is that the work of these councils should be accepted provisionally by the East, in a favourable light, as a positive element essential for a broader and deeper consideration of the questions involved. At the same time, the West should offer the East the same consideration of the councils and dogmatic decisions which this other part of the church is unanimous in judging to be equally important.

But from now on we have something better than the proposals of theologians. I produced the article mentioned in n.34 for the centenary of the Council of Lyons in 1274, but before the comments made by Paul VI. In his letter *Lugduni, in urbe Galliae nobilissima* of 5 October 1974, addressed to Cardinal Willebrands, his legate for the celebration of the centenary at Lyons, he wrote: '*Hoc Lugdunense Concilium, quod sextum recensetur inter generales synodos in Occidentali orbe celebratos*: this council of Lyons which is counted as the sixth general council celebrated in the Western world.'[39] The five preceding general councils were the four Lateran councils and the first council of Lyons in 1245. The same letter recognized that the 'union' of Lyons had not been 'received' by the Byzantine church.[40] To see how far we have come and the contribution to truth made by an authentic knowledge of history one need only compare what was said of this same Council of Lyons at Vatican I by Mgr Zinelli, in the name of the Deputation of the Faith.[41]

So, following Fr Louis Bouyer I have been led to recognize the compatibility of two different church orders at the level of the secondary norms of church life. I say secondary norms, for without minimizing their value and their importance, one must see them as being dependent on the primary norms, which are, first, the holy scriptures, and then the seven great ecumenical councils, the fathers and the tradition of the 'undivided church'. I am well aware of the questions that this position raises. They were raised at the time of the *Pro Oriente* colloquium.[42] I should say that this position offers an opening, a possibility. It should be criticized and sharpened by the work of our theological researches and our dialogues. For Roman Catholics this would end up in what I would call the 're-reception' of doctrines like those concerning the papal prerogatives, and of councils like Vatican I.[43] What is needed is reinterpretation and reception accepting what a better knowledge of history and openness to the truth of others through dialogue shows us that we should have accepted earlier. It is simply a question of a greater truth.

10

Diversity of Dogmatics in the Unity of Faith between East and West

At the beginning of this chapter it is worth quoting yet again some paragraphs from the Vatican II Decree on Ecumenism, because they illustrate what follows and lend it their support:

> What has already been said about legitimate variety we are pleased to apply to differences in theological expressions of doctrine. In the study of revealed truth East and West have used different methods and approaches in understanding and confessing divine things. It is hardly surprising, then, if sometimes one tradition has come nearer to a full appreciation of some aspects of a mystery of revelation than the other, or has expressed them better. In such cases, these various theological formulations are often to be considered complementary rather than conflicting. With regard to the authentic theological traditions of the Orientals, we must recognize that they are admirably rooted in Holy Scripture, are fostered and given expression in liturgical life, are nourished by the living tradition of the apostles and by the works of the Fathers and spiritual writers of the East; they are directed toward a right ordering of life, indeed, toward a full contemplation of Christian truth.
>
> This sacred Council thanks God that many Eastern children of the Catholic Church preserve this heritage and wish to express it more faithfully and completely in their lives, and are already living in full communion with their brethren who follow the tradition of the West. But it declares that this entire heritage of spirituality and liturgy, of discipline and theology, in the various traditions, belongs to the full catholic and apostolic character of the Church.[1]

This duality of tradition has not been a barrier to living for several centuries in a communion which has known moments of crisis, above all over questions relating to ecclesiastical figures. Pope John Paul II has also declared:

> At that time (the tenth century) the church of West and East was still united. However, it drew abundantly on two distinct traditions and belonged to two different civilizations, which was a great source of riches for the universal church.[2]

> For almost a whole millennium the two sister churches have grown up side by side as two great vital and complementary traditions of the same church of Christ, maintaining not only peaceful and fruitful relations but the care of an indispensable communion in faith, prayer and love which they have not wanted to endanger at any price, for all their different sensibilities.[3]

The most serious difference is over the expression of the truth on the procession of the Holy Spirit. However, today more than one Orthodox theologian recognizes that this difference did not hinder communion for several centuries and that it should not hinder the re-establishment of this communion. Mgr Damaskinos Papandreou, Metropolitan of Tranoupolis, Director of the Orthodox Centre at Chambésy and Secretary in charge or preparations for the forthcoming Pan-Orthodox Council has written: ' One can and should explain on the one hand the formulations of the Holy Greek Fathers and on the other those of the holy Latin Fathers and the *filioque*, bringing out their agreement but respecting to the full their respective originality. From the fourth century onwards the *filioque* came to be part of the Western tradition without ever having been considered an obstacle to union before this was broken for other reasons.'[4]

Is it not significant that authors who have studied the question in modern times seem to conclude that the difference in the doctrinal expression of the mystery, which they fully recognize, does not amount to an irremediable contradiction? This is the view held by scholars like M.-J.Scheeben and Fr Théodore de Régnon, both well versed in the Greek Fathers and sympathetic towards them,[5] as also by Christian Pesch.[6] Similarly, at the end of a rigorous study of 'the eternal relationship between the Spirit and the Son according to the writings of John of Damascus'[7] J. Grégoire concludes: 'Perhaps it might be asked whether the *dia Huiou* could not one day serve as a compromise between the churches of East and West. But would it not be better to draw the dogmatic consequence of the fact that the church lived for at least three centuries with divergent trinitarian

doctrines, even in the East, without producing schismatic disputes?'
Fr André de Halleux, one of the great experts on the question,
comes to the same conclusion.[8] This is also the position of Fr Louis
Bouyer, with his exceptional knowledge of the Fathers and the
spiritual traditions of the East.[9] And it is mine, at the end of a careful
study of the great witnesses of each of the traditions.[10]

Orthodox comments have come to meet us. Fr Sergius Bulgakov
expressed a conviction which I share and to which I attach great
importance.

> In practice the two parties... cannot prove the difference in their
> veneration of the Holy Spirit, despite their disagreement over the
> procession. It would appear very strange that a dogmatic diver-
> gence of such apparent magnitude should have no practical
> repercussions when normally dogma always has a practical im-
> portance and determines religious life. In the present instance,
> even the most extreme representations of the schismatic spirit
> have not been able so far to apply the pseudo-dogma to life or to
> indicate its practical consequences. One could say that neither
> the Eastern nor the Western churches have experienced active
> heresy over the Holy Spirit, which would have been inevitable
> had there been a dogmatic heresy.[11]

In fact, though there may be thematic differences which, taken to
extremes, have led to the charge of 'Christomonism' being levelled
against Roman Catholics by Orthodox theologians, we are nurtured
on the Fathers and the spiritual figures of the East. The experience
of the saints is comparable, even if, as is only to be expected, the
specific features of this experience vary depending on space and
time. The sacramental life is also comparable. Paul Evdokimov,
himself a great spiritual figure, could write: 'In the West the addition
of the *filioque* to the creed has become a liturgical tradition going
back over a millennium, but from the Eastern side as from the
Western side, despite the theological disagreement, one cannot in
practice discern any difference in the adoration of the Holy Spirit.
The lack of practical consequences indicates that the conflicting
formulae have an inadequate dogmatic basis.'[12]

This conviction held by very qualified Orthodox is bound up with
a profound and very important insight into the relationships between
faith and dogmatic formulation. Roman Catholics equally share this
perception. It is that the primary reality is not theoretical adherence
to dogmatic formulae, however useful and holy they might be, but
a vital trust of the heart, openness, and the total gift of all one's

being to Christ, our way towards God, the truth and the life. This
has been shown, for example, in the case of Theophilus of Antioch
(*c.* 180).[13] It led him to martryrdom. Perhaps the theological
expressions of the martyrs were imperfect, even in christology, but
their witness illustrated the truth of their faith over and above their
words. Möhler put great stress on that. But the most doctrinally
minded of Christians, because they are Christians first and foremost,
think in this way. 'I possess reality although I do not understand it',
says St Hilary.[14] 'The assent of faith does not end with the formula
but with the reality', says St Thomas Aquinas.[15] It is essential to the
nature of faith. When I say '*Credo* in (*Deum*), I believe *in* (God)',
I am expressing my movement of confident openness and self-
surrender. What follows is no more than making precise the conceptual content of my faith, features which belong to the Reality to
which I am bound. But the 'I' which professes this commitment only
exists in the confessing community of the church.

This confessing community lives out its faith by celebrating it. It
is no coincidence that in Scripture the doxologies are the best
expression of the dogmatic content of faith. The church prays, sings
and celebrates its faith. Dogma is only a landmark, holy though it
may be, in the church's experience of the fullness of its faith which
it attains by celebrating it.[16] There is nothing more profound and
decisive than faith lived out, expressed in spiritual life and prayer.
Now despite the difference in dogmatic formulae, that faith is the
same, and it is lived and prayed out similarly in both West and East.
To quote Mgr Damaskinos of Tranoupolis once again: 'When one
participates in the life of the church as a whole, one often recognizes
the identity of faith beyond the differences of theological vocabulary.
For the words are not prior to the life of the church; the life of the
church is prior to the words which express it. It is this life which
bears witness to life and the spirit which bears witness beyond the
word, and not the other way round.'[17]

Through the grace of God and by the very sure instincts of those
in charge, for fifteen years a dialogue of love has preceded the
theological dialogue between the Orthodox Church and the Roman
Catholic church. In parallel to this, the Orthodox Church has
pursued union with the Armenians and the non-Chalcedonian
churches 'beyond dogmatic formulae in the dynamism of the Spirit
of love'.[18]

The *filioque* was professed by the Latin fathers from the fourth
century (St Ambrose, though he was so dependent on the Greeks)
and in a number of councils from the sixth century, and was finally

introduced into the creed at a time when East and West were living in communion. The *filioque* is doctrinally necessary *in the Latin construction of the mystery* to preserve: 1. the distinction of the hypostases of the Son and the Spirit, since in the most common Latin interpretation, the persons are in reality distinguished only by an opposition of relationship, and that exists only through the processions.[19] 2. The full consubstantiality of the Son and the Father, with whom the Son has *everything* in common, apart from being Father. In fact, it was in its struggle with Arianism that the West developed this theology.

For Roman Catholic dialogue with Orthodoxy it is good to distinguish between the doctrine, which is shared throughout the West and for Roman Catholics is even the object of a dogma, and the insertion of the formula in the creed. In their exchanges with the Orthodox, the Anglicans have quite rightly made this distinction and kept the doctrine separate. That was the reaction of Pope Leo III in 810 to the demand of the emissaries of Charlemagne. We have the account of the audience, as detailed and precise as a stenographic report.[20] The Pope was in agreement over the doctrine but refused to make the insertion into the creed, while Charlemagne insisted on it. To confirm his position Leo III had the text of the creed without the interpolation, in Greek and in Latin, engraved on two silver scrolls which were hung on either side of the 'Confession', the high altar, in St Peter's, Rome, *pro amore et cautela orthodoxae fidei*.[21] It would have been a good way of celebrating the centenary of the council of 381, to which we owe the text of the Niceno-Constantinopolitan creed, had the successor of St Leo III repeated the gesture of his predecessor, thus 'receiving' the symbol as the West 'received it' sixteen centuries ago.

In its original text, the Niceno-Constantinopolitan creed does not express anything of the eternal relations between the Spirit and the Word-Son. We might wish that one day a completely ecumenical council could do this. A number of Greek Fathers have moved towards a role for the second Person in the procession of the third, but without developing it in their speculations, and always with a firm affirmation of the monarchy of the Father, which is also the Latin tradition. The procession *ab utroque* is even explicit in St Cyril of Alexandria. Otherwise we find three main themes in the East which set out to explain the relationship of the Spirit with the Son:

1. The procession of the Father 'by the Son, *dia tou Huiou*'. This is very common.[22] We know that the union of Florence accepted this formula, but in terms of the *filioque*, which missed the intention of

the Fathers, since it is doubtful whether they gave the Son a causal role. Maximus Confessor interpreted the Latin *filioque* along the lines of the Greek 'by the Son'. The road from Athens to the Piraeus is not entirely the same as that from the Piraeus to Athens! The two formulae are not completely interchangeable, but they have enough connections to be put together, perhaps in preparation for a common statement. But is that desirable? Is it possible, beginning from different conceptions and conceptualizations?

2. A number of Syrian epicleses, and sometimes the Greek Fathers, say that the Spirit proceeds from the Father and receives from the Son.[23] In this way they combine the two passages of John 15.26, 'who proceeds from the Father', and John 16.14, 'he will take of mine'. This last text, limited to v.14, concerns the economy ('he will glorify me', 'and share it with you'), in the same way as 15.26, but the sequel of the text has rightly been considered by the Latins as grounding the economy in 'theology' and as a support for the *filioque*.[24] In fact the sequence is: 'All that the Father has is mine. That is why I said, "He will take what is mine and share it with you."' If one wanted to complete the creed by saying *qui a Patre procedit et a Filio accipit* one would then risk coming up against the difference between the Orthodox, who understand the dependence on the Son at the level of the economy,[25] and Roman Catholics, who put it primarily on the eternal level of 'theology'.

3. St John of Damascus, who for the Orthodox is rather what Thomas Aquinas is for Roman Catholics, has the formula 'who proceeds from the Father and rests in the Son (as his radiant power)'.[26] He twice copies Pseudo-Cyril, who inserts the formula into the text of the creed.[27] This idea of resting in the Son is to be found among other Greek Fathers.[28] It is an expression of the circumincession or compenetration of the divine persons more than the relationship in being of the Spirit to the Son. St Thomas, who objects to this expression, responds without referring to circumincession.[29]

My own feelings on the matter are as follows. The obscurity which surrounds the redaction of our creed by the council of 381 is of little importance. We know that the text was attributed to it only by Chalcedon, in 451. Only the Greek bishops had been summoned by Theodosius and took part in the Council of Constantinople in 381. St Ambrose, who seems unaware of the dogmatic decision of the council, had complained about this neglect of Rome and the West in the matter of appointments to the sees of Constantinople and

Antioch: *non praerogativam vindicamus examinis, sed consortium tamen debuit esse arbitrii... cohaerere communionem nostram cum Orientalibus non videmus... Nec quaedam nos angit de domestico studio et ambitione contentio, sed communio soluta et dissociata perturbat... Postulamus ut ubi una communio est, commune velit esse iudicium concordantemque consensum*, 'we do not claim the prerogative of approval, but there must be consultation over judgment... we do not see our commuion joining with the East... Our disquiet is not over domestic matters or rival ambitions; what disturbs us is the disruption to communion... We ask that where there is one communion, judgment should be common and agreement shared.'[30] The West had 'received' the council of 381, which had translated its own faith; Pope Damasus had approved the affirmation of the consubstantial divinity of the Spirit.[31] However, from this time the West tended to suggest that the Spirit was dependent on the Son in his eternal procession. Ambrose himself, who owed so much to the Greeks, seems to have understood the *de meo accipiet* in this sense.[32] And we know how, first in Spain and then through the activity and in the empire of Charlemagne, the *filioque* introduced itself into the creeds, even that of Nicaea-Constantinople.

This is an irregular and anticanonical procedure. The East could quite legitimately use the words of St Ambrose that I have quoted. They have spoken quite as strongly and more polemically. I think that the centenary of the Council of 381 could have been celebrated by receiving the text of its creed as it was received by Damasus and Leo III, without the interpolation of the *filioque*. There could have been an account of traditional Roman Catholic doctrine, stressing the 'monarchy' of the Father which is so firmly believed in but which is not expressed in the *Filioque*. To quote Paul Evdokimov: 'It is not a matter of touching the text of the creed. However, it could be supplied with a theological commentary so that it could be used with one mind and one heart by East and West, reconciled to each other.'[33] Valuable preparations have been made for this, including those at the Council of Florence, though they cannot be used as they stand, any more than its formula of union.[34]

In these circumstances, if points of dispute were brought out into the open, looked at and overcome, the Roman Catholic Church could even withdraw the *filioque*. That is what was said by Mgr Sergius, at that time Bishop of Jamburg, Rector of the Ecclesiastical Academy of St Petersburg, who was to become the second holder of the restored title of Patriarch of Moscow, to the Old Catholics in 1903:

> When we are completely sure that in removing the *filioque* from their creed the Old Catholics are not just going through the motions in an attempt to smooth away canonical roughnesses, but really believe in the Trinity in as orthodox a way as the holy church, we shall certainly not ask them to sign the formula *a Patre solo*, but will leave them the above-mentioned *filioque* in the complete certainty that this formula is indispensable to the Western spirit for expressing the idea that we stress by means of the formula *a Patre solo*.[35]

Thomas Aquinas, on the basis of explanations already given by St Augustine, thought that the addition of *a Patre solo* would not rob the *filioque* of its truth.[36] However, this is what was recently written by Theodore Stylianopoulos, Professor of the Holy Orthodox Theological School of the Holy Cross at Brookline: 'The *filioque* is not a decisive difference in dogma but a serious difference in the interpretation of dogma which awaits resolution... The tragedy of the *filioque* is that, while not intended as a denial of the Catholic faith, and while yielding an Orthodox interpretation, it nonetheless gained a controversial significance... Finally, they (the Western theologians) must consider the removal of the *filioque* from the Creed both for the sake of the Catholic bond of love and with the anticipation that a future Ecumenical Council could very well incorporate the *filioque* into the Creed in mutually acceptable terms.'[37]

If only that could happen!

PART THREE

Looking towards the Reformation

11

Agreement on 'Fundamental Articles' or on the Positions of the Early Church

Erasmus (died 1536), faithful to the Christian faith but opposed to dogmatism and scholasticism, was foremost in a move towards reconciliation (R.Rouse and S.C.Neill, *A History of the Ecumenical Movement 1517-1948*, London 1954, 36). His view was that there is quite a large area of indifferent matters, not only in customs or even in morality, but in doctrine.

The notion of *adiaphora* played a considerable role in the Lutheran Reformation: 'It is not necessary for the true unity of the church that ceremonies instituted by men, should be observed uniformly in all places' (*Augsburg Confession* VII, 3: *Creeds of the Churches*, Atlanta, Ga [3]1982, 70). Melanchthon had no difficulty in giving references to the Eastern church, to the councils and to the Fathers of the early church.[1] However, in the course of the fifty years following the Augsburg Confession, discussions among Lutherans were focussed not least on the question of adiaphora. Were there not obligatory forms of worship and discipline? Under the pressure of a civil power or the social context, was it perhaps permissible to practise the Roman Catholic mass? The 1580 Formula of Concord is a reply to these questions. It bases the *adiaphora* on Christian liberty. As to the mass, *in casu confessionis* it is utterly impossible to practise what is contrary to the church.[2] In passing, in these long elucidations we should note a serious lack of awareness of the nature of the liturgy and a regrettable gulf between that and dogma or a sense of the Christian mystery.

Charity is needed in all things, necessary or indifferent, Luther had said in the second of the eight sermons which he preached at Wittenberg between 9 and 16 March 1522 in opposition to the 'prophets' of Zwickau and to Carlstadt, who, in his absence, had destroyed the images and prohibited private masses. Luther said:

There are two things (to consider). The first, which is necessary, that is to say, which must happen in this way and not otherwise, the second which is free and not necessary (*unnötig*), which one can observe or not without endangering the faith or the salvation of souls. In these two things love must be practised towards one's neighbour in the same way as we have received it from God; so it must follow the right way, without falling either to the right or the left.[3]

Luther is not the creator of the famous formula, cited again by John XXIII in his first encyclical *Ad Petri cathedram* of 29 June 1959 (no.38): *In necessariis unitas, in dubiis libertas, in omnibus caritas*: 'Unity in necessary things, liberty in doubtful things and love in everything.' However, he comes close to this idea, which has roots in St Augustine, the Fathers and tradition.

G.Krüger has established a genealogy or at least a chronological succession of occurrences of this maxim.[4] One antecedent, which would also hold for the notion of fundamental articles, can be found in a letter from King James I to Cardinal du Perron in 1612, edited by Isaac Casaubon. It was about an agreement between Anglicans and Catholics. This is the passage:

Quare existimat eius Maiestas, nullam ad ineundam concordiam breviorem viam fore quam si diligenter separentur necessaria a non necessariis. Et ut de necessariis conveniat omnis opera insumatur: in non necessariis libertati Christianae locus detur. (His majesty also thinks that there would be no shorter way than to separate carefully the necessary things from those which are not so; everyone should pay great attention to agreement in what is necessary and leave the rest to Christian freedom.)[5]

The climate was then favourable to an accord, at least between Protestants. In 1626, Petrus Meiderlinus published, under the name of Rupertus Meldenius, a *Paraenesis votiva pro pace Ecclesiae ad theologos Augustanae Confessionis*.[6] It has the formula with which we are concerned. He is the one who introduced it. It is perhaps inspired by the *Stratagemata Satanae* of James Acontius dedicated in 1564 to Queen Elizabeth of England.[7] In an Erasmian spirit, Acontius was opposed to the *rabies theologica*; he recommended mutual readiness to listen and an attitude of love. He distinguished between the articles of faith necessary to salvation and those of secondary importance. He reprimanded theologians, victims of the wiles of Satan, for *maxime necessaria negligere, eo quod non necessaria tractant*, 'of completely neglecting what was necessary and occupying themselves with inessentials'.

The formula has been quoted since. It can be found above all in Richard Baxter, who owed it to Meiderlin, in his dedication to the Bishop of Winchester of his *The True Way of Concord of all the Christian Churches*, 1679.

(i) 'Fundamental articles'

Dealing more specifically with 'fundamental articles', we may distinguish five or six groups of authors who each seem to have a particular context.

1. Context in church and dogmatics

The Protestant reforms of the sixteenth century were carried out 1. in the name of doctrine and by doctors often motivated by a sheer *rabies theologica*; 2. in a logic of 'Christendom', that is to say of a union between the position of the church – which was a *doctrinal* position – and the constraining authority of the magistrate.[8]

This double fact allows us to understand the fragmentation within the Reformation. I have tried hard to gain some idea of the disagreements and oppositions which for long prevailed between Lutherans and Reformed over the question of the eucharist and predestination. The colloquium of Marburg, 1-4 October 1529, had Luther and Melanchthon on one side opposed to Zwingli and even Bucer on the other on the question of the eucharist. 'You have another spirit than ours,' Luther had said. Moreover, among Lutherans, between 1546 (the death of Luther) and 1580 there were passionate discussions on the value of works, synergism, the existence among humanity of the justice of Christ (in his humanity?) and his place in our justice, the explanation of the real presence by ubiquity, the suspicion of crypto-Calvinism.[9]

It seems that Calvin had originally thought of fundamental articles because of his disquiet at the way in which the unity of Protestants was disturbed by the eucharistic question. This is evident from the first edition of the *Institutes* in 1536 onwards.[10] We can see clearly from his *Treatise on the Lord's Supper* that this is in response to the difficulties caused by the clash of eucharistic theologies.[11] Here is the most developed formulation, taken from the *Christian Institutes* of 1562, IV, 1, 12, which is a straight quotation of the text of ch.4 of 1536.

> When we say that the pure ministry of the word and pure celebration of the sacraments is a fit pledge and earnest, so that we may safely recognize a church in every society in which both exist, our meaning is, that we are never to discard it so long as these remain, though it may otherwise teem with numerous faults. No, even in the administration of word and sacraments defects may creep in which ought not to alienate us from its communion. For all the heads of true doctrine are not in the same position. Some are so necessary to be known, that all must hold them to be fixed and undoubted as the proper essentials of religion: for instance that God is one, that Christ is God, and the Son of God, that our salvation depends on the mercy of God, and the like. Others again, which are the subject of controversy among the churches, do not destroy the unity of the faith; for why should it be regarded as a ground of dissension between churches, if one, without any spirit of contention of perverseness in dogmatizing, hold that the soul on quitting the body flies to heaven, and another, without venturing to speak positively as to the abode, holds it for certain that it lives with the Lord? The words of the apostle are, 'Let us therefore, as many as be perfect, be thus minded: and if in anything you are otherwise minded, God shall reveal even this to you'(Phil.3.15). Does he not sufficiently intimate that a difference of opinion as to these matters which are not absolutely necessary, ought not to be a ground of dissension among Christians? The best thing, indeed, is to be perfectly agreed, but seeing there is no man who is not involved in some mist of ignorance, we must either have no church at all, or pardon delusion in those things of which one may be ignorant, without violating the substance of religion and forfeiting salvation. Here, however, I have no wish to patronize even the minutest errors, as if I thought it right to foster them by flattery or connivance; what I say is, that we are not on account of every minute difference to abandon a church, provided it retain sound and unimpaired that doctrine in which the safety of piety consists, and keep the use of the sacraments instituted by the Lord.

With Calvin, and also with his successor Theodore of Beza, the discussion is over what is necessary for there to be a church, that is to say, purity of the preaching of the word of God and the administration of the sacraments in accordance with it. At the colloquy of

Poissy in 1561, Theodore accepted the doctrine of the apostolic succession in the ministry 'on condition that it is conjoined with that of the prophetic and apostolic doctrine at least in substantial and fundamental points, and not otherwise'.[12]

Union with the Lutherans on the basis of the fundamental articles remained a preoccupation and a project for French reforms: e.g. at the Synod of Tonneins (1614) and after.[13] At the end of the sixteenth or beginning of the seventeenth century Lutheran theologians again took up the theme of fundamental articles, refusing to be content to hold that 'Christ is our saviour'. That was the view of Matthias Herfenreffer (1561-1619), Leonhard Hütter (1563-1616) and Balthasar Meisner (1587-1626).[14] At the beginning of the eighteenth century three Reformed theologians of Geneva, Basle and Neuchâtel, Alphonse Turretini (1671-1737), Samuel Werenfels (1657-1740) and Jean Frédéric Ostervald (1663-1747), sought a union of the Protestant, Lutheran and Reformed churches on the basis of fundamental articles ('reasonable orthodoxy').[15]

2. Erasmian context[16]

The most characteristic text by Erasmus himself is without doubt that of his letter to John Carondelet, Archbishop of Palermo, on 5 January 1523: 'The sum of our religion is peace and concord which can easily be maintained only on one condition: by defining the smallest possible number of dogmas, and in many matters leaving each person to his own judgment. In fact the obscurity surrounding many questions is enormous. Furthermore, it is an innate evil in the human spirit that men are incapable of yielding on a subject once it has been brought up for discussion.'[17] Erasmus accepted the dogmas as defined, but he attacked an intemperate scholasticism, multiplying qualifications, distinctions and discussions.[18] Erasmus argued for articles of faith, but he thought that there was a very large number of theories about which one could think differently. He himself made a list of them (not an exhaustive one) in the *Spongia adversus aspergines Hutteni*, 1523: 'For it is not a matter of articles of faith but of knowing if the primacy of the Roman Pontiff comes from Christ, if the college of cardinals is an indispensable part of the church, if Christ is the author of the creed, if the bishops, by their constitutions, can impose obligations on pain of mortal sin, if free judgment is important for salvation, if faith alone contributes to salvation, if any good work can be attributed to man, if the mass can be considered in some way a sacrifice. For these questions, which are a commonplace theme of scholastic debates, I would not dare to take a man's life if I was judge nor to risk my own life.'[19] One can see that that goes a long way.

This Erasmian spirit has inspired what one might call a third party in favour of the 'royal way', which goes through the middle without deviating to right or to left. Its mode of action has been colloquies (from 1540 onwards). That of Ratisbon in 1541 marked the most interesting advance towards agreement. But its final failure, the fact that the colloquies themselves were the occasion for theologians to argue even more vigorously, and finally the progressive polarization of differences and oppositions, led Cassander, in 1561, to take over this proposition from the Erasmus of the first years of the Reformation: would it not be possible to reach agreement on the essential points of faith, leaving the rest to the discussions of theologians? It is not just a matter of different opinions among the doctors, but of more or less serious differences which divide the churches as they are now constituted. Cassander formulated what would later be called the theory of 'fundamental articles'. He suggests that the churches should agree, in his own words, 'on the foundation of apostolic doctrine'. While keeping their particular opinions and ceremonies they will remain united among themselves by the bond of love.

> The whole Christ is head and body. One only separates oneself from the head by a doctrine of Christ as head which is false and contrary to scripture. One only separates oneself from the body, that is to say from the church, by lack of love, and never by a degree of diversity of rites and opinions.[20]

That presupposes an ecclesiology, however inadequate, since it introduces a break between Christ and his body the church. Its logic is that a personal faith in Christ held by the faithful is anterior to the church, which is formed by the faithful.[21] That allows the recognition of a universal church made up of specific churches which do not deny its christological and trinitarian foundation.

> Every church which rests on the foundation of the true and apostolic doctrine contained in the brief creed and which does not part company by an impious schism with the communion of other churches, I regard as the true church, a member of the true church and the Catholic church of Christ. And I say that not only of the Western churches, but also of the Eastern churches.[22]

That also led to the use of the early and apostolic church as a criterion. That had already been the position of George Wicelius/

Witzel, following the line of Erasmus, and is that of Cassander, who arrives at the criterion of Vincent of Lerins.[23] After the shock caused by the Thirty' Years War, i.e. from 1626, that was the position of George Calixtus (1614-1656).[24] Calixtus had been an intransigent Lutheran: for him, not only the papists but the Calvinists were the heretics. The Thirty Years War had horrified him and made him realize the evil of division. From now on he held that Catholics and Protestants belong to the same Catholic church on the basis of fundamental articles. These are the articles of faith necessary for salvation *necessitate medii*, necessary for Christian action. Calixtus found them in the creed, but from 1633 he attached himself to the *consensio quinquesaecularis*. No truths unknown to the early church, the church of the first five centuries, are necessary truths. These centuries were followed by a period of decadence, the excessive growth of the papacy, abuse, superstition. The Reformation, supported by a renewal of study, brought the church back to its purity, but to the degree that it also added to the fundamental articles, for example by holding a doctrine of the ubiquity of the humanity of Christ in connection with the eucharist, it produced divisions.

On this basis, Calixtus attempted a union on all fronts. He found sympathizers: Grotius, Duraeus (Durie) in England; Cyril Lukaris and Kritopoulos on the Orthodox side; Veron among the Catholics – though he incurred lively criticism from the Jesuit Ebermann of Mainz. Calixtus took part in the colloquy organized at Thorn in 1645 by Ladislaus IV of Poland.[25] That was a failure. Calixtus met very lively opposition in his own church, above all from Johann Hülsemann (1602-1661).[26]

3. In the context of Lutheran orthodoxy

If I understand things rightly, we do not find the idea of fundamental articles as doctrinal elements with Luther himself. Scripture is enough and, in scripture, only *was Christus treibt* is the word of God: scripture is the word of God only insofar as it speaks of Christ as my saviour.[27] The foundation of which I Cor.3.11 speaks is Jesus Christ as saviour. The *fides quae* is identical to the *fides qua*; that by which one is justified through practising a *fiducialis desperatio sui* to put all one's confidence in Jesus Christ.[28] In short, that is more a foundation than fundamental articles. We should note in passing that the Council of Trent, some days before the death of Luther, proclaimed as a 'firm and sole foundation' the Niceno-Constantinopolitan creed professed by all Christians (Denz.1500).

Melanchthon kept this affirmation and the reference to I Cor.3.[29]

He produces the famous formula *hoc est Christum cognoscere beneficia eius cognoscere*, 'to know Christ is to know his benefits' (*Loci of 1521*, 63). However, he betrayed Luther's insight by making faith a doctrine: *Fundamentum intelligit (Paulus) articulos fidei, hoc est summam doctrinae christianae et doctrinam de beneficiis Christi*, 'Paul understands by foundation the articles of faith, that is the sum of Christian doctrine and the doctrine of the benefits of Christ.'[30] We may note in passing that this primacy given to teaching, to doctrine, leads Melanchthon to see the church as a school or academy, and to miss its sacramental reality, its organic continuity. This objectivizing of faith and doctrine can be found among those who produced the 1580 Formula of Concord. The formula itself keeps the idea of the centre of faith, but in a doctrinal context, that of teaching.

This was the beginning of Lutheran orthodoxy, which developed a scholasticism very like that of the Catholic schools. Two levels or classes of error are distinguished there, and similarly two levels of truth. The Lutherans thus specify what marks them out from the Calvinists. Nicolas Hunnius (died 1643) indicates that these differences are not over the *fundamentum essentiale* but over the *fundamentum dogmaticum*. He gives thirteen negative and fifteen positive criteria for distinguishing between fundamental and non-fundamental articles.[31] He arrives at a distinction which could be summed up like this:

Fundamental articles

close to the faith = primary
(which cannot be ignored without loss of faith and salvation)

and therefore constitutive
(by which faith is directly caused)

apparent to faith = secondary (which can be ignored without imperilling salvation but which, when known, cannot be denied)

and therefore conservative
(necessarily secondary to the immediate cause of faith)

Non-fundamental articles

those parts of Christian doctrine which 'could be ignored and denied without damaging faith'. Examples are the visible or invisible church and the impossibility of forgiveness for the sin against the Holy Spirit.

Johann Hülsemann also makes distinctions which are explained by Keller and Hüschemenger (119-31). He attacks the plans for union on the basis of fundamental articles or the agreement of the first five centuries, whether put forward by Calixtus or Duraeus. Union is possible only on the principles of the confessions of faith which express the Lutheran conception of the faith itself: the fundamental article corresponds to the foundation. And that is my salvation by faith in Jesus Christ.[32]

4. The Anglican Context. Jurieu's systematization. The ecclesiological context

Bernard J. Verkamp has made a very fully documented study on the theme of adiaphora in the English Reformation up to 1554.[33] He cites Erasmus as having exercised a certain influence. The English partisans of the Reformation in this period sometimes applied the category of 'indifferent things' to doctrines: thus William Tyndale and John Frith applied it to transsubstantiation and to purgatory (94f.) That could lead to the idea of articles which must be known and believed, and others which need not. Two of the Thirty-Nine Articles of 1571 declare this:

VI. Of the Sufficiency of the Holy Scriptures for Salvation

Holy Scripture containeth all things necessary to salvation; so that whatsoever is not read therein, nor may be proved thereby, is not to be required of any man, that it should be required as an article of faith or be thought requisite or necessary for salvation.

XX. Of the Authority of the Church

The Church hath power to decree Rites or Ceremonies, and authority in Controversies of Faith: And yet it is not lawful for the Church to ordain any thing that is contrary to God's word written, neither may it so expound one place of scripture, that it be repugnant to another. Wherefore, although the Church be a witness and a keeper of Holy Writ, yet, as it ought not to decree any thing against the same, so besides the same ought it not to enforce any thing to be believed for necessity of salvation.

Richard Hooker (1554-1600), who might be called the Thomas Aquinas of the Anglican church, took care to shape a *via media* for this church between on the one hand the Puritans, against whom he maintained the value of traditions when they are not contrary to the church, and the Roman Catholics.[34] These were not excluded from salvation or from being recognized as the Christian church because their denial of the foundation of faith, Christ the saviour as witnessed to by the Scriptures (I Cor.3.2-12; I Tim.3.6), was only implicit and indirect. That denial arose from the theology of merit. Hooker thus distinguished between fundamental truths necessary to salvation and secondary customs, which it was permissible and convenient to practise. This position is common among the classical theologians of Anglicanism.[35]

The important thing for us is that the question of fundamental articles has become an article of ecclesiology in Anglicanism. The fundamental articles are seen as being what it is necessary, but sufficient, to hold to be a member of the Christian church: to be a Christian church.

The fact that Pierre Jurieu (1633-1713) received Anglican orders and that he served Anglican politics against the intolerant France of Louis XIV would in themselves justify our speaking of him here. But as far as I am aware, his 'system' has a very profound affinity with Anglican ecclesiology, as we shall see. It has antecedents well described by G.Thils, which I shall not stress here:[36] Philippe du Plessis-Mornay, King James I of England in his controversy with du Perron, Arminius, and finally I. d'Huisseau of Saumur, author of *La Réunion du Christianisme ou la manière de rejoindre tous les Chrestiens sous une seule Confession de Foy*, Saumur 1670.

Jurieu[37] put forward his views on the chapter that interests us in *Examen du livre de la Réunion du christianisme...*, Orleans 1671 (his titles are often very long); *Prejugez legitimes contre le Papisme...*, Amsterdam 1685; *le Vray Système de l'Église ou la Véritable Analyse de la foy*, Dordrecht 1686; *Traité de l'unité de l'Église et des points fondamentaux*, Rotterdam 1688.

Jurieu does in fact have an ecclesiology, but he approaches it, in accordance with Protestant logic, from the perspective of individual believers and what they believe. All those who hold the fundamental truths are united to Christ and thus form a universal church. As such, this is invisible, but it is specific and visible in the different communions or churches. Jurieu declares: 'by fundamental points we understand certain general principles of Christian religion in which distinct faith and credence is necessary to be saved and to be called Christian.'[38] Although scripture does not say that such truth is fundamental, we can infer it by using these criteria: that this truth is revealed, that it has weight and importance, and finally that it has a link with the ends of religion, namely the glory of God and the sovereign blessedness of man. By contrast, we are to see as non-fundamental truths those which, without being essential, contribute to the purity of the faith. Jurieu divides these into three categories: 1. 'The consequences which follow from the first principles of Christianity.' As our own minds are involved here, we shall not all come to the same conclusions. 2. The most distinct explanations of principles. The same holds. 3. Truths that do not necessarily follow from the general principles of Christianity but which are still religious truths.

The particular churches are distinguished by the non-fundamental truths which they profess and which are 'capital' for them. Thus 'the church is not enclosed within a single visible and external communion, but it can be extended in a number of communions so separate externally that they even mutually excommunicate themselves.'[39] These communions realize and display different degrees of purity. 'The mark of the universal church in general is conformity with the word of God in the fundamental truths and the mark of the purest church in the Christian communion is conformity with the word of God generally in all truths, that is, in those which are of some importance, even if they are not fundamental.'[40] The purest communion is the Reformed communion. By contrast, the Catholic church is the most corrupt. If it still preserves the fundamental points it is by a miracle, but its deductions, its explanations, and the enormous mass of what it has added mean that it cannot assure salvation.

Jurieu cannot provide a list of fundamental articles or points, any more than the other champions of the idea. He cites those who mention the creed, adding an 'and others like them' who leave the question open. Responding to Nicole, he makes his fundamental points equivalent to those articles of faith which Catholic theology thinks to be necessary.[41]

Without claiming that Jurieu expresses Anglican thought or that he influenced it, I think that the Anglican conception of unity is very close to that of Jurieu, by virtue of the basic categories which it uses.[42] There is a church which is one by virtues of the fundamental truths and institutions which it contains, but this one church exists in particular communions which in fact are not at present united: each one has its theological particularities, of worship, discipline and structures, but these particularities belong on the periphery of *diversum sentire* which is authorized by a *ius communionis*, to take up the terms of St Cyprian used by Charles Gore at the Malines Conversations. A comparison used by R.Hooker and, in more recent times, by C.Wordsworth and T.A.Lacey, seems to me to be striking: the church is one like the liquid mass of the ocean, but depending on where it is, it bears different names; it remains one under the barriers one can place on its surface.

The theme of articles or fundamental dogmas has been taken up more than once, in the modern and even contemporary period, in plans or suggestions for Christian union. I shall limit myself to a few references.[43] The very idea of diversities compatible with communion, or of the necessary but sufficient minimum of common doctrine to be held in common if unity is to be preserved, is in fact the object of all my research.

Before pursuing this it would be a good thing to arrive at a verdict on the idea of fundamental articles; what should be retained, and what cannot be accepted?

5. *Assessment*

Pius XI made a vigorous criticism of the idea of fundamental articles, in conjunction with what he called a plan of 'pan-Christianity':

> As to the dogmas of faith, it is a quite illegitimate distinction: it is the distinction which some have thought fit to introduce between articles of faith which are called fundamental and others which are called non-fundamental articles of faith, some being accepted by all, and the others being left to the free assent of the faithful. Now the supernatural virtue of faith has as its formal object the authority of the God who reveals, an authority which does not allow of any distinction of this kind. That is why all the true disciples of Christ believe, for example, in the mystery of the august Trinity with the same faith as in the Immaculate Conception, in that of the incarnation of our Lord and in that of the infallible *magisterium* of the Roman pontiff, of course as defined by the Vatican Council. and although they have been solemnly decreed at different times, even very recently, these truths are no less certain or worthy of faith: is it not God who has revealed them all?[44]

However, one could make a list of evidence establishing that from the seventeenth century to our day the Catholics have recognized the validity of the expression 'fundamental articles'. Pressed by Leibniz, Bossuet recognized that 'there are fundamental articles and non-fundamental articles... this proposition is not discussed between Catholics and Protestants'.[45] Reacting to Jurieu's incendiary letters, he explained: 'The Roman church affirms that there are certain principal articles which it is not permissible to ignore... but it does not say that one may deny the other points which are equally revealed and unanimously received.'[46] Newman, Franzelin, M.J.Scheeben, A.Tanquerey, L. de Grandmaison, and in more recent times P.Batiffol, M.Pribilla, A. Rademacher and Cardinal Hume, have recognized that there is a place for the category of 'fundamental articles'.[47]

While valid on its own level, Pius XI's criticism does not quite accord with reality. It is somewhat one-sided. Faith can be considered from two perspectives, either from that of its content, the objects to which it relates – I would say the *quod* – or from that of the formal motive, that is to say, what motivates us to believe – one might say the *quo*. In considering tradition, I have shown that in modern times Catholic theology increasingly constructed its account on the *quo*, the authority, rather than on the *quod*, the content.[48] I have already quoted the significant remark by Stapleton (died 1598): *in doctrina fidei non quid dicatur, sed quis loquitur a fideli populo attendendum est,*[49] 'in teaching the faith, the faithful people must pay attention not to what is said but to the one by whom it is said'. Now the question of fundamental articles relates to the *quid dicatur*, the material content: that is the aspect by which it belongs to the theme of the hierarchy of truths, to which we shall return shortly. From this point of view it is clear that the mystery of the holy Trinity is more fundamental and more important for the nature of Christianity than that of the Immaculate Conception, and the mystery of the incarnation more fundamental and more important than the infallibility of the papal *magisterium*! However, I have three other criticisms to put forward.

1. First comes an ecclesiological criticism. I agree that the basis of a common Christianity is the adherence in faith to some basic truths. That is the basis of ecumenism and of the 'imperfect communion' which exists between disunited Christians. However, I do not accept that *that* defines the church, or that the church is, as Jurieu says, 'composed of separate and even mutually self-exclusive communions' or is 'the sum of all Christian societies which retain the foundation'.[50] It is this syncretistic ecclesiology which, as G.Thils has shown, leads Nicole and Bossuet to formulate a 'new idea of unity', a unity of the church as a unique society.[51]

2. How does one decide on a list of fundamental articles? Who would make it? None of those who have maintained this position have been able to elaborate further on the subject. That would presuppose, as Tanquerey (col.2034) points out, an infallible authority to determine which articles are absolutely essential for faith.

To tell the truth, I do not think that a general consensus would be impossible. However, we can still be perplexed when we note the difficulty the World Council of Churches has in applying the 'basis' which it has formulated.

3. Newman distrusted the idea of fundamental articles. 'In fact it suggests that religious truth can be made to stand out like an object, that truth is on one side and the church on the other. Now Newman never accepted that religious truth could in this way be abstracted from the intimate life of the church.'[52] Anglican realism? This is a question that Henry Chadwick raises: 'To hold that the fundamental doctrines are of the essence of the church is to put the criterion for the existence of the church in doctrine and not in the continuity of the life of the community. The Roman Catholic thinks: we have the church, and that is why we keep the fundamental doctrines. The Protestant thinks: we keep the fundamental doctrines, and that is why we have the church. There is virtually no hope of a union or a compromise between these two attitudes.'[53] This difference in approach meets up with the one of which I have mentioned: does the church make Christians or do Christians make the church?

It is here that the Catholic criticism of fundamental articles joins up with the resolute rejection of them by Orthodox theologians. They say that not only does the proposed distinction have no foundation in tradition, not only are there no criteria for making it, and not only would it make the unity of the church unstable and fragile, but it fails to recognize the organic and basically unitary character of the church. 'Christian teaching,' writes Androutsos, 'forms a unified and organic whole, one doctrine presupposing another; the negation of certain doctrines, applied consistently, leads to the negation of the foundation and makes everything hypothetical'. 'The authority of the church embraces the whole, and it is infallible.'[54] Professor P.N. Trembelas thus arrives at the position I would favour:

> The distinction between fundamental and non-fundamental dogmas could only be accepted along with the formal emphasis that the latter are equally binding on all the faithful: their only difference in respect of fundamental dogmas (like the Trinity and the Incarnation) is that to deny the latter would make a Christian cease to be a Christian, whereas not to accept the others would only lead to heresy or heterodoxy.[55]

This orthodox reaction is so vigorous that it almost inspires one to reticence over the idea of a 'hierarchy of truths', established and fruitful though it is. The final report of the Moscow Conference between Orthodox and Anglicans held at the end of July 1976 made the following declaration (this is a question on which Roman Catholics are in agreement with the Orthodox, though not on the rejection of a 'hierarchy of truths'):

> We note that the Anglican members, while accepting the dogmatic decrees of the fifth, sixth and seventh councils, have for a long time been accustomed to put the main stress on the first four and believe that the concept of an 'order or "hierarchy" of truths' can be applied with profit to the decisions of councils. The Orthodox members find that this concept is in conflict with the unity of faith as a whole, though they recognize degrees of importance in matters of practice.[56]

However, the primacy of the first four councils is a basic datum of tradition. Better still, it has great ecumenical value, being common to the East, to Catholics, to Protestants and to Anglicans.[57] The fact is that these councils have established the truth on the very foundations of the faith: which makes the notion of fundamental truths or articles of abiding interest. However, as we shall see, we are not to suppose that this primacy devalues the other councils or that the doctrinal life of the church stopped at Chalcedon in 451. One indication of that is the fact that this council had to be supplemented, and even balanced, by the third council of Constantinople against monothelitism (680-1).

This structure of major realities of one kind which do not devalue other aspects can also be found elsewhere. The most interesting cases, also of great ecumenical value, are those of the major sacraments (baptism and the eucharist) and Paul VI's appreciation of the general councils of the Latin Middle Ages.[58]

(ii) The early church

Three further themes are very close to that of fundamental articles; so close that sometimes they are caught up with the *consensus quinquesaecularis* or the agreement on the first councils; they are the Vincentian canon and the *hierarchia veritatum*. I am going to develop them, adding, before the third, a criticism of the two first.

1. The consensus quinquesaecularis *or agreement over the first councils*

The humanists, very critical over scholastic discussions, recommended union on the basis of the faith of the early church.[59] Under the name of Hermann Bodius there was published, in 1526, a *Unio Dissidentium* which allowed the Fathers a major role, as an attempt to smoothe over the differences between the Reformation and the early church. Himself a humanist, Melanchthon very soon used texts from the Fathers to show that the early church, down to St Gregory (died 604), attested the authenticity of the Reformation.[60] Luther himself admitted in the Schmalkald articles (I a. 4: *Bekenntnisschriften*, 428) that the church had remained pure down to St Gregory. Dedicating the *Christian Institutes* of 1536 to Francis I, Calvin said, 'Were the contest to be decided by such authority, the better part of the victory would be ours.'[61]

It was George Calixtus who, after 1626, furthered agreement on the church of the first five centuries, which in general had remained pure, not only as a confessional justification but as a programme of union.[62] But the additions made by the Catholic church after this date had to be eliminated, in particular the *dominandi cupiditas* of the papacy, which had reached its climax with Gregory VII (*haeresis Hildebrandiana*).[63] Calixtus was vigorously criticized by the Catholic apologists; his attempts at union among Protestants were violently rejected by Lutheran orthodoxy.

The idea of the *consensus quinquesaecularis* has been particularly welcomed in England: the Anglican church was in fact concerned to maintain continuity with the early church, rejecting Roman innovations. People even spoke of the first six centuries, as did John Jewell in his *Sermon at St Paul's Cross* of 1559 and his *Apologia pro Ecclesia Anglicana* of 1562. Again, in 1904-05, Dr Wace, Dean of Canterbury, obtained 2,500 signatures for a manifesto aiming at reducing disputes in the Church of England; this said: 'Nothing can be accepted as truly Catholic which cannot claim the assent and the general practice of the Christian church before the end of the sixth century.'[64]

The same idea of an agreement on the faith of the early church is often expressed with reference to the councils: beyond the first four, which all accept (except that the Nestorians reject the third and the so-called Monophysites the fourth), the following have been admitted:

1. The first five, the fifth being Constantinople II (553), which condemned the Antiochene christology of the 'Three Chapters' (accepted by Calixtus).

2. The first six, the sixth being Constantinople III, against monothelitism, in 680-1. Following the colloquium of Poissy, in 1561, the Bishop of Valence proposed that the rule of faith should be

taken there.[65] Anglicans generally accepted it,[66] e.g. R.Field,[67] J. Hall (died 1656), H.Hammond (died 1660), J.Bramhall (died 1663), J.Cosin (died 1672) and even J.Jewell (died 1571), apologist of the Reformation. But Jurieu and even the Presbyterian Church of the United States, in the nineteenth century, also accepted the first six councils.[68]

Anglicans have usually terminated their agreement before the seventh council, that concerned with icons (Nicaea II, 787). Most considered the cult of icons to be an act of idolatry.[69] By contrast, as representative a figure as Charles Gore accepted the seventh ecumenical council and its doctrine.[70] At the Lambeth Conference of 1920, the Anglican bishops showed a degree of openness to the Orthodox delegation. More recently, Max Thurian, in *L'Unité visible des chrétiens et la Tradition*, 1961, suggested the consensus of the first seven councils as a criterion for the interpretation of revelation and a basis for Christian unity.

2. The Vincentian Canon

In 434, Vincent of Lerins wrote an aide-memoire, a *commonitorium*.[71] How, in a time of novelty and heresy, could one discern truth from error? Vincent is thinking of Nestorianism, which had just been condemned, but also of the Augustinian theories of grace. The sure criterion is Holy Scripture interpreted according to the norm of ecclesial and catholic opinion: this bears the triple characteristics of universality, antiquity and unanimity: *id teneamus quod ubique, quod semper, quod ab omnibus creditum est* (PL 50, 639).

Because Vincent appealed to an objective criterion, of the order of the *quod*, not the *quo*, and referred to the early church, before the frequent exercise of papal authority, he was to be accepted by Protestants, Anglicans, Gallicans and, more recently, Old Catholics. 'Although almost forgotten by the Middle Ages, it (the *Commonitorium*) had a prodigious success a millennium later: thirty-five editions in the sixteenth century and twenty-two translations; twenty-three editions in the seventeenth century and twelve translations; thirteen editions in the eighteeenth century and twelve translations; thirteen editions in the nineteenth century and twenty-one translations...'[72] Cassander cited the Vincentian Canon. Calixtus edited it in 1629 and 1655. It was particularly revered in the Anglican church. Again in modern times, the liberal heirs of the Oxford Movement have been fond of referring to it.[73] This was even more the case with the Old Catholics, who made it the principle and even the motto of their existence, the basis of their protestation.[74]

3. Critical appreciation

This applies as much to the use of the Vincentian Canon as to the appeal to the consensus of the first five or six centuries (the six or even seven first councils).

What is defined or acquired abides. But one cannot stop the life of the church in the truth at a past moment of its history. This is already the criticism which Hülsemann directed to Calixtus: new heresies have been produced since the sixth century which the church has to exclude. Jansen and Hessels made an analogous criticism,[75] as have several Orthodox theologians.[76] On the Anglican side, H.B.Swete pointed out that the Vincentian Canon, if taken as a principle for exclusion, would eliminate as not 'Catholic' things which are, like the prayers of the saints.[77] J.N.Figgis, like Fr Bulgakov, pointed out that the church has been inspired down through the centuries and that it always has a future, a creative power.[78] There is no point in saying that this is also the Catholic conviction: it is because the principle is too static that Vatican II avoided quoting it in its constitution *Dei Verbum* 8. This argument gets close to the heart of things. It substitutes the reality of the living church for a historical view, or rather, only half a view, because it is fixed. The canon of past centuries is a principle for intellectuals, for those who can study history. But those who know history well, like Harnack, find the canon unusable and false.

The canon has in fact been quite implacably criticized by modern ecumenists. Adolf Harnack demonstrated that the agreement of the first five centuries was a utopia based on an unhistorical ideal; furthermore, it would require Protestants to hold doctrines or positions that they reject.[79] That has also been argued in the case of the twofold papal dogma of Vatican I, which would call for qualification.[80] Does one stop the list of councils before the one one wants to reject? That is what the Nestorians and Monophysites have done.

Vincent of Lerins enunciated another principle in ch.23 of his *Commonitorium*: *Crescat igitur oportet vehementerque proficiat...* 'So it is necessary that it should grow and increase powerfully.' As J.-L.Leuba remarks, 'The inadequacy of St Vincent of Lerins consists in the fact that he did not sufficiently articulate either of the two rules that he formulated; he did not work out how one affects the other.'[81]

When we come more particularly to the criterion of the councils, it is necessary to see not only what they said but also what they represent in the life of the church and the manner of their pronouncements. The councils are ecclesiological facts. They enunciated dogmas, canons and anathemas. They exercised the normative teaching function of the church. They form its limits.[82] They used terms which are not in scripture but which do not betray its content. Even in a theology of *sobornost* and 'reception' they incorporate and translate the *sensus fidei* of the church which goes along with it all its life.

Having made these criticisms, one must welcome these proposed norms on the basis of antiquity, even beyond their practical value for theological ecumenism. Against a certain contemporary current which tends to identify tradition and magisterium, and to allow the content of the church's belief, attested in documents, to be swallowed up in obedience to the formal authority of the 'living magisterium', we must never forget:

1. This authority must necessarily refer to the content of faith as it has been transmitted and attested, and has no autonomy in this respect: 'The Vincentian Canon is a guideline for the teaching church itself.'[83]

2. The immense value of ancient tradition as such, as being a kind of classical period of the church.

3. Finally, the value of agreement as a manifestation of the truth and a sign of the action of the Holy Spirit, not only for apologetic but also for the church.

12

The 'Hierarchy of Truths'[1]

The Vatican II Decree on Ecumenism, *Unitatis redintegratio*, promulgated on 21 November 1964, which ranks among the great documents of Christian history, has a short passage in section 11 the importance and tenor of which were immediately seen to be decisive.[2] Here it is:

> *Insuper in dialogo oecumenico theologi catholici, doctrinae Ecclesiae inhaerentes, una cum veritatis amore, caritate et humilitate progredi debent. In comparandis doctrinis meminerint existere ordinem seu 'hierarchiam' veritatum doctrinae catholicae, cum diversus sit earum nexus cum fundamento fidei christianae. Sic via sternetur qua per fraternum hanc aemulationem omnes incitentur ad profundiorem cognitionem et clariorem manifestationem investigabilium divitiarum Christi (cf. Ep.3,8).*

Furthermore, in ecumenical dialogue, Catholic theologians, standing fast by the teaching of the Church yet searching together with separated brethren into the divine mysteries, should do so with love for the truth, with charity, and with humility. When comparing doctrine with one another, they should remember that in Catholic doctrine there exists an order or 'hierarchy' of truths, since they vary in their relation to the foundation of the Christian faith. Thus the way will be opened whereby this kind of 'fraternal rivalry' will incite all to a deeper realization and a clearer expression of the unfathomable riches of Christ (cf. Eph.3.8).

It was Mgr André Pangrazio, Archbishop of Gorizia in Italy, who in his speech on 25 November 1963, during the discussion of the schema on ecumenism, was responsible for the suggestion that the idea of a gradation within professed truths should be introduced, as an aid to better appreciation of the unity already existing between disunited Christians. This is what he said:

In the first place it seems to me very important to discover exactly what unity already exists between Christians and how much diversity can still be found alongside it. We must pay great attention to the hierarchical order which exists between the revealed truths by which the mystery of Christ is expressed and the ecclesiastical elements making up the church.

Even if all the revealed truths were believed with an equally divine faith, and all the constitutive elements of the church were held with the same fidelity, they would not all have the right to occupy the same place.

There are truths relating to the final order, for example the mystery of the Most Holy Trinity, the Incarnation of the Word and redemption, the love and the grace of God towards sinful man, eternal life in the kingdom of God, and so on.

Other truths relate to the order of means of salvation, as for example the seven sacraments, the hierarchical structure of the church, the apostolic succession, and so on. These are means which have been given by Christ to the church for its pilgrimage on earth and will disappear when that pilgrimage is ended.

The doctrinal differences between Christians are concerned less with the primordial truths, the final order, than with these last, related to the order of means, and without any doubt subordinate to the former.

One can say that the unity of Christians consists in faith and commitment relating to the final order.

If we gave explicit expression to this ordering of truths and elements, I think we would have a better perspective on the unity already existing between all Christians, who form a family already united by the primordial truths of the Christian religion.[3]

Mgr Pangrazio's suggestion had been taken up by Cardinal König in a well written *modus*, though the Latin was mediocre.[4] The *modus* put forward was incorporated as it stood into no.11 of the decree. There are truths – in the plural – but they are in hierarchical order following the relationship that they have to the foundation – in the singular – of the Christian faith. This faith, common to all Christians, is explicated in no.12 of the Decree: its content is 'God one and three, the incarnate Son of God, our Redeemer and Lord'. As to the hierarchy which the bond or relationship with this faith establishes in the truths of Catholic doctrine, the 'Reflections and Suggestions concerning Ecumenical Dialogue', issued by the Secretariat for Unity on 15 August 1970 'as an aid particularly to ecclesiastical authorities for application of the Decree on Ecumenism', comment: 'For example, the dogma of Mary's Immaculate Conception, which may not be isolated from what the Council of Ephesus declares about Mary, the Mother of God, presupposes, before it can be properly grasped in a true life of faith, the dogma of grace to which it is linked and which in its turn necessarily rests upon the redemptive incarnation of the Word.'[5]

This was one of the examples of *Mortalium animos*. There is no denial in any way that everything is related to faith, but there is a change from considering only the *quo*, 'by what authority?', to considering the *quod*, the content. That would suggest that Catholic doctrine is organized rather like a tree, the smallest branches of which are connected to the trunk by others. The trunk is Christ, God incarnate, the Redeemer, and therefore the principle of grace, involving Mary Mother of God and her privileges of grace. Everything is attached to one foundation (a trunk), which is the mystery of Christ the saviour, presupposing the mystery of the triunity of God.

Hence the theme of a hierarchy of truths – because they are related to the foundation – has something in common with the idea of the foundation in the Lutheran tradition. Note that the text says: *Cum diversa sit earum nexus cum fundamento fidei* christianae. Luther distinguished between the overall subject-matter of scripture and what is 'apostolic'. The apostolic element in scripture is what speaks of Christ, my saviour.[6] The criterion of apostolic authenticity is '*to preach and convey Christ*'. Whatever does not teach Christ is not apostolic, though it come from Peter or Paul; by contrast, whatever preaches Christ is apostolic, even if it come from Judas, from Annas, from Pilate or from Herod.'[7] There are countless texts in Luther, who uses 'analogy of faith' as a designation for the reference of everything to Jesus Christ, dead and risen for us, as the centre of revelation.[8] Very much in agreement with this, Gustav Aulén could write: 'A doctrine is not recognized as authentically Christian because it has excellent references or because it has been received by a large number of Christians. Everything depends on its intimate, organic and living connection with the fundamental fact of Christianity.[9]

This Lutheran view was clearly connected with a stress on the fiducial and saving character of faith, albeit to the detriment of its noetic and contemplative value. At the level of saving faith, the insight was a true one and could even be illustrated from texts of Thomas Aquinas.[10] Even the idea of a canon within the canon, which is the subject of much discussion today, is not lacking in either value or interest.[11] Its principle is the gospel, in the evocative sense that Luther gives to this term. There is also talk today of the 'middle' (or centre) of the gospel, Easter as the central fact in the history of salvation.[12] And it is true that the centre of our movement of faith is what St Paul calls 'the mystery of God' or 'the mystery of Christ' (Col.1.26; 2.2; 4.3; Eph.3.4; 6.19; cf. I Tim.3.16, etc.). It seems beyond question, however, that in later Protestantism Luther's insights led to a unilateralism of which Protestant thought is now seeking to be cured, thanks in particular to ecumenical confrontations. Lutherans are agreed today that what one might call the heart of the Gospel can be expressed with other New Testament ideas than that of justification, like reconciliation, new life, new creation. At the Waldenburg Week in 1930, Superintendent W. Zöllner said, 'In the sixteenth century we rediscovered the Epistle to the Romans. We are now rediscovering the Epistle to the Ephesians.'[13] One could cite dozens of similar testimonies.

Möhler said that 'the great work which reconciles man with God' is the essential content of the gospel.[14] Early Christianity said that that is what God has done by sending his Son in our flesh, that we might become sons of God. It has been demonstrated that between Tatian (the first to describe the Gospel of John as 'scripture', in 176) and St Irenaeus, and including the Muratorian canon (Rome, about 185), it was the Gospel of John that was taken as a kind of 'canon within the canon'.[15] It is probable that the Orthodox would be happy with this view.

So far we have been considering a hierarchy of truths from the perspective of their objective content. One can also find a *de facto* hierarchy arising from the way in which a particular truth is understood and lived out by a group, a school – one need only think of Alexandria and Antioch, of Africa between the third and fifth centuries, the schools of theology or spirituality – a given period, which is succeeded by another, or even a church and its particular cultural setting.

From a purely intellectual and logical point of view, any true statement of whatever kind is equal to another true statement. The character of truth is an absolute which, as such and in a formal way, cannot be either more or less true. From this point of view there could not be degrees in truth. But truth is truth *about something*, and is recognized and professed *by someone*. Because of the former, we have a hierarchy of truths depending on their more or less immediate or mediate relationship, depending on whether they are nearer to or further from the roots and the focal point of revelation and faith, the Christ, sacrament of our union with God. We need to pause a moment on the second aspect.

A truth has reality as such only as it is perceived and expressed by the mind. Only the uncreated Spirit of God and the human conscience of Christ perceive and express supernatural truth perfectly. However, they belong to the transcendent and metahistorical sphere. Here on earth, the perception and expression of supernatural truth, even by the church or the churches, are subject to a historicity which imposes limits on them. So it is possible for there to be differences in the perception and expression of Christian truths, either between churches or between different periods in the same church. The difference in the content of the 'canon within the canon' that we have already encountered, which certainly exists between the Protestant world and the Orthodox Eastern world, illustrates that well enough. Hence we can recognize a different form of 'hierarchy of truths' from the objective form, depending on a relationship to the centre of revelation, namely the historical forms of the dogmatic statements of the Christian churches.

In these expressions we necessarily find particular elements of culture, language and vocabulary, and of common philosophy. Thus a human element of interpretation, systematization and expression is combined with the perception of faith which may become dogma. As one instance, Fr Tavard suggested transsubstantiation as an expression of the real presence (284). As another, I would also venture to suggest the way of explaining the relationship of the Holy Spirit to the second person in the eternal and immanent being of God.[16] The theme of 'hierarchy of truths' would thus find a second application, in ecumenism. It would then play a part in the question of the comparison of creeds.

U. Valeske, Tavard and I, along with others, have shown that the ancient tradition, and more particular that of the heyday of Scholasticism, contained antecedents or equivalents of the notion of 'hierarchies of truths'. Let me recall two of them: the distinction between heresies, depending on their gravity and on how radical they are; and the distinction of two categories in the articles of faith.

1. Heresies differ in their seriousness, and in the harm that they inflict on membership of the church. The church basically rests on faith, a faith professed and sealed in baptism. This raises the question of the nature of the profession of faith which makes baptism true, and of what destroys its truth. This question was raised on the level

of the universal church at the council of Nicaea. In canons 8 and 19, the council gave two different solutions, one relating to the Novatians, who were dissidents over penitential discipline, and the other relating to the disciples of Paul of Samosata, whose doctrine did serious damage to trinitarian belief.[17] However, questions relating to Easter were settled on the basis of a very interesting principle, even if the specific application of the principle seems somewhat surprising. It distinguishes between heresy and trinitarian heresy, i.e. heresy involving trinitarian faith as sealed in baptism; there were heresies which radically destroyed this faith and others which did not. Thus there was a hierarchy of errors, and that presupposed a hierarchy of truths. This application was favourable to the Arians, who at least professed a Trinity of persons. It was possible for them to be reconciled after a profession of faith, and they were not rebaptized.

Once again, I am only recalling the principle involved: radical membership of the church on the basis of baptism which sealed a profession of faith in which the most essential truths were honoured. It seems to me that, given the illustration provided by the historical example I recalled above, the Vatican II statement about a hierarchy of truths is of interest not only in theological dialogue, but also in the ecclesiology of imperfect communion which needs to be perfected, a theme which underlies the ecumenism of Vatican II.

2. The most representative figures of thirteenth-century Scholasticism had a very vivid awareness of truths being centred on some principal articles, and therefore of an organic structure, as much of faith and its confession as of the revelation to which it is responding. For example, the position of St Thomas Aquinas has been expounded more than once, by myself among others.[18] Thomas distinguishes two categories among the truths of faith which have been primarily the object of revelation, those which directly have this character by reason of their content, *directe, per se*; and those which are indirectly such by reason of the relationship they have with the former, *indirecte, in ordine ad alia*.[19] Now when Thomas defines the content which puts a statement in the first category, he says, 'That by which man is attracted and made completely happy, that of which the vision will be given to us in eternal life, and that by which we can arrive at this eternal life: that corresponds specifically to the intrinsic mystery of God and of the Incarnation, theology and the economy.'[20] In the vocabulary of the Eastern tradition, which should have been familiar to the Latin West, there was talk of deification. However, one could just as well put salvation in this

category, since this is, through Christ and the Holy Spirit, the achievement or the success of man in God. St Thomas gives whatever is relevant to this salvation as the specific content of *sacra doctrina*, the term he uses to denote the totality of communications of revealed truth, scripture, tradition, preaching and theology.[21] Often, moreover, he explains, as did St Augustine before him[22]: *doctrina quae est de pertinentibus ad salutem*,[23] *doctrina salutaris*.[24]

We can find a prudent echo of this traditional doctrine in the dogmatic constitution of Vatican II on divine revelation.[25]

The texts of St Thomas which I have cited are an example of how the *credenda* may be reduced to the articles of the creed. What interests me is not so much this explanation as a scholastic technique, which I find quite artificial; it is the feeling behind it and the fact that it expresses an essential and central content of revelation, and therefore of dogma and the faith. God did not speak to teach us just anything, but to reveal to us the truth of our destiny in him. The Bible is not just a collection of disparate statements or stories. It has a centre, a kernel. And in that sense, there is an 'essence of Christianity'.

There is another traditional datum of theology, related to the previous one, which we must recall here: the truths which it is necessary to believe for salvation. The Schoolmen held that these truths are all contained in scripture.[26] The Reformers, e.g. Bucer, used this notion of *ad salutem creditu necessaria*, and connected it with the fundamental truths. In the Middle Ages scholars were dealing with a largely illiterate people and they had no printed books. A theology of implicit faith had also been developed.[27] Beyond question the notion was twisted to signify confidence in and pure obedience towards the church: the 'faith of the common man', a faith by proxy which the Reformers had to reject, staking everything on salvation by faith, and faith and trust in Jesus, my saviour. However, the great Schoolmen like St Thomas did not forget the aspect of knowledge and personal commitment. The question was not resolved by an appeal only to the *quo*; there was also a reference to the *quod*, to the content that everyone *could* attain in accordance with their condition and *should* know in accordance with their function, their *officium*. Among ordinary Christians, this was an explicit belief in the articles of the creed and the mysteries celebrated in the liturgical festivals.[28] Implicit faith would relate, on the one hand to this explicit faith, and on the other to what the *maiores* held explicitly, each according to his *officium*.[29] But there was no unconditional subordination of the *minores* to the *maiores*.[30]

Commenting on the passage in the declaration *Mysterium Ecclesiae* that I quoted above (n.5), Karl Rahner wrote: 'When the document goes on to say that "all dogmas must be believed with the same divine faith", this is too easy a way out; and the existential and ecclesiastical significance of the hierarchy of truths becomes illusory. Of course, a Catholic Christian cannot absolutely deny any dogmas. But does every Catholic have to affirm every single dogma with a positive, absolute assent? If we presupposed this, then the doctrine about the *fides implicita*, the theological question about the extent of what has to be believed as necessary for salvation, and the teaching about the hierarchy of truths as well, would in fact no longer have any practical significance.'[31]

Rahner's question certainly holds for individuals. It is hard to see how one could apply it to churches as such, at least if it were a question of basing unity or full communion with the Catholic church on a minimum. However, adherence to the Apostles' and Nicene Creeds, held by all the classical churches, marks out an area of faith which is the basis for a communion. What should it be called? People of God, brotherly communion of Christians? There is incorporation in Christ, there is communion in the *res* of salvation without complete communion in the *sacramentum* instituted to bring about this *res*, for this *sacramentum* is not only the act of baptism, but is the church with its profession of the whole faith, and the celebration of the eucharist.[32] The churches or ecclesial communities are moving towards eschatological plenitude. Those involved in the ecumenical movement have by virtue of that a *votum unitatis, votum catholicitatis*, which gives to their present belief a dynamic dimension in which their intention of plenitude is fulfilled.

This is the inspiration for what the World Council of Churches represents, *koinonia ton ekklesion*. It gives the Council a real ecclesial value, difficult though that may be to define.[33]

13

Tradition and Traditions

The member churches of the World Council have become aware that although they have the same orientation on scripture and an equal concern to make it the norm of their dogma and their lives, they still have different confessions of faith, liturgies, ecclesiastical structures and theologies. Thirty years ago, Paul Evdokimov wrote: 'Catholics, Protestants, Orthodox, we are all grouped round the Bible. The closed Bible unites us; as soon as we open its pages, the open Bible disunites us. We read it differently, we read different truths in it.'[1] Perhaps that goes too far, because today there is quite a large degree of agreement at an exegetical level. However, it remains true that no church lives by scripture pure and simple. Each church lives by scripture in and through a certain tradition. The awareness of this fact, made explicit from the time of the Third World Conference of Faith and Order, held at Lund from 15-28 August 1952, even led to the formation of a commission to study the question of tradition. This commission published a provisional report in 1961: *The Old and the New in the Church*. Then the two sub-commissions or sections, one North American and the other European, each produced a very interesting preparatory rport for the Fourth World Conference of Faith and Order, held at Montreal from 12 to 26 July 1963.[2]

These reports are a landmark. They have expressed a vivid awareness of the historical character of the church, with its two aspects of continuity and newness. Christianity did not begin in the sixteenth century; it has been handed down since Christ and Pentecost. Equally, the reports have demonstrated the need to reconsider relations between scripture and tradition. They criticized the slogan *scriptura sola*. At the same time (November 1962) these questions were discussed at Vatican II; Fr R.Rouquette could write that the vote taken there on 20 November marked the end of the Counter-Reformation.[3]

The synthesis aimed at for the Montreal conference had been prepared for by a Faith and Order document (no.40, Geneva 1963). It is the Montreal Report which is of interest to us.[4] It analysed and sharpened up the distinctions, suggested by the reports, between three understandings of the word tradition:

The content of Tradition (with a capital T) is 'the revelation of God and the gift which he has made of himself in Christ, his presence in the life of the church' by the power of the Holy Spirit (nos.45,46). Scripture is the written form or the written testimony to this (no.50).

By contrast, tradition (with a small t) is the fact of the transmission of Tradition (no.46). Catechetical teaching is an essential vehicle of it (no.74), but so too are the word and the sacraments (no.56 end). 'Tradition can be a faithful transmission of the Gospel, but it can also disfigure it'(no.48).

The traditions 'are the expressions and manifestations under different historical forms of the one truth and the one reality which is Christ' (no.47). These historical expressions and forms characterize the different 'confessions' or existing groups: there is the Presbyterian tradition, the pietistic tradition, the Roman tradition, and so on. So the word can designate either the form of expression or the 'confession' which hands it on and is characterized by it (no.47). It is clear that geographical, ethnic, historical and cultural elements find their way into these specific expressions which are characteristic of a group, being conveyed through history and seeing to the continuance of the group. These traditions are in fact the specific vehicle of Tradition: they can transmit it all. That this happens in the case of fundamental matters is the basis for a Christianity common to all the communions, the fact which makes ecumenism possible. However, should we not recognize that all the churches, in their specific and historical reality, are incomplete realizations and expressions of Tradition? That applies even to the Orthodox Church and to the Roman Catholic Church. That is also the basis and the appeal of ecumenism.

What will be the criterion for the fidelity of tradition and traditions to the Tradition? The Montreal Conference identified it as scripture (no.49), the scriptures correctly interpreted. But what is 'correct interpretation' (no.51)?[5] 'The question of interpretation arises as soon as one resorts to written documents' (no.49). 'This problem has been regarded in various ways by the different churches' (no.53), a statement which is followed by the main approaches. This is too complex a question to be discusssed in a few words, and in any case it is not directly relevant.

By contrast, I would want to keep one of the expressions relevant to the theme of this book: diversity in a degree of unity. In ecumenism I constantly welcome the expression that 'the others' make the traditions in which they live out Christianity. And we make our starting point the division between elements of doctrine and 'non-theological' (ethnic, historical and cultural) themes of division. The report of the American section commented here:

> Pluralism is evident throughout the history of the church. The diversity of traditions must be recognized, even when the integrity of the Tradition is professed. This diversity cannot be eliminated by a simplistic return to New Testament Christianity, to the *consensus quinquesaecularis*, to the Vincentian canon or to an elementary paradigm, like the idealization of the thirteenth or sixteenth centuries. No tradition of itself has the authority to disinherit the others. All have a fundamental right to be examined in the light of the intention that they profess to obey the tradition.[6]

That is the dossier, the challenge or the paradox of ecumenism. It is on the move towards the final eschatological revelation and communion. An impossible task? It is enough to know that we are summoned to perform it. That is a necessity.

14

Theological 'Agreements'

As theological agreements are produced almost every year, and as their 'acceptance' is a process which involves time, I need to date the writing of the present chapter. It was written in the middle of December 1980. I shall talk only of theological agreements and not of theological dialogues or conversations which can end up in communiqués, not to mention agreed conclusions, but do not have the character of formal declarations of agreement.[1] The levels on which these agreements are reached and the qualifications made to them differ. We need to apply a very simple criterion to them.[2]

We have either declarations or doctrinal formulae presented on the highest authority which commit the churches. Among these declarations I would include the lifting of the anathemas between Rome and Constantinople (which go back to 1054), which was promulgated simultaneously on 7 December 1965 at Istanbul (by Patriarch Athenagoras) and at Rome in the General Session of the Second Vatican Council (Mgr Willebrands, in the name and in the presence of Paul VI);[3] the joint declaration between Paul VI and Dr Michael Ramsey, Archbishop of Canterbury, at the inauguration of the dialogue between the Roman Catholic Church and the Anglican Communion on 24 March 1966 (DC 1469, 682); between Paul VI and Dr Coggan, Archbishop of Canterbury, on 29 April 1977 (DC 1720, 458); and between John Paul II and Robert Runcie, the present Archbishop.

These are declarations with a practical concern. By contrast, there is at least one declaration the content and tenor of which relates to dogma: that between Paul VI and the Coptic Patriarch, Pope of Alexandria, Shenouda III, on christology (10 May 1973, DC 1633, 515). It is a model ecumenical document: in fact it expresses the christological faith of Chalcedon without using the formulations of Chalcedon, which the Copts reject. This encounter between two heads of churches was followed by the institution of a joint commission which, among other things, took up this christological question.[4]

In addition to authorities which commit the churches, there are agreements prepared and voted on by commissions. There are two or even three different kinds of these:

1. Joint commissions the members of which are officially nominated by the church authorities at a world level. These can be bilateral or multilateral.

2. Commissions, the members of which are officially nominated by the authorities at a national level. The perfect example of this is the commission between Catholics and Lutherans in the United States; it has done quite remarkable work.

3. Commissions or working parties not officially mandated and, in that sense, private. I shall make some more specific comments, beginning with this third group.

3. The Dombes Group is well known in France, not to say famous.[5] Its first beginnings, due to Abbé Paul Couturier, date from 1937. Its theological intervention in the ecumenical sphere extends over two periods: 1956-1970, when each week of common prayer and work ended with theses which were accepted unanimously; and 1971 and the following years, when work ended in agreements or elements of agreement bearing on the principal sacraments which mark out church life.[6] Texts of this kind tend to look for a form of expression which accords with the views and sensibilities of both Protestants and Catholics, and yet is situated outside (or within?) certain confessional statements which, in the case of Roman Catholicism, derive from mediaeval Scholasticism or the Counter-Reformation. Questions are raised and even criticisms are made in this connection.[7]

The Dombes Group is a private group, the members of which are co-opted. However, many of them hold responsible positions in their churches, and indeed bear authoritative titles, so that they deserve to be taken seriously. The published documents are notable for their weight of wisdom and seriousness; they have a worth and credit going far beyond those of a private document.

Ecumenical Institutes in German universities: there are three Protestant and three Catholic Institutes. In 1973 they published a document on 'Reformation and Recognition of Ministries in the Churches'.[8] The preparatory studies for the document were published with it. Many people have found its basis inadequate and not sufficiently serious – indeed, it has been said to be somewhat adventurous. It remains as testimony to the thoughts and proposals of men of indisputable worth and ecumenical zeal.

2. In France, in 1968 the Joint Catholic-Protestant Committee issued a 'Declaration on the so-called Problems of Intercommunion and Reflections', along with 'Reflections and Questions relating to the *communicatio in sacris*', submitted to authorities and theologians of the Catholic church and the Reformed churches in France. In 1972, the same committtee published a common declaration on baptism (*DC 1623, 22*) *and a doctrinal agreement on marriage (DC* 1623, 24) which is obviously very important. Then, in 1975, came a 'Note on the Ecumenical Celebration of the Baptism of Children of Mixed Marriages' (*DC* 1673, 318ff.).

In Switzerland, in 1971-3, an interconfessional commission worked out an agreement for the mutual recognition of baptism, and the same thing happened in Belgium in 1971 (*DC* 1600, 35).

The Commission for the Union of Catholics and Lutherans in the USA is a model of methodical work, and is remarkably progressive. The first study was on The Nicene Creed as an Ecumenical Document (1965); this was followed by Baptism for the Remission of Sins (1966); The Eucharist as Sacrifice (1967); Church and Ministry (1970); Papal Primacy and Universal Church.[9] In 1978 there was a discussion of the delicate question of 'Teaching Authority and Infallibility in the Church'. The subjects are linked, and agreement on the preceding issue served as a stepping stone towards the next, as at Dombes. Each time an agreed text was established, and then each party made its own statements; note was taken of the differences which remained or of points on which agreement still had to be reached. This work is probably most advanced with the Lutherans.

1. That is also true at the level of Joint Official Commissions at a non-local level which in this sense are universal. From the Catholic side, members are appointed by the Roman Secretariat for Unity. With the World Lutheran Federation, after the meetings begun in 1967, this has led to the so-called Malta Report on the Gospel and the Church (1971). Athough it is obviously imperfect, and open to many questions which still need to be resolved, it is quite a remarkable basis for substantial agreement. Then the Joint Commission produced a volume *Das Herrenmahl*, Paderborn and Frankfurt 1978, on the eucharist.[10]

The initials ARCIC denote the Joint Commission between the Anglican Communion and the Roman Catholic Church. It, too,

links its working themes. It has produced the following joint
declarations: on the Eucharist, the so-called Windsor Report; on
the Ministry, Canterbury 1973; on Authority in the Church, Venice
1976. A commission on the theology of marriage with reference to
mixed marriages (1967-1975) published its conclusions in 1976.

A Joint Commission of the Catholic Church and the Reformed
World Alliance, formed in 1970, published at the end of 1976 a joint
report on 'The Presence of Christ in the Church and in the World'.
One might add a tripartite report produced by the Roman Catholic
church, the World Lutheran Federation and the World Reformed
Alliance on the theology of marriage and the problem of mixed
marriages.

Criteriology or theological evaluation

1. In 1977, the Roman Secretariat for Unity defined the meaning of
expressions in the languages most frequently used relating to the
area with which we are concerned. They are:

Convergence: this is more a matter of a dynamism towards a goal
than of a substantial agreement.

Agreed Statement (*point d'accord, Einzelüberstimmung*): agreement on a particular point, leaving more or less profound differences
on others.

Consensus (*Konsens*) or Full Agreement (*volle Übereinstim-
mung, accord plénier/total*): a total agreement at least in content, if
not in expression.

Substantial agreeement (*accord substantiel, substanzielle Über-
einstimmung*): this relates to a basic nucleus without which the
message of salvation is not transmitted in its integrity, while accepting that neither doctrinal elaborations nor practice correspond
entirely among the partner churches. The essentials are assured,
and there is the same shared intention of faith.

2. Even the agreements of category 1 are only, for the moment, the
agreements of theologians. Certainly these are men of the churches,
aware of their responsibility in that role. Those designated by the
Roman Secretariat are presumed to be men of sound doctrine.
Where the relevant pastoral authorities have not adopted agreements, these are the sole responsibility of the commissions which
have published them. Theologians can commend practical decisions
which pastors in office do not follow, for example those in the United
States which argued for the possibility of intercommunion or con-
celebration between Catholics, Episcopalians and Lutherans.[11]

Acceptance by the grass roots is yet another question, beginning with the extent to which people are kept informed of the agreements proposed.

3. It is conceivable, and I for my part would think it desirable, that the authorities concerned should note publicly at the highest level that in certain terms, on particular points, there is no (or there is no longer any) difference. They could indicate issues which need to be elucidated and the lines which should be pursued. Speaking to the Secretariat on 8 February 1980, John Paul II said: '[Once agreements by commissions and by the experts have been concluded] the Catholic church could make an official pronouncement and draw the conclusions for the next step.'[12]

However, it should be noted here that the partners do not have the same structure of teaching authority, nor even always the same demands or the same possibilities of reference to a normative doctrine. From the Catholic side these points are clear enough in principle: certainly, a papal declaration is law. However, even on the Lutheran side, where there is more of a common doctrine – the same confessional documents are recognized throughout the world; there is the same concern for pure doctrine - there are the difficulties recognized in the Malta Report.[13] These difficulties are even greater with other partners. Fr Hamer quotes an example which I have also noted (art. cit., 571). The so-called Windsor Agreement with Anglicans on the Eucharist says (no.6): 'Communion with Christ in the Eucharist presupposes his true presence, effectually signified by the bread and wine which, in this mystery, become his body and blood.' This is language which accords with Catholic doctrine: it talks of 'bread and wine' on the level of the sacrament, the sign, but these have become the body and blood of Christ. By contrast, the agreement between Anglicans and Lutherans on the same question is expressed in Lutheran terms: 'In the eucharistic action, including consecration and reception, the bread and wine, while remaining bread and wine, become the means whereby Christ is truly present and gives himself to the communicants.'[14] This is an expression of what is called impanation. Now I personally do not think it evident that this theory is incompatible with the faith of the undivided church, though many people do; one can see how the same church can hold two different formulas. That involves any agreement concluded with it in a degree of uncertainty which stands in the way of any final settlement.

4. The very status of the agreements arrived at in ecumenical dialogue means that their texts do not embrace completely any of the normative texts to which, rightly or wrongly, there has been opposition so far. Were there complete agreement, it would be a unity of belief and union. Rather, there tends to be a certain detachment from confessional texts, which has come about, to take up the question once again, from fresher sources and a situation of openness. Commenting on the ARCIC agreement on the eucharist, Bishop Butler said: 'Our work has consisted in leaving aside for the moment both Trent and the Articles (without, of course, denying either their authority or their truth) and turning towards the Bible and the "common tradition" shared and revered by our two communions in the course of the centuries preceding the Reformation.'[15] This is what has sometimes been called the 'metadogmatic' method. This work is not at the level of conclusions, but at that of dynamic process or of a movement which is intended progressively to lead there. Basically, the term 'agreement' is somewhat ambiguous. The English word 'statement' is more neutral. These are stages on the way to 'full agreement'. That is why I can only feel that 'agreements' would be devalued by a critical evaluation made in the name of the more precise formulae of dogma, not to mention Catholic theology, as Fr Bertrand de Margerie has suggested in connection with agreements relating to the eucharist, the 'priesthood' and ministries.[16] It is worth reminding ourselves of these demands, without always making them. But the 'agreements' are there, on a road on which we encounter other Christian traditions tending towards a unity which embraces the value of these traditions.

In this connection the French Episcopal Committee for the Unity of Christians has published a precise and subtle note on the subject of the important Dombes Group document: 'Towards the same eucharistic faith'.[17] It notes certain inadequacies of expression and specifies the more abstruse conclusions, but first it comments:

> The Committee considers this document to be an important stage in a broad approach towards a doctrinal agreement. However, by definition movement is not the end-point. So it is necessary to appreciate the stages that have been gone through in relation both to the starting point and to the goal (no.2).
>
> An attempt at ecumenical expression of the faith necessarily obliges us not to take as starting points doctrinal formulations which in the past have been points of dispute, not to mention polemic. For this reason, the Dombes document often avoids

particular formulae to which many Catholics are used and which contribute to the structure of their faith (no.5).

Is it not precisely by virtue of this aspect of consensus yet to be achieved, or perhaps incapable of achievement, that the 'agreements' are of particular interest to the general theme of this study, 'diversity and communion'? They are one element of it, at least provisionally, by forming a stage.

The ecumenical process is obviously concerned with more than the relationship of other communions to the Catholic Church. It is also concerned with the relationship between these other communions. That is an enormous area, of immense diversity. There can be no question of cataloguing it here.[18] I have chosen to limit myself to a single instance, the agreement between Lutherans and Reformed on the question of the eucharist.

The starting point was an age-old opposition between the two schools, relating to their general views on predestination and above all on the eucharistic reality, in connection with certain christological theses (the *extra Calvinisticum*). Despite attempts at union, and even the highly dubious creation of a 'United Church' by the King of Prussia in 1817 – a third confession! – there are numerous Lutheran affirmations to the effect that union would be easier with the Catholics than with the Reformed. People have come much closer together. However, in signing the fine Barmen Declaration of 1934, the Lutherans noted that they did not recognize it as a confessional document expressing a church union because it did not touch on the question of the eucharist. Nevertheless, the firm confession which it made of a sole Lord had a dynamism of its own, which was recognized in Halle in 1937. It was impossible to prevent intercommunion between the three confessions! It was necessary to provide a theological basis for this practice. The assembly of the Protestant Church in Germany at Treysa in 1947 also decided to open up conversations on this question.[19] They took place, in a series of six sessions, at Arnoldshain, from 1947 to 1957, and resulted in the Arnoldshain Theses (2 November 1957) which were presented to the Protestant Church in Germany on 25 July 1958.

These were the theses and the conclusion of *theologians*, and it was necessary for the churches to receive them.[20] However, even the theologians themselves differed on how to read them. H.Gollwitzer and W.Kreck saw in the receiving of the Lord's Supper what the Lord *does* or *gives*, not what he *is*; Peter Brunner, a classical but open Lutheran, stressed that the gift and the giver are identical: Jesus is given in person in the sacrament. Another more 'confessional' Lutheran, E. Sommerlath, had refused to sign. The VELKD (Vereinigte Evangelische-Lutherische Kirche Deutschlands: United Protestant Lutheran Church of Germany) saw the theses only as a study document. In fact they were vigorously discussed. However, they were put forward for acceptance by the Reformed Churches of Europe in a much broader document concerned also with the understanding of the gospel, justification by faith, christology, predestination and baptism. After discussion, this document was accepted at Leuenberg in 1971.[21] The churches had to adopt a position on this agreement: the date they were given as a deadline was 1 March 1973. Of the eighty-nine Protestant churches of Europe, seventy-one signed; some refused, for example the synod of the Lutheran Church of Finland.[22] The fact remained that the Concord was not a confession of faith by the church. All it signified was that the Protestant churches of Europe could make a joint confession on the Lord's Supper, the expression of a fellowship of churches of different confessions which, for the moment, wish to remain such, but a confession which is thought sufficient to allow intercommunion.

By definition, intercommunion is not communion pure and simple.

15

A Catholic 'Recognition' of the Augsburg Confession?

Charles V had a deep desire to re-establish the religious unity of his empire. At the diet of Augsburg, the princes and cities which had supported Luther's movement were required to present to him an apologia or 'confession of faith' in response to his proposal for peace. This was the Augsburg Confession, composed by Melanchthon on the basis of various professions of faith or anterior articles, approved by Luther, albeit with some reservations, and read before the emperor on 5 June 1530.[1] Despite a substantial approach, in particular from the Commission of Fourteen, and although the *Confutatio* produced by the Catholic theologians, including Johannes Eck, found hardly anything to take up in the purely dogmatic sphere, there was a stalemate. Soon positions hardened and became involved in the political conflict, and the Confession was read not in its own irenical and traditional perspective but in the context of polemic and violent pamphleteering. And so the centuries went by.

Now, however, in the climate of a confident and constructive dialogue carried on over about fifteen years, Vincent Pfnür has put forward the idea that a 'recognition' of the Augsburg Confession by Catholics is at last possible![2] Pfnür's teacher, J. Ratzinger, echoed him in a lecture given in Graz in January 1976.[3] Since then the question has been studied and discussed; a large number of publications, of great scholarly value, were issued on the occasion of the 450th anniversary of the Augsburg Confession.[4] Almost all that can be said has been said. The question is of very positive relevance to the theme of the present work. In fact it meets up with the idea of 'reconciled diversity' put forward by Harding Meyer and adopted by the assembly of the World Lutheran Federation at Dar-es-Salaam in June 1977. The idea would be to accept that the Augsburg

Confession is an expression of the Catholic faith acceptable as such, and therefore that the churches whose dogmatic basis it represents are a variety of Catholicism.

But what does 'recognition' mean?[5] It is a term that can be found in all the documents of the World Council from the Toronto Declaration (1950) to the Nairobi Assembly (1975). But it is always made precise or specific: 'recognize as church', 'recognize as bishop', etc. To 'recognize' is not to accept the reality in question as one's own; it is less strong than 'receive' (acceptance consists in making one's own a resolution framed by someone else). The other keeps a degree of otherness or autonomy, but is considered as belonging to the same family. The Augsburg Confession would be seen by the Roman Catholic Church as one possible and legitimate expression of a common Catholic faith. That would obviously mean that the Lutheran churches, which sometimes call themselves 'the church of the Augsburg Confession', represent a variety of the main Catholic church.

There are many reasons for recognizing the Augsburg Confession. Its formal intention was to express a possible position in a Catholic church which had not yet arrived at the Council of Trent, Vatican I, the mariological dogmas of 1854 and 1950, the Counter-Reformation, the anti-revolutionary Restoration, the Syllabus or the anti-modernist reaction. The Augsburg Confession assumes the faith of Nicaea and Chalcedon; the confessional Lutheran writings begin with the Apostles' Creed, the Niceno-Constantinopolitan Creed and the so-called Athanasian Creed. Luther and the Reformation kept the dogma of the ancient church.[6] The *Confutatio* does not find much to object to in the first twenty-one articles, which are about doctrine; those which follow criticize (often in an excessive way) abuses which Lutherans today recognize as no longer existing. Bossuet produced for the Duke of Saxe-Gotha an appreciation of the Augsburg Confession which, using Melanchthon's apologia, and passages from other credal writings and from Luther himself, showed the accord of this Augsburg Confession with Catholic doctrine and the Council of Trent.[7] At this very council, in 1561, the Cardinal of Lorraine proposed taking the Augsburg Confession as a basis of reconciliation.[8] In our day many Catholics have allowed the possibility of a recognition, albeit with differences and qualifications: Bishop Martensen of Copenhagen, J.Ratzinger, W.Kasper of Tübingen,[9] H.Fries of Munich,[10] H.Schütte, V.Pfnür and Fr Daniel Olivier, the best Catholic authority on Lutheranism.[11] In their pastoral letter for the Week of Unity in 1980, the bishops of the

Federal German Republic expressed their joy at the fact that the Augsburg Confession represents 'a consensus over the central truths of our fatih'. All recognized that the Augsburg Confession had its faults, but also that the progress of dialogue has begun to remedy them. The joint commentary on the whole of the Augsburg Confession has taken account of present ecumenical developments and the results of dialogues. Its title is significant.[12] Such a mode of procedure is legitimate: it moves the Augsburg Confession in the direction of its formal intent, namely to manifest its agreement with the traditional church, once that has itself undergone purification.

It is clear that so long as a 'recognition' was neither grudging nor excessively reticent, it would have an unforeseeable impact on general attitudes. It would stir things up, and would open up unsuspected possibilities in the direction of an organic unity.

Of course, considerable difficulties remain. They have not been hidden in the publications that I have come across. First of all, one cannot isolate the Augsburg Confession either from the church whose fundamental text it is, with the riches of its four centuries of history; or from the other confessional writings of this church – the Apology, the Catechisms of Luther, the Schmalkald articles, the Formula of Concord; or from Luther himself, who cannot be reduced to Melancthon's work.[13] A Catholic 'recognition' would call for reciprocity. Is the Lutheran church ready to recognize that it is Catholic in a communion with the Catholic Church as it has become and as it is?

The Augsburg Confession has weaknesses. It is not just that it does not mention the Pope or purgatory; its theology of eucharistic celebration and its ecclesiology are unsatisfactory. It suffers from a lack of sacramental sense. Here Orthodox criticism joins up with our own. Very little of what the Greeks see in mystery, the presence of eschatological realities in the life and celebrations of the church, can be found here. It has been shown that the *satis est* of Article VII is not exclusive and that the minister has his place, but the church of the Augsburg Confession remains that of a humanist professor. The very genre of the sixteenth-century confessions of faith lends itself to this kind of discourse.[14]

We cannot fail to note the risk that a 'Recognition' of the Augsburg Confession would unleash indignation among Catholic conservatives who remain strangers to the movement of ideas and specifically to ecumenism. The healing of a rift could produce a schism. I am very sensitive to such painful possibilities.

However, I also appreciate the well-founded and serious possibility that by the grace of God immense progress can be made on the road of reconciliation. It will be a progress not against the truth but for it and towards it. In the course of his reception for representatives of the other churches in Paris on 31 May 1980, His Holiness John Paul II said: 'I take most seriously the anniversary that you are celebrating this year, the 450th anniversary of the *Confessio Augustana*; yes, very seriously indeed. I experience it in a way which is incomprehensible to me because it is someone who experiences it in me. "Someone will lead you": I think that the words which the Lord said to Peter are perhaps the most important of all the words he ever heard: "Someone will lead you".'[15] Less mysteriously, in the General Audience of 25 June 1980, the precise anniversary of the day on which the Augsburg Confession had been read before Charles V, the pope said: 'I would like to encourage all the faithful, and above all the theologians, begging them in fidelity to Christ and the Gospel, in fidelity to the "earliest church", in fidelity to the Fathers of the Church and to the Ecumenical Councils, to search with our brothers and sisters for the Christian heritage which unites us, and to rediscover the mutual blessings of faith.'

What future should we envisage? In 1979 H.Fries argued in favour of a 'recognition' which would consist in 'considering and validating the Augsburg Confession as a legitimate interpretation of the faith and thus saying that this confession bears witness, in its own way and in its own language, to the same content of faith as that to which the Catholic church bears witness: it is a legimate expression of Christian truth.'[16] That would presuppose that important points of doctrine were brought out in a sense of substantial agreement. In these conditions, the Lutheran expression of the common faith would represent a development in response to a particular charism. It would make clear the message of salvation by pure grace, of Christian liberty in the faith, of the sovereignty of the Word of God, and finally of a theology of the cross. It would be a school not only recognized as such, but one which kept its parochial and organizational structure, though henceforward in reconciliation and unity.

Is that possible?

16

'Reconciled Diversity'. How would Möhler have Reacted?

In its assembly at Dar-es-Salaam in June 1977, the World Lutheran Federation adopted the proposal of 'reconciled diversity, *Versöhnte Verschiedenheit*'. That had been proposed by the Concord of Leuenberg, which allowed the joint possibility of different doctrinal theses between the Lutheran church and the Reformed churches, although for centuries, above all on the Lutheran side, these points had been thought irreconcilable. The idea of reconciled diversity could be extended and become the formula for ecumenism, even between the Lutheran Church and the Catholic Church.[1]

However, in the World Council itself, it has come up against the idea of unity developed by the Faith and Order Commission under the title 'conciliar community'. That in effect sets out to be a synonym for organic unity and presupposes that unity of faith and sacramental life has been achieved at the local level.[2] Thus there is a tension at the heart of the World Council between this ideal of organic unity and the maintaining of 'confessional families', among which the Lutheran one affirms itself with a particular vitality. In fact all the Lutheran churches have had the same confessional writings from the start, and these play an active and decisive role among them: doctrine, *'reine' Lehre*, fixed in the confessional writings of the sixteenth century and with its reference to the same founding fathers (with Luther the colossus!), provides the climate for a very strong confessional awareness. A 'reconciled diversity' would allow this confessional existence to be retained within a rediscovered communion.[3] However, Faith and Order find it rather different from organic unity. Granted, they have a somewhat inaccurate understanding of 'reconciled diversity', seeing in it 'the description of the persistence of the coexistence of separate confessional groups' (cf. n.2). The Lutherans reply to this criticism, explaining their idea in a sense which brings it close to what I myself would see as diversity in unity.[4] I would still have difficulties to report and requests to make.

They are those which Fr de Montcheuil already expressed in 1938, in a tribute to Möhler:

> It is by virtue of this complex conception of unity that the church has always rejected these attempts at ecumenism which at root are only an attempt to realize a federation of schisms, each of which agrees to recognize the legitimacy of the others. This is to misunderstand true unity in two ways: the unity that people attempt to reconstitute in this way is only a deliberate agreement between different groups; it does not consist in being grafted on to a common trunk to live one's life; one reconciles the churches, but does not make one church. Besides, it is not enough to recognize the right of the other groups to exist: what is needed is to assimilate the truth possessed by each of the others, excluding their exclusiveness. To do that would be to dissolve the groups as groups, so that they could return to the church, assuming that one believes with Möhler that heresy appears when one gives an absolute value to a particular aspect.
>
> But also – and this lesson is now addressed to Catholics – Möhler teaches us that there is nothing more contrary to true Christian unity than the quest for unification. This always consists in wanting to universalize one particular form, to enclose life in one of its expressions. It is always an individuality – that of a man or a group – which denies its limits and seeks to impose on the others. It is negation of diversity among those who are its protagonists; unification estranges those who submit despite themselves from the unity that is needed. There is always, everywhere, a conflict between egoistic particularism and the universalism of the church. But to add to it a conflict between the legitimate tendencies to diversity spontaneously produced in members by the common life and the demands of unification born of a zeal which has not been properly clarified is to risk a break at a point where reciprocal wrongs and equivocation over the themes which have dictated separation make the return to the fold more difficult. Born of pride and provoking defiance, unification would seek to produce unity by moves compromising it at its very source. That would be to 'cling to externals, to reject what is worth most, namely faith and love' (*Einheit*, para.48, 124).[5]

The problem with the Lutheran theme is that it starts from the division which is expressed in the diversity of confessions and not from the reality of the undivided church which carries within itself a fullness to which, in all truth, its dogmatic or theological formulas give only very imperfect expression. I would say that to start from the situations and confessions fixed in the sixteenth century can only be an approach. It is doubtless a necessary manoeuvre for the Protestant churches, since they begin from this situation. But they should ask themselves, with reference to the *reality* of the church inherited from the very beginnings, what there is specifically in that church which is common to the Catholic church and the Orthodox church. The drama – and that is what we must catch today, remedying its consequences – has been that, though they set out only to reform the existing church, the Reformers were led to define, by written works, the status of a confession.[6] Obviously the existing church has a very grave responsibility in that. However, that is our drama.

Möhler (he died in 1838), whom Fr de Montcheuil invokes, had a very lively sense of relationships betwen unity and diversity in the living unity of the church. For him, 'the integrity of the faith does not consist in the sum of all the truths but in the living exchange, within the church, of doctrinal truths which manifest in different ways the one reality lived in faith and charity.'[7] For Möhler, the church is a living reality. On the one hand it is made up of living subjects, who give and express faith and love in a limited, imperfect fashion; on the other hand, it is an organism given life by the Holy Spirit. Now life is not uniformity, monotony; it requires diversities, which it harmonizes. When it comes to the church, what is needed is not uniformity but universality, that is to say, the unity of diversity which constitutes an organic totality. It is here that Möhler is inspired by Schelling and doubtless by Adam Müller (*Lehre vom Gegensatz*, 1804). The *Gegensätze* are contrasted positions which express different aspects of reality. When they are held in the living unity of the church which embraces them, each one is corrected by at least a potential openness to the complementary aspect. They interpenetrate in such a way that they have a mutual relationship. These are diversities in unity. Heresy arises when a subject or group is isolated (Möhler calls this egoism) and develops its *Gegensatz* outside communion with the others. It then turns this into a *Widerspruch*, a contradiction. The restoration of unity does not come about by a reconciliation of contradictions among themselves, as in Hegel, but when false oppositions turn into authentic contrasts *in* the church, in the reality of the church which pre-exists them.

Only there do they rise to consciousness and are brought out into the open (*Einheit*, 46).

What interests me is the notion of unity that these somewhat idealistic analyses outline. One cannot avoid seeing the church as plenitude. The unity which Jesus asks for the church in his 'high-priestly prayer' is that of a unity of plenitude, the image of unity existing between Father and Son.[8] It is not a unity by poverty, by reduction to a single element. Pluralism will find a place there. A redefined confession, according to H.Meyer's formula, that is to say one which has looked again at its confessional principles both critically and positively, in the light of the scriptures expounded and lived out in the Christianity of the fathers and the undivided church, could find a place there. There it would represent its own values, but healed of all contradictions through communion with other values. That precisely would be the fulfilment of the results of our dialogues, for it is with that in view that they take place and in that light that they have already made substantial advances. Of course, all the churches have to make progress in this way. As to the Catholic church, the terms *metanoia*, reform, 're-reception' represent more than a programme: they are already facts. The moves everyone needs to make are primarily spiritual. The dialogues and explanations are necessary, but they must be backed up by a great vitality of prayer and love. There again Möhler is a guide: 'It is at the heart of the distinctive life of each church that we must work; reunion cannot flourish from outside, but can only be the effect of a necessity tested by life. Otherwise it will only be a union concealing a hypocrisy, like all those attempted hitherto. In the primitive church, unity extended outwardly from the inner life; broken unity will only be restored in the same way.'[9] It is also necessary that redefinitions, openness to others, should affect the body of the faithful. So it will be a long process, co-extensive with the life of the church, the churches...

The idea of 'reconciled diversities' thus remains a question mark for us. The Synod of the Dioceses of the German Federal Republic asked itself 'to what degree a union would be possible in the sense that a church respected and recognized the tradition of the other as a possible explanation of revelation, even if this church did not want to adopt it for itself.'[10] That is our problem; it is that of a possible 'recognition' of the Augsburg Confession.

Appendix

Harding Meyer on the Idea of 'Reconciled Diversity'

1. Ecumenical experience and new ecumenical developments have led us to the point where the old conception of a fundamental antagonism between confession and ecumenism, between confessional identity and Christian unity, prove to be out of date and in need of revision if:

2. Confessional assertions can be liberated from the condemnations which have been associated with them down to the present and which have separated the churches; if:

3. The different confessional assertions are rooted in the church and if by virtue of this fact they have a universal Christian impulse, demanding and favouring ecumenical community. [If we are in such an ecumenical situation,] then Christian unity must be understood in such a way as to include confessional identities, instead of abandoning them or seeking to fuse them: in that case it is a matter of creating a concept of Christian unity which is no longer governed by the letter but by the essence of community.

It is in fact very interesting to see how within the ecumenical movement what are sometimes very important currents move neatly towards such a conception of Christian unity.

First of all there is the concept of the conciliar community of churches as it has been recently developed at the World Council, in particular within the Faith and Order Commission. In fact this view of a united church is characterized by the fact that it does not seek a 'monolithic unity' (Nairobi, Section II, no.4) but aims at linking unity and plurality. It would then be appropriate for all the churches, Catholic, Anglican, Orthodox, Lutheran, in short all the confessional churches, to find their place in this conciliar community. However, we must not disguise the fact that this does not seem to be what the Faith and Order Commission, and more recently the Nairobi Assembly, seemed to have in mind when they spoke of Christian unity. It is said in that context that the churches which form the conciliar community are local churches, themselves authentically united. Or, as was said at the session of the Faith and Order Commission at Accra (1974): 'The conciliar community presupposes organic union' (Accra 1974, *Beiheft* to *Oekumenische Rundschau* 27, 67). So the conciliar community is possible only to the degree that confessional identities have already been transcended and suppressed on the local level by the formation of unions of churches and to the degree that there are no longer confessional churches. Thus the concept of conciliar community is still marked in principle by the ancient anti-confessional approach. It is not really in the line of an ecumenical community of confessions.

The concept of unity developed in the European conversations between Lutheran and Reformed, and in the Leuenberg Concord, i.e. the concept of ecclesial communion, is rather different. This in effect envisages an ecumenical community in which the churches keep their confessional identity while being involved in complete communion in preaching, the eucharist, the ministry, witness and service on the basis of a new agreement relating to the conception of the gospel and the abolition of former condemnations. Of course one may again have some reservations or want to raise some questions about the Leuenberg Concord and the communion between the Lutheran and Reformed churches which it seeks to promote. However, that does not in any way alter the fact that here there is a concept of Christian unity which seeks to maintain a union between confessional identity and Christian unity, and also to realize it in practice.

From the Catholic side, ecumenical thought and effort also tend increasingly towards a conception of unity the essentials of which take the same line. The conclusions of the Episcopal Conference of the Federal German Republic in December 1974 included a statement on the theme 'Unity of the Church, the Ecumenical Objective' to the following effect: 'From the beginning, it has been clear that in the church the fullness of the one faith has developed in a larger variety of testimonies of faith' (4,13). 'It is only when the unity of the faith is seen and affirmed at the same time as the plurality of its forms that it is possible to give an objective definition of the aim pursued in seeking the unity of the church' (3.34). Under the title 'Plurality in Unity', the text follows this up in a more precise way: 'In the reconciliation and reunion of churches and ecclesial com-

40rAppendix Harding Meyer 155

munities which have previously been separated these can not only keep their own traditions and riches but integrate them into a greater whole... It is appropriate that one can recognize different confessions in the plurality of traditions... a legitimate plurality, and evaluate them in a positive way. The synod sets its hopes on an evolution which would abolish and surmount the oppositions which have hitherto separated the churches and which would make these once separated churches the bearers of this plurality in the one church of Jesus Christ' (4.32f.).

The declarations of Cardinal Willebrands, in which he takes up and develops the idea that different churches represent different *typoi* which should not be abandoned but kept within the community of the one church of Christ have also found a very lively response. He goes on to define the concept of *typos*: 'We find the reality of a *typos* in the existence of a long and coherent tradition, inspiring love and loyalty in men and women, forming and maintaining an organic and harmonious totality of complementary elements, each of which supports and reinforces the other.' A *typos* is made up of the following elements: a 'characteristic theological method and perspective', a 'characteristic canonical discipline', a 'tradition of spirituality and devotion', a 'characteristic liturgical expression'. And Willebrands declares: 'The life of the church has need of a great variety of *typoi* which show the plenitude of the catholic and apostolic character of the one holy church' (Cardinal Willebrands' Address in Cambridge, England, 18 January 1970, in *Documents on Anglican/Roman Catholic Relations*, 1972, 39ff.)

It is in the *Working Paper on the Ecumenical Role of World Confessional Alliances*, elaborated in 1974 by the Conference of Secretaries of World Confessional Alliances, that we find what is probably the most striking expression of a Christian unity in which the confessional identities are not to be either abandoned or fused but maintained in total communion with one another. This is the expression of 'reconciled diversity'. Let me quote one of the most important passages of this document (I recommend that you should read all of it, or at least Chapters I, IV, V): 'We regard the multiform confessional heritage as being legitimate because the truth of the one faith seeks a great variety of forms of expression in history. We do not forget that these forms of expressing the faith are also marked by errors which have threatened the unity of the church. Furthermore, it is necessary to see that a heritage transposed adequately into new historical situations remains legitimate and must be safeguarded. If that happens, this heritage remains a precious vehicle of the riches of the life of the entire church. In its encounter with other heritages, the contribution of a certain denomination can lose its exclusive character. That is the reason why it is not necessary to make the faith and ecclesial constitutions uniform in order to achieve unity and communion among the churches; these must leave the field free for the plurality or the diversity of convictions and traditions. This idea is as old as the ecumenical movement itself, but it is only in the course of the last ten years that it has been taken seriously... Based on this old idea, a new conception of relationships between confession and ecumenism has developed. Confessional loyalty and ecumenical commitment are not contradictory, but, paradoxical though it may seem, are one and the same thing. When the differences existing between churches no longer separate them, we have a vision of unity with the character of a reconciled diversity' (no.30).

In recent times the concept of reconciled diversity has been both warmly welcomed and criticized. Those who have criticized it – e.g. at the Faith and Order meeting in Accra in 1974 – only see this concept as 'the persistence of the coexistence of separate confessional groups'(sic) (Accra 1974, *Beiheft* to *Oekumenische Rundschau* 27, 67). That is of course a flagrant misunderstanding. But we know – as the discovery of America proves – that errors can also have their merit; and this could contribute to our seeing the concept of reconciled diversity even more clearly; for that to happen it would be necessary above all to reinforce the element of reconciliation.

The working paper has not failed there, though we should certainly continue to develop this point. So it is, for example, that the document calls for fundamental acts of reconciliation like a covenant formula by which the partners bind themselves to one another, the mutual recognition of baptism, the realization of eucharistic communion, the mutual recognition of ministries, common witness and service. These ultimately classic acts of reconciliation, which are in fact a feature of a true and committed ecclesial community, are also the mark of a community of reconciled diversity.

However, if we are to understand the concept of reconciled diversity properly, it is important to note that the Working Paper stresses with great determination that reconciliation between the hitherto separated confessions is inconceivable without renewal and change at the heart of the different confessional identities themselves. A dialogue between the confessions aimed at their reconciliation cannot fail to affect the form in which they have been transmitted. So reconciled diversity does not purely and simply sanction the *status quo*. It has to result in true change and renewal which must not be limited to relations between confessions but must be found first and foremost at the very heart of the confessions.

What does this involve? Surely not a simple smoothing over of confessional differences. It is not easy to combine the reciprocal integration of confessional particularities and the specific confessional convictions of others with the aim pursued. Neither of these corresponds to the idea of a reconciled diversity. In fact this concept itself tends to show another way than that of progressive fusion.

The defence of change and renewal implied in the concept of reconciled diversity is concerned, rather, with a process that could be described as a redefinition of the confessions by dialogue. This redefinition would have a double aspect. It would involve eliminating the elements which have disfigured, distorted and exaggerated the confessional traditions and which, by superimposing themselves on their legitimate and authentic form, have transformed the diversity of confessions into differences separating the churches. It is precisely by this process of change and renewal, which has to be accomplished in dialogue, that the confessions will rediscover their authentic faces and will be able to recognize one another, affirming themselves as legitimate expressions of faith, witness and Christian life. This is the way in which reconciliation of diversities will come about. It is not a matter either of reconciliation or community achieved by the abandonment of confessional identity, or by reciprocal integration of confessional convictions. Still less is it a matter of a tolerant coexistence which would not deserve to be called either reconciliation or community. It is rather a matter of reconciliation and community through the vigorous affirmation of the other with his otherness *redefined*, in a way which shows its legitimacy.

If this reconciliation and this community are to be given specific form in the life of the churches, it will be important to sustain them by specific acts of reconciliation which would doubtless include the classical acts of reconciliation mentioned in the working paper. But at the same time there would be a need for acts of reconciliation oriented even more specifically on a community of reconciled diversity, corresponding to its particular form. It seems to me that these acts could be as follows:

1. A statement saying that the community is based on a common conception of the church, and thus showing that the diversities rest on a common basis capable of supporting them;
2. A theological affirmation explaining why the diversities are

legitimate expressions of Christian faith and church order and why for this reason they must be maintained in one community;

3. A declaration stipulating that the condemnations pronounced in the past no longer apply to the partner whose identity has been redefined;

4. Finally, and this is not the least of the demands, it would be necessary to create, or rather develop, a ministry of unity, whatever its concrete form might be, specifically charged, at the local level as at the level of the universal church, with safeguarding the community in diversity.

PART FOUR

Towards a Conclusion

17

Our Present Situation

At the end of a largely historical enquiry we are confronted with ecumenical reality today. That leads us to ask how one can conceive the unity aimed at by the ecumenical movement with which this century has been graced, at this moment of very human history, which is nevertheless animated by a hope which comes from God. I feel very small and very inadequate. The current issues in world problems are monumental and extremely difficult. Who could claim to have the key to them? All I can offer are some reflections which arise out of more than half a century of study, experience and prayer. Of course they are open to question, but they do also incorporate some certainties and even some evidence.

No church or communion has succeeded in convincing the rest that it is in possession of *the* truth. Despite the profundity of its tradition and its constant affirmation that it is the solution to all our problems, the Orthodox Church has not succeeded in convincing the rest of us that we must return to its fold. Nor has the Catholic church, despite its wealth of arguments, succeeded in convincing others of its papal dogma. Despite their learning and the vitality of their faith in Jesus Christ as saviour, the Protestants have not convinced others that they *are* the *Reformed* church. Nor has the Anglican communion, despite its concern to unite Reformed and traditional Catholicism, effectively been the bridge church which it claims to be. We are still in a position of being face to face or side by side, though to some degree we are also together and even incorporated.

Even if one could point out some hitches, we would have to say that the Catholic church has ceased to see and above all to commend union purely in terms of 'return' or conversion to itself. It has learnt something; it has become converted to ecumenism. We have abandoned the attitude which made J.A.F.Maynard say: 'After all,

Rome does not want any of us except as fuel for its ecclesiastical machine'; that was in 1938.[1] We have made progress since. History has contributed to that. Just as in the fifteenth century the experience of internal schisms helped to make the Latin church more receptive to its sister in Constantinople, so now the experience of our differences makes us more open to the legitimacy of pluralisms in unity. The important Toronto Declaration made by the World Council of Churches in 1950 noted that all churches recognize that there are Christian elements in the others. No Christian church can any longer conceive of this unity as the reduction of the others to itself. Even the Orthodox Church, in which one can find so many declarations to this effect – I have noted a great many of them – is preparing to declare in its Pan-Orthodox Council:

> Aware of the importance of the present structure of Christianity, our Holy Orthodox Church, though being the one holy, catholic and apostolic church, not only recognizes the ontological existence of these Christian churches but also believes firmly that all its relationships with them must be based on as rapid and objective elucidation as possible of the ecclesiological problem and the whole of their doctrine. It also recognizes that encounter with them will take place on a basis the centre of which will be the theandric structure of the church.[2]

Confronted with the humanly insurmountable difficulties of the *unitatis redintegratio* and what might be thought to be very moderate results of hundreds of approaches over the course of several centuries, some scholars think an organic unity impossible: there is no point in seeking it or desiring it. They leave it to eschatology. At the end of a study of the 'birth of ecclesial unity' in the time of St Paul, E.Trocmé wrote:

> Do we need a detour by way of primitive Christianity to understand that the quest for institutional unity is a mirage, since true unity can only exist before God on the last day?[3]

Again very recently, in an ecumenical colloquium, the venerable André Gounelle so stressed the fact that no formula, no structure is adequate, that his account gave the impression of defeatism:[4] 'It seems to me probable that this ecumenism will only work out, in one way, eschatologically'; it provoked reactions from other Protestant theologians like, 'Having listened to you, I no longer know what ecumenism could be';[5] 'Though we must recognize the depth of the differences which emerged at the time of the Reformation, that is

no reason for despairing of our ecumenical task. Does it not consist
precisely in seeking to recognize the Catholic faith among others
under the confessional form which is their own, and showing it to
them in our own particular form? Such a dialogue, which would
involve Constantinople as well as Rome and Geneva, would seem
to me to be the best way towards the *magnus consensus* that we must
all seek[6]... What a marvellous proposal!

Other theologians involved in ecumenism have also criticized this
leaving of unity to eschatology, e.g. Adolf Deissmann,[7] and J.J.von
Allmen, who denounces it as 'a kind of ecclesiological docetism'[8]
and a quite false way of fobbing off on God the drama of the schism.[9]
It is again Lesslie Newbigin, Bishop of the Church of South India,
who wrote: 'There is a way of bringing the eschatological perspective
to bear on our present perplexities which relieves them at no cost to
ourselves, which allows us to rest content with them because in the
age to come they will disappear. That is a radically false eschatology.
The whole meaning of this present age between Christ's coming and
his coming again is that in it the powers of the age to come are at
work now to draw all men into one in Christ.'[10]

That having been said, it is true that eschatology has some
significance for the unity of the church and thus for ecumenism. It is
significant in three ways:

1. Because, without giving way to defeatism over our present
task, it is true that perfect unity will be *given*, eschatologically in the
cosmic Easter when God destroys all temples 'made with hands',[11]
Garizim or even Jerusalem; when he abolishes every human practice, every barrier erected from the human side (cf. Eph.2.11,14).
All our work will cease on this sabbath when God becomes all in
all.[12] 'May grace come and this world pass away'.[13]

2. Because, as Lesslie Newbigin says, the powers of the world to
come are at work in terrestrial history looking towards the *unitatis
redintegratio*, the sovereign power being the Holy Spirit, the eschatological gift. He has been at work from Pentecost, which ushers in
the last days (Acts 2.17). It is not, strictly speaking, a matter of
hoping for the new Pentecost, but of realizing the eschatological gift
by new 'missions' of the Holy Spirit.

3. Work for unity implements the realities which derive from the
historical incarnation and its consequences – the Tradition! – but it
envisages a consummation and can only be understood as a tension
towards eschatological plenitude. In a succinct and profound med-
itation, Paul Evdokimov showed that the church as it exists in its
dogmatic, sacramental and canonical structures is historical, but

that ecumenism, which goes beyond these structures without devaluing them, relates to its further eschatological dimension: 'Without conflicting in any way with the historical church, which we cannot leave even for a moment, the ecumenical experience brings us unity not in the historical Christ but in the *Christ of Glory, who is to come*. It is not a question of a union of historical churches but of the formation of the total, universal, eschatological body of Christ.'[14] Will this body be represented on earth? One might well ask. Lesslie Newbigin has written: 'The nature of the church is never to be finally defined in static terms, but only in terms of that to which it is going. It cannot be understood rightly except in a perspective which is both missionary and eschatological.'[15] Here we are at the heart of the ecumenical task and we can welcome the valuable elements in certain propositions which I have expounded and in some cases criticized.

I have already quoted St Bernard's comment on the church: *ante et retro oculata*, looking both forward and backward,[16] and that has met with some success. I am going to take up its substance. Here I shall pick up the positive side of the study by E.Trocmé which I have already quoted (above, n.3). While pointing out the indications of tensions and even opposition in the church of apostolic times, Trocmé sees at work in it a principle of unity consisting in a reference on the one hand to Christ who is at the same time historical Jesus and glorious Lord, and on the other to eschatology. Those are in fact my points of reference, with the proviso that we do not separate from Christ the apostolic and ecclesial communication of what comes from him. These two references to the Alpha and the Omega govern what I have recently called the two plans of fidelity,[17] a theme which I shall take up in the present setting. One could just as well express it in terms of 'truth', since that is not exhausted by matching up to existing formulae: it seeks to attain what has yet to be recognized.

Retro oculata

This is neither preoccupation with the past nor an inability to move, but a matter of Christian identity, of the continuity of the church with its roots or its source. The roots and source must be seen to be the *reality* of the church as people of God, body of Christ, living temple of the Holy Spirit. These cannot be reduced to what exegetes can derive from canonical texts: they are the reality of the river, the total *traditum*. Consequently I would accept the validity of the various proposals I have outlined:

The distinction made by the 1963 Montreal Conference between Tradition (transmitted by tradition) and traditions. Each of these traditions aims at transmitting the totality of Tradition. Thus in all the churches there is a common basis which contains the substance of Christianity. It has been rightly connected with baptism, with baptismal faith. The ecumenism of Vatican II, elucidated by Cardinal Bea,[18] is based on the unity of Christian baptism (numerous agreements have focussed on a mutual recognition). This was already the position of Catholic ecumenists at the time of Pius XII.[19] This basic unity of the faith in which we are baptized occurs again in the communal witness of martyrdom. Among the 1886 Uganda martyrs there were Anglicans who made the supreme act of witness alongside Catholics. The Orthodox Church counts among its martyrs a large number of Turks. But even today, a great many Baptists and Orthodox in the USSR, and a great many Catholics and others under dictatorial or unjust regimes, give testimony to their life for the gospel. Is this not the expression of a basically common faith? Baptism then presupposes a christological and trinitarian faith, but it is received in a specific church which has its own confession of faith and its own catechism. It is not certain that these coincide with St Irenaeus' rule of faith, or that of the 'undivided church' of the first millennium, when West and East lived out a communion which was often threatened and even damaged. It remains the fact that without going back on the criticism I have made of 'fundamental articles', the Vincentian Canon and the *consensus quinquesaecularis* or the criterion of the first Councils that what 'the undivided church' believed is a positive and valuable point of reference. It is not an exclusive criterion, but it can illuminate the course of an ecumenical conversion. A healthily critical knowledge of this past and a good application of the idea of a 'hierarchy of truths' are the necessary means of ecumenism. A 'hierarchy of truths' does not signify the elimination of secondary truths, as if they were no longer truths. But, as O. Cullmann has rightly pointed out,[20] that could be the basis for an important shift in values and balance. In some historical contexts central truths have become peripheral, and vice versa. The history of mediaeval Catholicism is an illustration which is all the more important because it was essentially against certain of its accretions that the Reformation reacted. Moreover, Orthodoxy wants to have nothing to do with it. So a criticism of mediaeval Catholicism is essential. Unfortunately, however, a break in real ecclesial continuity has not been avoided. The efforts at reunion which use criteria from the past – the first five centuries, the first councils – have been made from a predominantly theological and intellectual perspective, as if the 'undivided church' were only a collection of theses which need only to be recognized to be in touch with the reality of the church. The greatest possible integrity and the clearest possible knowledge must be put at the service of an openness and a desire for communion with the living reality of the church. That is an immense task, and can only be a long and patient process of self-criticism and self-transcendence, of rediscovery and renewal. It is the aim which J.J.von Allmen put in these words: 'Unity can only come about if the different confessions die to themselves in order to be reborn, through a purification which will affect them all differently, in unity, holiness, catholicity and apostolicity.'[21]

Ante oculata

The church (or the churches) will be polarized by the future, by the call to which they must respond. This is certainly eschatology, but it is an eschatology which gives history its meaning and its tasks. Specifically, the two principles of these tasks are mission and ecumenism. Their connection is intrinsic to their very nature, as the consequences of the phrase 'that the world may believe' (John 17.21), and from the very beginning the World Council of Churches has expressed it in its conception, its title and its structure. For the churches that implies the recognition of *open* realities. What they have to be is not determined solely by what they see behind them. God calls them to be a single people not only with their own present loyalties; they need to embrace other denominations on the basis of the already substantial degree of common Christianity which we have recognized. But what ecumenical unity must embrace extends to particular modes and therefore, all things considered, to the specific ways in which a particular tradition has lived out and formulated the original *traditum*. Unity will embrace a pluralism. That is clearly subject to the demands of unity and at the same time imposes its legitimate demands on it (*licet, salvo iure communionis, diversum sentire*).

Looking forward, towards eschatology, allows the church (the churches), or rather imposes the need on the church, to appreciate its historical manifestations and the very forms – its traditions – in which it now expresses the original unique *traditum* in a critical way, recognizing their relativity. In the same movement, and by virtue of the same principle, the church would recognize the legitimacy of other expressions in other circumstances, obviously *salvo iure communionis*, 'the requirements of communion being saved'. Beyond question it is the characteristic absence of an eschatological perspective in pre-conciliar Catholic ecclesiology which has hindered ecumenical openness and has imposed on it the theme of 'return', however nuanced by friendly proposals and a feeling of humility. When he arrived in Rome in 1968, Patriarch Athenagoras said: 'We hope that we will succeed in recognizing exactly the articles of faith which we ought necessarily to profess in common so as to distinguish them from those other elements of church life which – while not affecting the faith – can determine freely and in accordance with the tradition specific to each church aspects of their lives which the other would respect.'[22]

18

The Unity of the Faith and the Unity/Diversity of its Formulation

We all agree in affirming that the unity of the church can only be realized in the unity of faith. Faith is primarily this inward and personal movement by which we open ourselves and deliver ourselves to God, to Christ. But one has to adhere to something. This movement presupposes a proposition, an announcement (cf. Rom.10.14, 17), and expresses itself in a confession. As God and Christ and the proclamation of them which is made to us are intrinsically relevant to all men, proclamation and confession are public. They are matters for the church. The unity of the faith, too, is not only that of the *fides qua*, the movement of personal gift and confidence in Christ, but that of the *fides quae*, i.e. the content of the truth – or truths – professed. The principle has often been expressed among Catholics in the rejection of 'false eirenism' and in the affirmation of a concern not to sacrifice any dogma.[1] At the same time, however, it is said that dogmas can be interpreted and even formulated anew. Or, as Cardinal Hume put it: 'There can be a pluralism of doctrine, but there cannot be pluralism in the faith.'[2] Everyone recognizes that there are some differences between the truth(s) of faith and the formula(e) in which they are expressed. That brings us to the difficult problems of relationships between the truth, the concepts that we form and the way in which they express the truth.

Every formula aims at expressing the truth perceived, but the perception itself already falls short of the reality. There are therefore two reasons why our statements of the *fides quae* are inadequate. The objects of faith are expressed in formulae which, while being true, and expressing in their own way something of the truth, are not copies of reality. In this sense, they have a symbolic aspect. St

Thomas, of course, adopted this definition of the article of faith: *perceptio veritatis tendens in ipsam*: 'a perception of truth aiming at the truth itself.'[3] First faith, and then theology on its own level (one degree below), are for Thomas participation in eschatological knowledge, the knowledge which the elect in heaven have of God and his will. Faith and – at its own level and in its own way – theology thus have a proleptic character, to take up an expression of H.G.Gadamer's. It is their nature to tend towards eschatology. 'When we have reached you, these words that we multiply without reaching you will cease.'[4] The gap which there is between our truest expressions and the reality towards which they strive allows for a plurality of expressions. They strive for the same reality, but they do so from different approaches, using different resources. For example, there are numerous definitions and numerous approaches to what we call a sacrament. One can express an authentic christological faith without using the Chalcedonian definition.[5] Or again, every dogmatics accepts a self-revelation and self-communication of God to the sanctified faithful, while at the same time recognizing that the inner nature of God could never be totally grasped by the creature. However, there are several ways of expressing that, in different intellectual constructions: Palamism is one of them.[6] There are similarly numerous approaches to the mystery of the tri-unity of God. In an earlier chapter we considered the key question of eternal procession of the Holy Spirit. In connection with what all these examples illustrate one could cite the principle of 'equivalences' as expounded by Fr Maurice Villain.[7]

Secondly, this diversity in the one aim of faith is related, as Fr G.Dejaifve has shown, to the fact that faith is lived out and expressed by human subjects.[8] It is the faith not just of individuals but of human groups or particular churches characterized in their 'particularity' by a culture, a tradition, a language peculiar to them. We have seen the importance of an East-West duality. But there are more than two cultural spheres: the Slavonic world is not the Greek world, England is not the Mediterrannean, Anglo-Saxon is not Latin American, and so on. And to these we must add the areas of Africa or Asia which still find too little expression in Christianity. Furthermore, diversity is not only geographical and cultural, it is also historical. The majority of territories have experienced successively a number of cultural changes – for example, in the West, from Latin-Roman culture to Germanic, and so on;[9] they have sometimes also experienced quite marked reactions to great times of change:

for example the Counter-Reformation, with the Society of Jesus, or Ultramontanism against episcopalist currents. By 'great times of change' I understand such important facts as the emergence of Luther and the Reformers, leading to new expressions of Christianity which were embodied in confessions and churches which have developed a history of a quite considerable complexity.

All the dogmatics which have multiplied in this way are focussed on the fullness of God's communication of himself in revelation and the covenant. None of them can express it adequately. The faithful live by it without ever exhausting it. As the body of Christ the church contains it in the terms of St Paul's mysterious evocation of its growth into the fullness of Christ (Eph.4.13-16; cf. Col.1.19f.). But the church, the body of Christ, contains it, by the gift of God, in a way that is not exhausted by the manner in which it is expressed. Between these expressions and the fullness of the gift there always remains the margin which we have recognized between every element or form of the historical life of the church and eschatology. It is in this margin that the enterprise of ecumenism is inscribed.

This enterprise involves going from the one to the one through the many. The original one is the undivided church, which is, alas, divided. It exists in the Catholic church of East and West. My profound conviction is that this is the same church of Christ and the apostles which exists in the Orthodox church and the Roman Catholic church. We know that the Orthodox reject this idea. For Roman Catholics it is a certainty. I have noted dozens of texts in which the Orthodox affirm that their church – which we love – is *the* church pure and simple. But their participation in the ecumenical movement has already shown them a reality which they have to incorporate into their dogmatics. The Pan-Orthodox Council will be an occasion of grace in that respect.

The Catholic church professes that 'the separated Churches and communities as such, although we believe that they suffer from the defects already mentioned, have been by no means deprived of significance and importance in the mystery of salvation.'[10] What does the movement for the restoration of unity, beginning from historical divisions, suppose or demand of them? What does it suppose or desire of us? We are told that 'well before Vatican II, Soloviev had an intuition that a distinction could be made between on the one hand the truths of faith proclaimed in an infallible manner by the ecumenical councils, which are to be believed by all, and on the other hand dogmatic propositions which can be formulated differently according to the particular traditions of the churches (e.g. the *filioque*); finally, there are theological opinions, these last remaining the object of free discussion.'[11] If there is a universal requirement of adherence to the truths of faith proclaimed by the councils of the 'undivided church' down to the Second Council of Nicaea in 787, there is also need for a hermeneutic or a criteriological appreciation of at least some of their definitions. The East would need to do this for the Second Council of Nicaea (icons), and Roman Catholics would need to do it for Florence, Trent, Vatican I, etc. The Roman Catholic Church would insist on the following three points:

1. A full recognition of the historicity of the features which govern the life of the church. This is not a ploy deriving from bad liberalism but a condition of the greatest truth. Its absence leads to the abuse of 'dogmatism'.[12] While the motives which inspire them may be respectable, some ultra-conservative attitudes are in fact rejections of the truth. For example a stubborn observation of the Julian calendar and a refusal to adopt the Gregorian calendar is objectively a rejection of a truth of creation and shows a misunderstanding of history, and even more of historicity. Roman Catholics need to progress in recognizing the historicity of the papacy and the hierarchical structures of their church.

2. There is a need to envisage a 're-reception' on the part of churches which have conciliar or pontifical decrees in the form of 'credal writings', and normative confessional experiences which are expressed in the form of traditions which in practice govern their lives. In particular, I have in mind: in the case of the Catholic church, some constructions inherited from Scholasticism and the Vatican I constitution *Pastor aeternus*; in the case of the Lutheran churches the Augsburg Confession; in the case of the Orthodox church Palamism; and these are only examples. These doctrines have been 'received', that is to say, the churches find them beneficial and have lived according to them.[13] It is not a matter of abandoning them but of giving them a new context and the equilibrium of scriptural witness, what T. Sartory calls, 'a repatriation of dogmas in the light of the overall witness of the Holy Spirit';[14] it is a matter of thinking them and living them out, taking account of the knowledge we have acquired of the historical, cultural and sociological conditioning of the decision in question, of the current needs of the cause of the gospel which we seek to serve, of the connotations which have accrued since the first reception of the decision or doctrine, and finally of the criticisms and valuable contributions received from others. For example, Fr André de Halleux makes the

following point: 'The history of the schism between East and Christian West can be summarized as the development of divergent theologies in a purely dogmatic disagreement. So all true reconciliation must pass through the inversion of this dialectic, each of the two churches agreeing to recognize each in the tradition of the other an equally authentic interpretation of their common faith.'[15]

Re-reception could make a profound difference to the circumstances of a reconciliation and reunion, since the church involved in the union would look different from the church as it had been known during times of opposition. For example, the papacy that Roman Catholics would require Orthodox and Protestants to recognize would no longer be that of Gregory VII, Boniface VIII and Pius IX, which they would find impossible. The Augsburg Confession that Roman Catholics could 'recognize' would be explained and supplemented by the perspectives and agreements achieved during the intense dialogue of the last fifteen years. And so on.

Implemented by both sides in this way, with each side coming to meet the other, a 're-reception' could lead to the joint reformulation of doctrine of which Fr Pierre Duprey so happily speaks.[16] It would be like a fragmentary anticipation of a future joint Council.

3. Should a church, beginning with the Catholic church, make it a condition of union that others should 'receive' definitions or, to put it more precisely, dogmas, defined by it in the absence of others? Must one, can one, require non-Chalcedonians to accept Chalcedon, the Orthodox to accept the dogmas of 1854, the Immaculate Conception,[17] the *Pastor aeternus* of 1870, the Assumption of 1950, not to mention the *filioque*? We have already considered this question. The questions raised are tricky ones. They have already been touched on and discussed. Their importance demands that we pause over them. First of all let us consider the papal dogma. Here are some declarations made by Orthodox theologians.

Hamilcar Alivisatos: 'As I have recently explained in articles published on the occasion of the encyclical of His Holiness John XXIII, I cannot find any other solution to this great problem than a return to the coexistence of two systems of church authority such as existed before the schism. It is beyond question that while in the West the supreme authority of the pope was fully developed, he never involved himself in the affairs of the Eastern church.'[18]

Evangelos Theodorou: 'From the Orthodox side one could express the following opinion. While the doctrines or institutions of our Roman Catholic sister church (like, for example, the doctrine establishing the pope's primacy of jurisdiction and infallibility) no longer claim validity and universal application and are invalidated by a symbolic interpretation, valid only in the sphere of the Roman Catholic Church, my own personal opinion is that this symbolic interpretation could be considered acceptable in view of the unity of the Orthodox Church and of theology.'[19]

Mgr Damaskinos Papandreou, Director of the Orthodox Centre of Chambésy (Geneva), designated Secretary for the preparation of the Pan-Orthodox Council: 'If Rome were unconditionally to accept communion with the East – of course after an agreement with all Orthodoxy, that would presuppose an explicit recognition of the legitimacy of the episcopal structure of the East. That would be *ipso facto* recognition that the East should not be obliged to accept Western developments in the exercise of the primacy.

For its part the East would recognize that despite the doctrine of primacy, the West has not in principle abandoned the episcopal structure of the ancient church, even if it has adopted a new factor which the Orthodox Church does not feel to be necessary.'[20]

Two Catholic theologians put forward convergent proposals in the context of the Koinonia colloquium organized by the Viennese *Pro Oriente* foundation in April 1974:

The dogmatic definitions made by Vatican I, which are binding on Catholic faith, should not be abolished. They must be recognized for what they are: definitions which have been made without the participation of the sister church of the East. By virtue of that, on the one hand they are to be observed by Western Catholics, and on the other hand they need to be rethought in the light of the development and the tradition peculiar to the East as this has been recognized by the Decree on Ecumenism and accepted by Paul VI by sanctioning a consistent theology of sister churches. Long fraternal explanations will certainly be needed if we are to arrive at mutual understanding in the sphere of this twofold ecclesiological tradition.[21]

At this stage, or later, there must be a declaration by the Apostolic See of Ancient Rome that the dogma of the primacy of this see and of the infallibility of doctrinal decisions taken by the pope as doctor of the universal church must be understood with the additions already made by Vatican II, concerning the *magisterium* held by all bishops and the participation of the whole people of God in the witness perpetually given to the truth in love, and, moreover, in the light of the whole tradition of the undivided church. As to the papal definitions of 1854 and 1950 concerning the Immaculate Conception of the Blessed Virgin Mary and her Assumption, it seems equally the case that the same Apostolic See should and could without difficulty declare that these definitions are themselves to be understood as expressions of the simple truths that the Orthodox church itself has not ceased to believe: the perfect purity of the Mother of God and her close association, after her dormition, in the victory of her son over death itself...[22]

That is precisely my proposal for 're-reception'. At the same Vienna Colloquium, the Catholic views I have just quoted were discussed by Fr J.Ratzinger and Fr W. de Vries.[23] They are obviously novel and cannot be justified by any accepted criteria. However, it seems that ecumenical experience is moving in this direction. Numerous Catholic ecumenists think that one cannot impose dogmas defined without the participation of others and without any root in their tradition as a *sine qua non* for communion. That was the view of Otto Karrer, who added that a time of approach in patience and love should be arranged.[24] Heribert Mühlen called for the anathema on the rejection of these dogmas to be removed, which would amount to removing their binding and obligatory character.[25] Fr Avery Dulles also proposes this in connection with the dogmas of 1854 and 1950, which have only indirect foundations in the Bible.[26] J.M.R.Tillard similarly says:

The Catholic Church cannot require *complete* assent to the 'dogmas' it defined independently, above all where the East shows itself to be reticent. That is to say that the points of basic faith are less numerous than Catholic 'dogmas'. Where refusal to accept such Catholic dogma (for example the Immaculate Conception) is not bound up with a passionate condemnation of those who accept it but has arisen from an unequivocal recognition of freedom to accept or reject it, there is no necessary reason for supposing that all visible unity is impossible. Only a rejection which goes against the fundamental content of the faith has to be recognized as being incompatible with a true communion... The possibility of restoring visible unity can be ruled out only in the case of major differences; it does not arise out of differences caused by circumstances (doctrinal or theological) which came about after the period of the stabilization of the *depositum fidei* in the awareness of the church.[27]

These are bold proposals. Some will think them rash or frivolous. Fr Bertrand de Margerie has made a vigorous criticism of the comments by Avery Dulles on the suppression of anathemas, [28] and has been even more critical of those by the American Lutheran A.C.Piepkorn,[29] who envisages 'the day when it is accepted and recognized that *the whole* was not consulted before (the definitions of) 1854 and 1950, that the *whole* church did not accept or assent to these definitions and that, whatever the degree of their canonical validity for those who accept the authority of the Bishop of Rome, they remain open questions for the *whole* church'. Fr de Margerie has no difficulty in showing that the church has never adopted such a method: it affirms its belief and does not ask the opinion of those who do not belong to it and therefore exclude themselves from it. That has been its attitude in the past.

However, I am not sure whether this discipline does not vitiate the question. We cannot compare the great Christian divisions of today with ancient heresies relating to a particular article, the only positive feature of which is what they take from the church as they part company with it. The great divisions with which we are concerned are the forms of Christianities which have shown great vitality and have dissociated themselves from the historical form of a church which they accuse of adding human elements to the purity of original Christianity.[30] The dogmas of 1854 and 1950 claim that their content is part of revelation, which is the property of all Christians, but they do not indicate how this is so. Moreover, what is at issue is not the precise conditions on which individuals may belong to the Catholic church *as it is*, but differences which may or may not stand in the way of restoring communion between Christian churches inspired by the new movement of reunion, raised up by the Holy Spirit in circumstances which the past could not know. What does God want to say to us by inspiring this movement at a time when Christianity as such, and its innermost essence, is put in question by theoretical or practical atheism, by an indifference to anything beyond the creature comforts of individuals, or by the more or less aggressive competition of 'religions'? Does God not want to bring us back to essentials, to basics? Karl Rahner thinks that in future dogma will no longer develop in the direction of the expression of new propositions but as an intensive deepening of the nucleus and the essence of what God has revealed (and is still revealing) to man.[31] That seems to him to be of decisive importance for the ecumenical cause. He has returned to the question often:

The best ecumenical theology is Christian theology for today's pagan.[32]

The theological questions which divide the Christian churches cannot be resolved by sterile discussions in the style of traditional controversies. They can only be resolved if theologians concentrate their attention on the present and the future and seek to rethink and preach the traditional gospel message about God, Jesus Christ and his grace in such a way that it can be heard and received by the pagan world today. If the theologians and all the churches succeeded in making the gospel real today, they would preach the same message, for they would make the same response to the situation in which they all have a share.[33]

That would not happen in isolation, because dogmatics makes an impact on responses: this Rahnerian anticipation needs to be supplemented by a common practice of the service of humankind aimed at human liberation, the achievement of human dignity, the transcending of all that opposes and oppresses the majority of humankind. If the church is the sacrament not only of union with God but of the unity of the whole human race, it must demonstrate the truth of Gal.3.28: 'There is neither Jew nor Greek, bond nor free, man nor woman.' That is the context of a practical ecumenism, whose benefits I recognize while rejecting the view that it devalues and even eliminates theological, spiritual and institutional ecumenisms.[34] One thing is certain: if the churches act together, performing the same action in the service of humankind in the world, they are bringing a community into being and at least realizing the beginnings of unity.[35] However, perhaps I may be forgiven for concentrating my attention on the doctrinal dimension of the ecumenical task, since that is clearly decisive. I return to Karl Rahner.

Rahner thinks that in terms of dogma union is possible between the Protestants of the great churches and Rome.[36] I would not disagree. There is still not enough agreement on essentials, even in Mariology, the profound perceptions of which I believe to be a dimension of the mystery of Christ and the church. But so many human voices involved in the service of Christ and the church focus our attention on a unity in what is essential and fundamental, and that must be a serious possibility. Let us listen once again to Mgr Damaskinos Papandreou. I would support his approach, which relates to the question of union between the Orthodox Church and the Roman Catholic church, though in my view it applies to all plans for unity:

Eucharistic communion, the expression and crown of perfect communion, is impossible where there is still a division in the substance of the *pistis*, the faith, that is to say in the fundamental confessions of faith of the great councils of antiquity. It is no longer possible where the fundamental structure of the church, that is to say, continuity in the apostolic succession with the primitive church, has not been preserved. We cannot separate these elements from each other.[37]

I end this book on a note of hope, in the words of John Paul II, who, in his meeting on 17 November 1980 with the Council of the Protestant Church in Germany, took up the words of the German bishops in their pastoral letter of 20 January 1980, 'Thy Kingdom Come'.

'Let us rejoice that we can affirm, not a partial consensus on some truths, but an agreement on the central truths of the faith. This allows us to hope that we shall attain unity in the spheres of our faith and our life where we are still separated.'[38]

ABBREVIATIONS

AAS	Acta Apostolicae Sedis
AKG	*Archiv für Kulturgeschichte*
AKK	*Archiv für Katholische Kirchenrecht*
APAW	Abhandlungen der preussischen Akademie der Wissenschaften
BEvTh	Beihefte zur *Evangelische Theologie*
BFCT	Beiträge zur Förderung Christlicher Theologie
BHT	Beiträge zur *Historische Theologie*
Bibl	*Biblica*
BOO	*Bulletin d'Orientation Oecuménique*
CQR	*Church Quarterly Review*
CSEL	Corpus Scriptorum Ecclesiasticorum Latinorum
DACL	*Dictionnaire d'Archéologie Chrétienne et Littéraire*
DC	Documents Catholiques
Denzinger	H.Denziger, *Enchiridion Symbolorum*
DS	H.Denziger and A.Schönmetzer, *Enchiridion Symbolorum*
DTC	*Dictionnaire de Théologie Catholique*
EJC	*Ephemerides Juris Canonici*
ER	*Ecumenical Review*
ET	English translation
ETR	*Études théologiques et religieuses*
EvTh	*Evangelische Theologie*
FTS	Freiburger Theologische Studien
GCS	Griechischer Christlicher Schriftsteller
GOTR	*Greek Orthodox Theological Review*
Greg	*Gregorianum*

IKZ	*Internationale Katholische Zeitschrift*
ITQ	*Irish Theological Quarterly*
JEH	*Journal of Ecclesiastical History*
JES	*Journal of Ecumenical Studies*
JTS	*Journal of Theological Studies*
KuD	*Kerygma und Dogma*
LM	*Lutherische Monatsschrift*
MGH	Monumenta Germaniae Historica
Mus	*Le Muséon*
NeV	*Nova et Vetera*
NovT	*Novum Testamentum*
NRSM	*Nouvelle Revue de Science missionnaire*
NRT	*Nouvelle Revue Théologique*
NS	New Series
OC	*Orientalia Christiana*
OrC	*Oriente Cristiano*
OeR	*Oekumenische Rundschau*
PG	Patrologia Graeca
PL	Patrologia Latina
PO	Patrologia Orientalia
POC	*Proche-Orient chrétien*
RAC	*Rivista di Archeologia cristiana*
RCE	*Revue catholique des Églises*
REB	*Revue des Etudes Byzantines*
REG	*Revue des Etudes Grecques*
RHE	*Revue d'histoire ecclésiastique*
ROC	*Revue de l'Orient chrétien*
RQH	*Revue des Questions historiques*
RP	*Revue philosophique*
RSCI	*Rivista di Storia della Chiesa in Italia*
RSLR	*Rivista di Storia e Letteratura religiosa*
RSPT	*Revue de Science et Philosophie théologiques*
RSR	*Revue des sciences religieuses*
RT	*Revue Thomiste*
RTL	*Revue théologique de Louvain*
SBAW	Sitzungsberichte der königliche preussische Akademie der Wissenschaften
SC	Sources chrétiennes
SLT	*Slavorum litterae theologicae*
TDNT	*Theological Dictionary of the New Testament*
ThBl	*Theologische Blätter*
TLZ	*Theologische Literaturzeitung*

TQ	*Theologische Quartalschrift*
TS	*Theological Studies*
TU	*Texte und Untersuchungen*
TuG	*Theologie und Glaube*
TvT	*Tijdschrift voor Theologie*
WA	Weimarer Ausgabe (edition of the texts of Luther)
ZR	*Zeitschrift für Rechtsgeschichte*
ZKG	*Zeitschrift für Kirchengeschichte*
ZPF	*Zeitschrift für philosophische Forschung*
ZWT	*Zeitschrift für wissenschaftliche Theologie*

NOTES

Introduction

1. *Foi et Vie*, January-February 1978, 55.
2. As presented by André Thérive, 'Dossier oecuménique', in *Écrits de Paris*, March 1966, 86.
3. W.A.Visser't Hooft, at Montreal, 21 July 1963.
4. And Vatican II, *Unitatis redintegratio*, nos.4, 14-17: Abbott, 456f., 464-7.
5. Cf. e.g. G.Dejaifve, 'Diversité dogmatique et unité de la Révélation', *NRT* 89, 1967, 16-25; id., 'Hors de l'"impasse" oecuménique', *NRT* 111, 1979, 498-509; E.Lanne, 'Pluralisme et unité: possibilité d'une diversité de typologies dans une même adhésion ecclésiale', *Istina* 19, 1963, 171-90; J.M.R.Tillard, 'L'expression de l'unité de foi', *Proche-Orient Chrétien* 28, 1978, 193-201; id., 'How do we express Unity of Faith?', *One in Christ* 14, 1978, 318-27.
6. Text in *DC* 69, no.1621, 3 December 1972, 1061-66; in *Documents on Anglican/Roman Catholic Relations*, 1972, 39f.
7. Thus Avery Dulles, *Models of the Church*, Garden City 1974; id., *The Resilient Church*, Garden City 1977, 173ff.; Harding Meyer, at the meeting of diocesan delegates for ecumenism at Chantilly: 'Les modèles d'unité que nous trouvons actuellement dans l'église', *Unité des Chrétiens* 27, July 1977, 16-21.
8. Cf. *Irénikon* 49, 1976, 189f.
9. R.Mehl, 'L'Unité conciliaire de l'Église', in *Die Einheit der Kirche. Dimensionen ihrer Heiligkeit, Katholizität und Apostolizität*, Festschrift Peter Meinhold, Wiesbaden 1977, (69-79) 76f.
10. J.Delumeau, 'Une crise inédite', *Le Monde*, 5 June 1979, 2.
11. *Irénikon* 50, 1977, 374-8; H.Meyer, 'Versöhnte Verschiedenheit', *OeR* 27, 1978, 377-400.
12. Memorandum of the Comité épiscopal français pour l'unité des chrétiens on the Dombes Group document, 'Vers une même foi eucharistique', *DC* no. 1669, 2 February 1975, 126.

182   *Notes to pages 9–15*

PART ONE

1. Diversity and Unity according to the New Testament

1. However, V.Subilia, who comes very close to Käsemann in his view of unity through reference to the same heavenly head, writes: 'The diversity of perspectives threatens to disrupt the unity of the primitive church. Two separate churches are not formed, but there is simply an agreed division of spheres of activity (Gal.2.1-10)', 'L'unità della Chiesa secondo il Nuovo Testamento', *Protestantesimo* 19, 1964, (129-56) 148. Tertullian had already referred to the agreement between Peter and Paul, *De praescr.* 23.

2. E.Käsemann, *Das Neue Testament als Kanon*, Göttingen 1970.

3. I.Frank, *Der Sinn der Kanonbildung. Eine historisch-theologische Untersuchung der Zeit vom I.Clemensbrief bis Irenäus von Lyon*, Freiburg 1971.

4. L.Goppelt, 'Die Pluralität der Theologien im NT und die Einheit des Evangeliums als ökumenisches Problem', *Evangelium und Einheit* I, Göttingen 1971, 109-15.

5. Cf. P.-H.Menoud, 'L'Unité de l'Église selon le Nouveau Testament', *ETR* 21, 1946, 265-82; id., 'Mia Ekklesia', in *Hommage et Reconnaissance à Karl Barth*, Neuchâtel and Paris 1946, 87-91.

6. R.Pesch, 'Were there Parties in the New Testament Church?', *Concilium* 8.9, 1973, 26-36.

7. J.Colson, *L'Évêque dans les communautés primitives. Tradition paulienne et Tradition johannique de l'Épiscopat, des Origines à saint Irénée*, Unam Sanctam 21, Paris 1951.

8. For this theme cf. my 'Église de Pierre, Église de Paul, Église de Jean. Destin d'un thème oecuménique', in *The Ecumenical World of Orthodox Civilization. Russia and Orthodoxy*, III, Essays in Honour of Georges Florovsky, La Haye 1973, 163-79.

9. E.Junod, 'Observations sur la réulation de la foi dans l'Église des II\u1d49 et III\u1d49 siècles. La pluralité doctrinale et la tendance à l'uniformisation', *Le Supplément* 133, May 1980, 195-213.

10. Cf. F.J.Theunis, 'Omtrent Kanon en Schrift', *Bijdragen* 41, 1980, 64-87.

11. See my 'L'Esprit des Pères d'après Möhler', in the first edition of *Esquisses du mystère de l'Église*, Paris 1941, 134-6. L. Bouyer, *Le Consolateur*, Paris 1980.

12. G.Ebeling, 'Das Neue Testament und die Vielzahl der Konfessionen', in *Wort Gottes und Tradition, Studien zu einer Hermeneutik der Konfessionen*, Göttingen 1964, 144-54.

2. Diversity and Communion in the Early Church

1. In addition to Hefele-Leclercq, *Histoire des conciles* I, 133-51, cf. the dictionaries: 'Pâques', *DACL* XIII/2, cols.1531f., by H.Leclercq; *DTC* XI, cols.1948-70, by G.Fritz and Fliche-Martin, *Histoire de l'Église* II, 88f.; III, 87-93; IV, 342-44; cf. M.Richard, 'La Question Pascale au II\u1d49 siecle', *L'Orient chrétien* 6, 1961, 117-212; P. Nautin, *Lettres et écrivains chrétiens*

des IIe et IIIe siècles, Paris 1961; V.Peri, 'La Data della Pasqua segno d'unità e occasione di scandalo', *Vita e Pensiero* 48, 1963, 664-86; id., *La date de la fête de Pâques*. *Note sur l'origine et le développement de la question pascale*, Vatican 1968. And see below, n.10.

2. B.Botte, 'La Question Pascale. Pâque du vendredi ou pâque du dimanche?', *La Maison Dieu* 41, 1955.1, 84-93, with reference to F.E. Brightman and O.Casel. See also no. 67, 1961, 36f., 39f. G.Lohse holds that the Quartodeciman mode of celebration was primitive and that it was entirely oriented on the expectation of the parousia. It would have been Pope Sixtus who, about 115, gave Easter the significance of a commemoration of the passion and the resurrection: *Das Passafest der Quartodecimaner*, Gütersloh 1953.

3. Apart from J.Schmid, *Die Osterfestfrage auf dem ersten allgemeinen Konzil von Nicäa*, Vienna 1905, and E. Lohse, cited above, cf. B.J.van der Veken, *Sensus Paschalis in saeculo secundo*. *Objectum Paschalis Quartodecimanorum et Romanorum apud auctores praecipuos ultimorum annorum (1919-1959)*, Postel 1962; N.Brox, 'Tendenzen und Parteilichkeiten im Osterfeststreit des II. Jahrhunderts', *ZKG* 83, 1972, 291-324.

4. *Inter Cypriani Epist.*, Ep.75.6.

5. Canon 1: Mansi 2, 471, and cf. F.Cabrol, 'Annonce des fêtes', *DACL* I/2, cols.2230f.

6. Innocent I, *Epist.* 14, PL 20, 517f.: *Curato, ut dignum est, unitatem Ecclesiae custodire, idemque omnes pariter et sentiamus et pronuntiemus...*

7. *Epist.* 96: *Ad praecipuum religionis nostrae pertinet sacramentum, ut in festivitate paschali nulla sit toto orbe diversitas... ut quorum in fide est una confessio, sit etiam in hac festivitate una devotio* (PL 54, 945AB); *Ep.*121.1 and 3 (cols. 1056A; 1058A); *Ep.* 122 (1059C); Ep.138 (1101B).

8. In Socrates, *HE*, 1,9. Cf. Kirch, *Enchiridium Fontium Historiae ecclesiae antiquae*, no.412. Cf. V.Grumel, 'Le Problème de la date pascale aux IIIe et IVe siècles', *REB* 18, 1960, 163-78. For an earlier study, L.Duchesne, *RQH* 28, 1880, 22-26; *Bessarione* 7, 1900, 369-91.

9. *Epist. de Synodis* 5: PG 16, 688.

10. Cf. F.Heiler, *Altkirchliche Autonomie und päpstlicher Zentralismus*, Munich 1941, 152f.; J.Ryan, 'The Early Irish Church and the See of Peter', in *La Chiesa dei Regni dell'Europa occidentale e i loro rapporti con Roma sino all'800*, Spoleto 1960, II, 549-74; id., in *Mediaeval Studies presented to A. Gwynn*, Dublin 1961, 14f.

11. Cf. P.Grosjean, 'Recherches sur les débuts de la controverse pascale chez les Celtes', *Analecta Bollandiana* 64, 1946, 200-44.

12. Narrative in Bede, *Historia ecclesiastica Gentis Anglorum* III, 25; ed. C.Plummer, Oxford 1896, 188, or PL 95, 163.

13. B.Colgrave, *The Life of Bishop Wilfrid by Eddius Stephanus*, Cambridge 1927, 24; L.Saltet, *Les Réordinations. Études sur le sacrément de l'Ordre*, Paris 1907, 88f.

14. Documentation can be found in H.Vinck, 'Une tentative de Pie X pour fixer la date de Pâques. Quelques documents inédits', *RHE* 70, 1975, 462-8. This gives the text of a brief manuscript note of St Pius X.

15. Conclusions published in *Proche-Orient chrétien*, 1969, 354-8. Cf. also *Irénikon* 42, 1969, 547-50.

16. The report has been published in *Istina* 20, 1974, 457-62. This fascicle also contains reports by D.P.Oguistski (462-71) and Fr Liviu Stan (471-85), both Orthodox.

17. *Istina*, ibid., 485-7.

18. E.Wolf, 'Verlorene Einheit', *EvTh* 8, 1948-49, 141-51; '*Communio sanctorum*. Erwägungen zum Problem der Romantisierung des Kirchenbegriffs', *ThBl* 21, 1942, 12-25 (reprinted in *Peregrinatio. Studien zur reformatorischen Theologie*, Munich ²1962, I, 279-301).

19. W.Bauer, *Orthodoxy and Heresy in Earliest Christianity*, ET Philadelphia and London 1972. I have only seen reviews of H.E.W.Turner, *The Pattern of Christian Truth: A Study in the Relations between Orthodoxy and Heresy in the Early Church*, London 1954, which criticizes Bauer. Among the reviews of Bauer see also that by H.D.Simonin, *RSPT* 25, 1936, 342-5.

20. *Adv.haer.* I, 10,2 (PG 7, 552; Harvey I, 92).

21. W.Elert, *Abendmahl und Kirchengemeinschaft in der Alten Kirche, hauptsächlich des Ostens*, Berlin 1954, 45f.

22. L.Duchesne, *Églises separées*, Paris 1896, 164f. P.M.Jugie in *Le schisme byzantin. Aperçu historique et doctrinal*, Paris 1941, 9, counts 217 years of schism represented by seven ruptures between 337 and 843.

23. E.Wolf, cited above n.18; H.Frick, *Romantik und Realismus im Kirchenbegriff*, Tübingen 1929 (a mediocre work).

3. Diversity has always been Accepted

Bibliography

L.Duchesne, *Autonomies ecclésiastiques, Églises Séparées*, Paris 1905

L.Bréhier, 'Avant la séparation du XIᵉ siècle: les relations normales entre Rome et les Églises d'Orient', *Istina*, 1959, 352ff.

E.Rösser, *Göttliches und Menschliches, Unveränderliches und Veränderliches Kirchenrecht von der Enstehung der Kirche bis z. Mitte des 9. Jahrhunderts*, Paderborn 1934

P.Batiffol, 'Les Trois Zones de la *potestas* papale', in *Cathedra Petri*, Unam Sanctam, Paris 1938, 41-79; cf. H.Marot, *Concilium* 1.7, 1965, 9ff.

F. Heiler, *Altkirchliche Autonomie und päpstlicher Zentralismus*, Munich 1941

F.Dvornik, *National Churches and the Church Universal*, London 1944

E.Lanne, 'Les Différences compatibles avec l'unité dans la tradition de l'Église ancienne', *Istina*, 1961-62, 227-53

H.Marot, 'Unité de l'Église et diversité géographique aux premiers siècles', in *L'Épiscopat et l'Église Universelle*, Unam Sanctam 39, Paris 1962, 565-90

C.Vogel, 'Unité de l'Église et pluralité des formes historiques d'organisation ecclésiastique du IIIᵉ au Vᵉ siècle', ibid., 591-636

P.Meyvaert, 'Diversity within Unity. A Gregorian Theme', *Heythrop Journal* 4, 1963, 141-62

Y.Congar, *Istina* 1959, 187-236, and 'De la communion des Églises à une ecclésiologie de l'Eglise universelle', in *L'Episcopat et l'Église univer-selle*, Paris 1962, 227-60

Y.Congar, *L'Ecclésiologie du Haut Moyen Age*, Paris 1968
Concilium 8.9, 1973, Ecumenism

E.Lanne, 'Pluralisme et unité: possibilité d'une diversité de typologies dans une même adhésion ecclésiale', *Istina*, 1969, 171-90

V.E.Devadutt, 'What is Indigenous Theology?', *ER*, Autumn 1949, 40ff.

J.Vodopivec, 'Unity in Diversity. The Problem of Reunion in Missionary Perspective', *Euntes docete* 13, 1960, 459-512

G.Schille, 'Erwägungen zur urchristliche Kirchenbildung', in *Theologische Versuche*, Berlin 1966, 66-82 (geographical areas)

E.Lanne, 'Unité de la foi et pluralisme théologique. Dimensions oecumé-niques du document de la Commission internationale de théologie', *Irénikon* 46, 1973, 207-13

1. *Dial.* XLVII,2.
2. In Eusebius, *HE* V, XXIV.
3. Firmilian, *Inter Epistolas Cypriani, Ep.* LXXV, VI.
4. We know that in arguing against the Donatists, who referred to the martyr bishop, Augustine was fond of stressing that Cyprian had kept communion with those who thought and acted differently from himself: cf. *De baptismo* I, 18,28; II, 5,6 and 6,7; III, 3,5; IV, 8,11; V, 17,23 (PL 43, 124,130,141,161,188); *C.Crescon.* II, 28.48-49 (43, 496-7); *Epist.* 93,41 (PL 33,341).
5. *Sententiae episcoporum de haereticis baptizandis*, Hartel I, 435.
6. *De baptismo* III, 3,5 (PL 43, 141-2).
7. C.Gore in W.Frere, *Recollections of Malines*, London 1935, 110-19. Reply by P.Batiffol, 'Unité de communion et unanimité de foi. A propos d'un mot de S.Cyprien', *RSPT* 17, 1928, 616-32.
8. *Epist.* 54,2,2 (and 3): PL 33, 200 (201); reproduced by Gratian C.11 D.XII (Friedberg, 29f.). Cf. *Ep.* 55, 18, 34 (cols. 220-1); *Ep.* 36,9,22 to Casulanus: *Sit ergo una fides universae quae ubique dilatatur Ecclesiae, tanquam intus in membris, etiamsi ipsa fidei unitas quibusdam diversis observationibus celebratur, quibus nullo modo quod in fide verum est impeditur* (PL 33, 146). The text of this letter was cited by Cervini at the Council of Trent, in the debate on traditions, 23 February 1546. Seripando also appealed to St Augustine in the same debate (*Concilium Tridentinum*, ed. Goerresgesellschaft XII, 517-24): cf. H.Holstein, 'La Tradition d'après le Concile de Trente', *RSR* 47, 1959, 367-90, and *La Tradition dans l'Église*, Paris 1960, 181, 289.
9. *Ep.* 71 to Lucian, in 399: PL 22,672.
10. Cf. E.Lanne, 'Les Différences compatibles avec l'unité dans la tradition de l'Église ancienne', *Istina*, 1961-62, 227-53.
11.*Reg.* I, 57, 18 (MGH, *Epp.* I, p.42; PL, *Ep.* I, 43; 77, 497).
12. *Reg.* XI, 56a (MGH, *Epp.* II, 332f.; PL *Ep.* XI, 64: 77, 1187). The authenticity is put in question by S.Braechter, *Die Quellen zur Angelsach-senmission Gregors des Grossen*, Münster 1941. There is a favourable response by P.Grosjean, *JEH* 10, 1959, 1-49; cf. M.Deanesley, *JEH* 12,

1961, 231-4. The question does not appear to be completely settled. Cf. also P.Meyvaert, 'Diversity within Unity. A Gregorian Theme', *Heythrop Journal* 4, 1963, 141-62.

13. *Ep. ad Senarium* XIII: PL 59, 406.

14. PG 102, 604-5.

15. Mansi 17, 489, translated M.Jugie, *Le Schisme Byzantin*, Paris 1941, 143.

16. Cf. my *Ecclésiologie du Haut Moyen Age*, 131.

17. Cf. C.Munier, *RSR*, 1966, 113-26.

18. *Ep.* 3: PL 141, 192; translation in V.Seumois, *La Papauté et les missions au cours des six premiers siècles*, Paris-Louvain 1953, 162.

19. *Confessio fidei* III, 26, *inter opera Alcuini*, PL 101, 1072.

20. Accusations against the Latins, 15: PG 126, 245b. Cf. M.Jugie, op.cit., 243-5.

21. First letter to Cerularius in September 1053, no.29, edited by Humbert: Jaffé 4302, PL 143, 764; C.Will, *Acta et Scripta de controversiis saec.XI*, Leipzig-Marburg 1861, 181. Humbert, alas, did not apply his principle to the marriage of Greek priests!

22. Yvo of Chartres, *Panormia* II, 155 (PL 161,1119); *Decretum* IV, 223 (col.313) and V,44 (339).

23. *De sacramentis Ecclesiae* 1, PL 158, 552D; *Opera*, ed. F.S.Schmitt, II, 240.

24. Gregory VII, *Reg.* VIII,1; ed. Caspar, 513. Anselm, *Epist. de sacrificio azimi et fermentati* 1: *De sacrificio in quo idem Graeci nobiscum non sentiunt, multis rationibus catholicis videtur quia quod agunt non est contra fidem christianam. Nam et azimum et fermentatum sacrificians panem sacrificat* (Schmitt II, 223). Cf. Petrus Venerabilis to St Bernard, *Inter Bernardi Epist.* 221, 9 (PL 182, 403).

25. *Latinos dicere tres personas credendas in una substantia, Graecos vero non minus fideliter tres substantias in una persona confiteri*, *Ep.* II, 83 (Schmitt III, 208); *Monologium*, Prol. (I, 8); *Epist.* II, 204 (IV, 96f.); *Ep. de Incarn. Verbi*, ch. 16 (II, 35).

26. Cf. my 'Unité de Foi, diversité de formulation théologique entre Grecs et Latins dans l'appréciation des Docteurs occidentaux ', *RSR* 54, 1980, 21-31, or in the third volume of *I Believe in the Holy Spirit*, 174-84. I could now add a great deal of other evidence, e.g. Richard of St Victor, *De Trinitate* IV, 20 (PL 196, 943C): *Sed absit ab eis (Graeci et Latini) diversas credere, et hos vel illos in fide errare! In hac ergo verborum varietate intelligenda est veritas una, quamvis apud diversos sit nominum acceptio diversa!*

27. Cf. my *L'Église de S.Augustin a l'époque moderne*, Histoire des dogmes III/3, Paris 1970, 131f.

28. *ST* II, 2 q. 93 a.1 ad 3. Leo XIII (*Providentissimus*, 18 November 1893, DS 3289) cited the text of II *Sent.* d.2 q.1 sol.3: *in his quae de necessitate fidei non sunt licuit sanctis diversimode opinari sicut et nobis.* Rupert of Deutz already said *licuit semperque licebit cuique dicere, salva fide, quid senserit* (prologue of *De divinis officiis*).

29. *Opus tripartitum* II, ch.29: Mansi 24, 129.

30. 'Men must not be generally constrained by the positive determinations of popes to observe and to accept a manner of government or things which do not take into account whether indirectly or directly the truths of our faith and the law of the gospel': Prince Augustine Galitzin, *Sermon inédit de Jean Gerson sur le retour des Grecs à l'unité*, Paris 1859, 41.

31. Cf. M.Seidlmayr, '*Una religio in rituum varietate*. Zur Religionsauffassung des Nikolaus von Cues', *AKG* 36, 1954, 156f.

32. The comment by C.Courtois is strict, but is it so wrong? 'Rome, which only conceived of the universal under the multiple form of its own image', *Les Vandales et l'Afrique*, Paris 1955, 112. The work of F.Heiler, *Altkirchliche Autonomie und päpstlicher Zentralismus*, Munich 1941, is still valuable.

33. *Decr. ad Gallos*; E.C.Babut, *La Plus Ancienne Décrétale*, Paris 1904, 78. C.Pietri, in *Roma Christiana. Recherches sur l'église de Rome, son organisation, sa politique, son idéologie, de Miltiade à Sixte III (311-440)*, Rome 1976, cites Damasus and Innocent I and continues: 'the popes confused two spheres which today would come into a dogmatic treatise or a colleection of canon law'(1472 n.).

34. *Epist*, 6,3,5: PL 13, 1166.

35. E.Rösser in *Göttliches und menschliches, unveränderliches und veränderliches Kirchenrecht von der Entstehung der Kirche bis zur Mitte des neunten Jahrhunderts*, Paderborn 1934, 136 n.20, gives this series of declarations: Celestinus I, *Ep*. 18.3 (Coustant I, 1158), *fides quae una est*; *Ep*. 25, 17 (1217) *quia una fides necesse est uniter praedicatur*; Sixtus III, *Ep*. 1,2 (1234), *Romana ecclesia...in ipsa fidei praedicatione unam semper sententiam servavit*. St Leo, *Ep*. 29(7), ed. Schwartz, *Acta Concilia* 2/4, *fides quae non nisi una est, in nullo potest sui esse dissimilis*; *Ep*. 33 (12), *per totum mundum una... fides et una eademque confessio*; *Ep*. 35 (5), *Sancti Spiritus... una est eruditio eademque doctrina, quem quisque non recipit, non est membrum corporis Christi*; *Ep*.161 (101), *catholica fides, quae vera et una est, nulla se patitur diversitate violari*. Hormisdas, *Ep*. 137,2 (Thiel I, 960), *Neque enim possibile est, ut sit diversitas praedicationis, ubi una est forma veritatis*.

36. *Ep*. 14, 1 (PL 20, 517), in 414 in a fine vocabulary of communion.

37. *Epist*. 25,1, of 19 March 416 (Jaffé 311): PL 20, 551. G.Malchiodi, *La lettera di S.Innocenzo I a Decenzio vescovo da Gubbio*, Rome 1921, but above all the critical edition, with translation and commentary by R.Cabié, Louvain 1973 (I am sorry that I knew of this too late to be able to use it).

38. *Ep*. 9, PL 54, 624f. And cf. P.A.McShane, *La Romanitas et le pape Léon le Grand*, Paris and Montreal 1979, 212, 290.

39. *Ep*. 87 (13), ed. Tangl, 198: PL 89, 951f. (Jaffé 2291). There is a comparable reaction from Leo IV (847-855), who writes to Abbot Honoratus that if he gives up Gregorian chant he will be excommunicated, *quoniam convenit vos ea sequi salubriter, que Romana ecclesia mater omnium et magistra vestra non spernit, sed appetit atque insolubiliter tenet*, MGH, *Epp*. V, 604.

40. *Reg*. VII, 11, letter of 2 January 1080 to Duke Vratislav II, Caspar, 473.

41. *Reg.* 1, 64; Caspar, 93f.: 19 March 1074. Cf. P.Kehr, *Das Papstum und die Königreiche Navarra und Aragon bis zur Mitte des XII. Jahrhunderts*, APAW 1928, phil.-hist.Kl.4, 19f.

42. P.M.Gy, 'L'Unification liturgique de l'Occident et la liturgie de la Curie romaine', *RSPT* 59, 1975, 601-12. The clergy and the faithful in Castile offered some resistance to this introduction of the Roman liturgy: A.Becker, *Papst Urban II*, Schriften der MGH 19, Stuttgart 1964, I, 231. It was thought that the popes should not argue like this. Once there is great stress on authority of a monarchian type, there is a tendency to uniformity, as with Constantine (cf. E.Rösser, *Göttliches und Menschliches...Kirchenrecht...*, 1934, 139). In his imperial programme of unification, which even included the liturgy, Charlemagne insisted that there must be one *ordo psallendi* as there was one *ordo credendi*, *Libri Carolini* I, ch.6: PL 98, 1021CD: cf. my *Ecclésiologie du Haut Moyen Age*, Paris 1968, 271; also C.Vogel, 'La réforme liturgique sous Charlemagne', in *Karl der Grosse* II, 1965.

43. Above all Pius IX, *In suprema Petri*, 6 January 1848 (*Acta Pii IX*, I/1, 78-91); Leo XIII, *Orientalium dignitas*, 3 November 1894 (*Acta Leonis* XIII, vol.XIV, 358-70). A large number of texts may be found in A. d'Avril, *Documents relatifs aux Églises de l'Orient considérées dans leur rapport avec le Saint-Siège de Rome*, Paris 1862, 27-60; Petreni, *De relatione iuridica inter diversos ritus in Ecclesia catholica*, Rome 1930, 14-25; J.Schweigl, '*De unitate Ecclesiae orientalis et occidentalis restituenda, documentis S.Sedis ultimi saeculi (1848-1938) illustrata*', in *Periodica de re morali, canonica, liturgica* 28, 1939, 209-32, cf. 230 n.18.

44. There is of course the action on the part of Dom Guéranger in favour of the Roman liturgy.which led to uniformity. His pupil J.B.Pitra has some frenzied pages to the same effect, 'Vie du Vén. P.Libermann', 192f., quoted in A.Battandier, *Vie du Cardinal Pitra*, Paris 1893, 249.

45. To the Armenian Catholics, 20 May 1870.

46. Apostolic letter of 6 January 1862; d'Avril, op.cit., 53, and text in *Collectio Lacensis* II, 558ff.; cf. also *In suprema Petri Apostoli Sede*, 1848.

47. *Orientalium dignitas*, 30 November 1894; *Actes de Léon XIII* (B.Presse), V, 140.

48. AAS 11, 1919, 97-99.

49. 1 November 1923: AAS 15, 1923, 573.

50. *Motu proprio Sanctae Dei Ecclesiae*, 25 March 1938, AAS 20, 1938, 155.

51. AAS 36, 1944, 138.

52. Thus the speech of 13 November 1960, DC 1960, col.1475.

53. Cf. *Sacrosanctum Concilium*, 4 and 37-40; *Lumen Gentium*, 13 and 23 end: *Unitatis redintegratio*, 4 and 14-18, stressed particularly strongly in no.15; *Ad Gentes divinitus*, 8,9,16 and 22; *Gaudium et Spes*, 44 and 58. 3; *Orientalium Ecclesiarum*, 2, which cites nineteen pontifical documents extending from the eleventh to the nineteenth century; and cf. 5,6.

54. *Tomos Agapis*, Vatican-Phanar, 1958-1970, Rome-Istanbul 1971, nos.172, 374.

55. To the Coptic delegation, 22 June 1979, *Irénikon* 52, 1979, 377.

4. Pluralism in Ethnic and Cultural Areas

1. 'Do not use any zeal, do not advance any arguments to convince these people to change their rites, their customs and their manners, at least if they are not clearly contrary to religion and morality. What is more absurd than to transport France, Spain, Italy or some other part of Europe to the Chinese? Do not introduce among them our countries, but the faith, this faith which does not reject nor hurt the rites or customs of any people provided that they are not detestable, but on the contrary wishes them to be kept and protected. It is as it were inscribed on the nature of all men to think, to aim and to value above all else the traditions of their countries and their countries themselves. So there is no more powerful motive for alienation and hate than to introduce these changes in the customs peculiar to a nation, principally those which have been practised as long as the elders can remember' (op.cit., n.2, I, 16 and quoted by S.Delacroix, *Histoire universelle des missions catholiques*, Paris 1957, II, 156).

2. Cf. *Le siège apostolique et les missions*, II, 183, 219, 242; III, 365f., Union missionnaire du Clergé, ²1959.

3. Decree *Ad Gentes divinitus*, nos. 16,17,21,22,26,34. Cf. *Gaudium et Spes* 58, 3; *Lumen Gentium*, 13,17.

4. *Le Monde*, 2 August 1969 and the audience of 6 August, *DC* 51, no.1546, 16 September 1969, 756. This is the original text: 'Your evangelistic work raises a question which remains very much alive and arouses a great deal of discussion, namely the adaptation of the gospel, the church, to African culture... Must the church be European, Latin, Oriental, or should it be African? The problem would seem to be difficult, and indeed it can be. But there is a ready solution, with two answers. Your church must be above all Catholic. In other words. it must be entirely based on the identical, essential, determinative heritage of the same doctrine of Christ, professed by the authentic tradition and authorized by the one true church. That is a fundamental demand which is beyond discussion. But given this first answer, we must move on to the second: the expression, that is to say the language, the way of expressing the one faith, can be multiple and consequently original, conforming to the language, the style, the temperament, the genius of the culture which professes this one faith. In this perspective pluralism is legitimate and even desirable. An adaptation of Christian life in the areas of pastoral care, ritual, teaching and spirituality is not only possible, but is encouraged by the church. That is what is expressed, for example, in liturgical reform. In this sense you can and should have an African Christianity. Certainly you have human values and characteristic forms of culture capable of development to their own fulfilment, which may well find in and through Christianity a richness of authentic African expression... If you can avoid the possible dangers of religious pluralism, and consequently refrain from making your Christian profession a kind of local folk-lore, exclusivist racism, egotistical tribalism or even arbitrary separatism, you can remain sincerely African even in your interpretation of the Christian life; you can formulate Catholicism in terms which are completely appropriate to your culture, and you can bring to the Catholic church the precise

and original contribution of negritude which, at this moment in history, it especially needs.'

5. *DC* 77, no.1787, 1 June 1980, 504f. Cf. the speech to the bishops of East Africa on 7 May, ibid., 534, and to the young people at Yamoussoukro on 11 May, ibid., 547f.

6. Thus I.J.Luzbetak, *L'Église et les cultures. Une anthropologie appliquée pour l'ouvrier apostolique*, Brussels 1968; J.Bruls, 'La Mission et les cultures', in R.Aubert et al.(eds), *Nouvelle Histoire de l'Église* 5, 1975, 465f.

7. Books include: *Personnalité africaine et catholicisme*, Paris 1963 (in the context of the council); Anselm Titianma Sanon, *Tierce Église, ma mère, ou la conversion d'une communauté païenne au Christ*, Paris 1972; Aylward Shorter, *African Christian Theology*, London 1965; *The Churches of Africa: Future Prospects*, Concilium 106, June 1977; R.Luneau, *Voici le temps des héritiers*, Paris 1981. Of the colloquia see especially *Civilisation noire et Église catholique*, Paris and Dakar 1978.

8. The constitution *Sacrosanctum concilium* gives the main ones, nos.37-40, 65. Cf. Boniface Luykx, 'Culte chrétien en Afrique', *NRSM* 1974; Anselm Titianma Sanon, 'L'Africanisation de la liturgie', *Maison-Dieu* 123, 1975, (108-25) 108f.n.1 (the bibliography also gives some titles relating to Asia).

9. R.Laurentin, *L'Évangélisation après le quatrième synode*, Paris 1975, 50.

10. Op.cit. (n.7), 166,212.

11. J.-P. de Jong, *L'Eucharistie comme réalité symbolique*, Cogitatio fidei 65, Paris 1972, 61; R.Luneau, 'Une Eucharistie sans pain ni vin?', *Spiritus* 48, February 1972, 3-11.

12. References in my 'L'Économie', *Irénikon*, 1972, 172 n.3.

13. Cf. *Spiritus* 60, September 1975; 'Vie de famille et mariage des chrétiens en Afrique subsaharienne', Dossiers *Pro mundi vita*, Brussels 1976; M.Legrain, 'Les Africains peuvent-ils espérer une autre législation matrimoniale?', *L'année canonique* 22, 1978, 81-147; id., *Mariage chrétien modèle unique? Questions venues d'Afrique*, Paris 1978; V.Mulago, 'Mariage traditionnel africain et mariage chrétien', *Studia Missionalia* 27, 1978, 53-134.

14. E.Hillman, *Polygamy Reconsidered. African Plural Marriages and the Christian Churches*, Maryknoll 1975; id., 'Polygyny Reconsidered', *Concilium* 3.4, March 1968, 80-9; M. Legrain, *L'Année canonique*, 136f.

15. There is a summary of the debate in R.Laurentin, *L'Évangélisation après le quatrième Synode*, Paris 1975, 58-61. Cf. K.A.Dickson and P.Ellingworth, *Pour une théologie africaine*, Yaoundé 1969.

16. R.Laurentin, op.cit., 78f.

17. *DC* 71, no.1684: 19 October 1975, 584.

18. I Cor. 10.3f. Cf. Augustine, *In Ev.Ioan.* XXVI, 12f.

19. Augustine, *Epist.* 110, 5f. (PL 33, 858) and other texts; Thomas Aquinas, *III Sent.* d.13 q.2 a.2, qa 2 ad 4; d.40 a.4, qa 2 ad 2; *IV Sent.* d.8q.1a.2, qa 2 ad 1; *De verit.* q.14a 12; *ST* Ia IIae q.103 a.4; q.107 a.1 ad 1; IIa IIae q.1 a.2 and 7; q.4a 6 ad 2; IIIa q.8a. 3 ad 3; *In Symb.* a.9.

20. *Sessio* XXI c.2: DS 1728.

5. 'Pluralism', Intrinsic Value of Unity

1. There is a substantial bibliography on pluralism; I have noted about fifty titles. Here I mention only P.Delhaye, 'Unité de foi et pluralisme des théologies dans les récents documents pontificaux', *Esprit et Vie* 41, 1972, 561-9; 42, 593-9. Y. Congar, 'Unité et Pluralisme', in *Ministères et Communion ecclésiale*, Paris 1971, 229-60.

2. *De Trinitate* II, 2 (PL 10,51).

3. *De Synodis* 62 (PL 10, 522).

4. *III Sent.* d. 25 q.1 a. 1 q. I obj 4; ST IIa, IIIae q.1 a.6.

5. Cf. P.J.Labarrière, 'Place et fonction de la "recherche" dans l'Église', *Études*, February 1980, 235-48. However, he has also a 'Critique du pluralisme', *Études*, June 1977, 773-86: he prefers to speak of plurality.

6. Cf. e.g. J.Rémy, 'Conflits et dynamique sociale', *Lumen vitae* 24, 1969, 26-50; F.Houtart and J.Rémy, *Église et Société en Mutation*, Paris 1969; *Concilium* 109, November 1975: 'Vie chrétienne et conflits' (no English ed.); J.M.R.Tillard, 'La Communauté Religieuse', *NRT* 94, 1972, 428-519; 95, 1973, 150-87.

7. 'Qu'appelons-nous unité?', *Terre Entière*, March-April 1969, 93f.

8. Cf. among many other texts (which contain full bibliographies) my 'Le Dialogue, loi du travail oecuménique, structure de l'intelligence humaine', *Chrétiens en Dialogue*, Unam Sanctam 50, Paris 1966, 1-17; Langdon Gilkey, 'L'Esprit et la découverte de la vérité par le dialogue', in *L'Expérience de l'Esprit*, Mélanges E.Schillebeeckx, Paris 1976, 225-40.

9. In *Irénikon* 52, 1979, 377.

10. See my account in the colloquium *Ecclesiam suam*, 'Situation ecclésiologique au moment d'*Ecclesiam suam* et passage à une Église dans l'itinéraire des hommes'.

11. Cf. my 'De la communion des Églises à une ecclésiologie de l'Église universelle', in *L'Épiscopat et l'Église Universelle*, ed. Y.Congar and B.-D.Dupuy, Unam Sanctam 39, Paris 1962, 227-60.

12. I have already cited texts in the study quoted in n.11, p.238. I have noted a number of others since. However, it is most important to be aware of the true sense of the expression which Paul VI again used to sign the documents of Vatican II, a sense established beyond any possible doubt by H.Marot, 'Note sur l'expression *Episcopus Ecclesiae Catholicae*', in *La Collegialité Épiscopale*, Unam Sanctam 52, Paris 1965, 94-8; it is 'bishop of the authentic church which is at Rome'.

13. *Lumen Gentium*, no.123, with a quotation from St Cyprian in the note.

14. Cf. *Lumen Gentium*, no. 26.1; *Christus Dominus*, no 11.1; *Sacros. Concilium*, no.41; *Ad gentes divinitus*, ch.III.

15. J.Hamer, 'La Terminologie Ecclésiologique de Vatican II et les ministères Protestants', *DC* 53, no.1589, 4 July 1971, 625-8; C.J.Dumont, 'Eucharistie et Ministères. A propos des "Accords des Dombes". Essai de critique constructive', *Istina* 18, 1973, 155-207.

PART TWO

6. Some Relevant Eastern Concepts

1. *Epist. ad Michaelem*, PG 120, 812f.; cf. M.Jugie, *Le schisme byzantin. Aperçu historique et doctrinal*, Paris 1941, 227.

2. For this plan of Barlaam's, cf. C.Giannelli, 'Un progetto di Barlaam Calabra per l'unione delle Chiesi', in *Miscellanea Giovanni Mercati III*, Studi e Testi 123, Rome 1946, 154-208, which contains an edition of the first (185-201) and second (202-8) discourses given in Avignon in 1339. There is a French version in J.Meyendorff, 'Un mauvais théologien de l'unité au XIV⁰ siècle: Barlaam le Calabrais', in *1054-1954, L'Église et les Églises*, Etude et travaux offerts à Dom Lambert Beauduin, Chevetogne 1955, II, 47-64.

3. PG 151, 1337; Meyendorff, 50.

4. I am amazed that in his very interesting 'Réflexions sur le rétablissement possible de la communion entre les Églises orthodoxe et catholique. Perspectives actuelles', *Istina* 20, 1975, 112-5, Fr Louis Bouyer has written: 'As a third stage it should be promulgated by the authorities of East and West that the faith defined is the same on both sides and that doctrinal differences relate only to those controversial points which have not yet been the object of immutable decisions, so that one finds oneself confronted only by theologoumena over which a common agreement must be reached without the differences involved leading to any breach in the unity of faith' (113). I subscribe to the idea of a unity of faith in two different constructions. But it seems to me inadequate to call the doctrine of the *filioque* a 'theologoumenon'. For Roman Catholics it is a dogma, and one which has found its way into the creed, the solemn confession of faith. Fr Bouyer's position is supported by what he says a little later: 'As a fourth stage, it should be recognized by both sides that only the seven great councils of the undivided church could formulate definitions of faith on which one should not go back in any way.' On the one hand, this fourth stage would seem presupposed by the first; on the other, what it represents poses many very delicate problems. But I am sure that they can and even should be raised. I am very aware that Fr Bouyer has had the courage to raise them and to do so lucidly.

5. Evangelos Theodorou, 'Unité et pluralité du témoignage du Christ', *Istina* 20, 1975, 12-22.

6. Ibid., 138f.

7. The main studies I have consulted in addition to pages or appendices of monographs devoted to different authors are: W.Gass, 'Das patristische Word oikonomia', *ZWT* 17, 1884, 465-504; A. d'Alès, 'Le mot oikonomia dans la langue théologique de S.Irénée', *REG* 32, 1919, 1-9 (criticized by Moingt, 896); G.L. Prestige, *God in Patristic Thought*, London 1952, 68-76, 98-104 (cf. Moingt, 893); O. Michel, *TDNT* 5, 154f.; A.Houssiau, *La Christologie d'Irénée*, Louvain-Gembloux 1955, 93-104; J.Reumann, 'Oikonomia = "Covenant": Terms for Heilsgeschichte in Early Christian Usage', *NovT* 3, 1959, 282-92; G.W.H.Lampe, *Patristic Greek Lexicon*, Oxford 1961, 940-3; O. Cullmann, *Salvation in History*, London 1967, 75-

8; J.Moingt, 'Théologie trinitaire de Tertullien, III', *Théologie* 70, Paris 1966, 891-932; H. de Lubac, *La Foi Chrétienne. Essai sur la structure du Symbole des Apôtres*, Paris 1969, 88-92. Note too the typescript dissertations by O.Lillge, *Das patristiche Wort Oikonomia, seine Geschichte und seine Bedeutung bis auf Origenes*, Erlangen 1955 (cf. *TLZ*, 1955, col.239); M.Widmann, *Der Begriff Oikonomia im Werk des Irenäus und seine Vorgeschichte*, Tübingen 1956). I have used here pp. 174-88 of my article 'Propos en vue d'une théologie de l'"Economie" dans la tradition latine', *Irénikon* 45, 1972, 155-206.

8. Lampe includes in this meaning the use of the term in the trinitarian theology of Hippolytus and Tertullian. J. Moingt shows that with these authors 'economy is the dispensation of the plan of God in several activities, successive and co-ordinated, and the distribution of these activities among a number of persons who thus show themselves to be distinct and united' (909).

9. Cf. J.Reumann, 'Oikonomia as "ethical accommodation" in the Fathers and its Pagan Background', *Studia Patristica* III, ed. F.L. Cross, TU 78, Berlin 1961, 370-9.

10. On 'condescension' see H.Pinard, 'Les Infiltrations païennes dans l'ancienne Loi d'après les Pères de l'Église. La Thèse de la condescendance', *RSR* 9, 1919, 197-221; F.Falbi, 'La "condiscendenza" divina nell'ispirazione bibblica secondo S. Giovanni Crisostomo', *Bibl* 14, 1933, 330-47; K.Gründer, *Figur und Geschichte. Johann Georg Hamanns "Biblische Betrachtungen" als Ansatz einer Geschichtsphilosophie'*, Symposium. *Philosophische Schriftenreihe*, Freiburg-Munich 1958, 28-92, who gives a bibliography of Protestant theology from the sixteenth to the eighteenth century (65 n.18, bibliographies of Protestant studies which appeared on this theme in the Fathers, between 1741 and 1821). The Dogmatic Constitution of Vatican II on Revelation (*Dei Verbum*, 13) took up the theme with reference to John Chrysostom, *In Genesim*, Hom. 17.1 (PG 53, 134), but was preceded by the encyclical *Divino afflante* of 30 September 1943 (Denziger 2294, not included in DS).

10a. Cf. Gregory Nazianzus, *Orat.* 42, 14 (PG 36, 473C).

11. Athanasius, *Epistola ad Palladium*, PG 26, 1168D. Cf. B.Pruche, Introduction to Basil, Treatise on the Holy Spirit, *Traité du Saint-Esprit*, SC 17, Paris 1945, 12-23; K.Duchatelez, *NRT* 92, 1970, 288f., 290 n.70. Newman was fond of evoking these arrangements which first God and after him the Church and the Fathers, had used in the communication of the faith: cf. *Apologia pro Vita Sua*, London 1945, 18; J.Guitton, *La Philosophie de Newman*, Paris 1933, 7.

12. First Canonical Letter = *Epist.* 188, about 373, can. 1 (PG 32, 669); I.B.Pitra, *Juris eccl. Graecorum Monumenta* I, Rome 1864, 578f.; M.Jugie, op.cit., n.16 below, 121f.

13. Second Canonical Letter = *Epist.* 199. can.47 (PG 32, 751): Pitra, 593f.; Jugie, 122.

14. J.Lebon, 'Textes inédits de Philoxène de Mabbug', *Mus* 43, 1930, 185.

15. Cf. M.Nicol, 'The Byzantine Reaction to the Second Council of

Lyons, 1274', in *Councils and Assemblies*, ed. G.J.Cuming & D.Barker, Cambridge 1971, 119, 126f.; however, that is precisely a sphere where according to Mgr Kotsonis (op.cit., infra, 153f.) oikonomia would not apply. The example of the Fathers shows that it is not so simple!

16. There is a history of this practice and positions taken or justifications given, in A.Palmieri, 'La Rebaptisation des Latins chez les Grecs', *ROC* 7, 1902, 618-46; 8, 1903, 111-43; T.Spacil, 'Doctrina Theologiae Orientis separati de Sacramento Baptismi', *OC* VI, 4, Rome 1926, 211-55 (a rich bibliography on the application of the theory of economy to this case); M.Jugie, *Theologia dogmatica Christianorum Orientalium*...III, Paris 1920, 117-25; J.Kotsonis, 166ff.; K.Duchatelez, both quoted in the next note.

17. I have read: (*a*) Orthodox: C. Dyovouniotis, 'The Principle of Economy', *CQR* 6, 1933, 93-101; H. Alivisatos, extracts from a memorandum, in *Dispensation in Practice and Theory*, London 1944, 25-43; G.A.Galitis, 'Le Problème de l'intercommunion sacramentelle avec les non-orthodoxes d'un point de vue orthodoxe. Étude biblique et ecclésiologique', *Istina* 12, 1969, 197-219; Jerome Kotsonis, *Problèmes de l'économie ecclésiastique*, Gembloux 1971 (the original Greek dates from 1957). (*b*) Western authors, among whom one finds references to and accounts of studies which have appeared in Greek, Roumanian and Russian; William Palmer, *Dissertations on Subjects relating to the 'orthodox' or 'Eastern Catholic' Communion*, London 1853 (I know this only through Thomson, 370, quoted below); M.Jugie, 'Une nouvelle dogmatique orthodoxe. Trois théologiens grecs en présence', *Échos d'Orient* 11, 1908, 146-54, 257-64; F.Gavin, *Some Aspects of Contemporary Greek Orthodox Thought*, Milwaukee-London 1923, 262-7, 292-303 (reissued London 1936); J.A. Douglas, *The Relations of the Anglican churches with the Eastern-Orthodox*, London 1921, 55-69; id., 'The Orthodox Principle of Economy and its Exercise', *Theology* 24, 1932, 39-47, and *The Christian East* 3-4, 1932, 99-109 (excessively dependent on K. Dyovouniotis); P.Dumont, 'Économie ecclésiastique et réiteration des sacrements', *Irénikon* 14, 1937, 228-47, 339-62; id., 'Anglicans et Orthodoxes. La Faculté de Théologie d'Athènes et les Ordres Anglicans', *Irénikon* 17, 1940, 50-79; *Dispensation in Practice and Theory, with Special Reference to the Anglican Churches*, London 1944; P.Rai, *Essai sur l'Économie en Droit canon byzantin des origines jusqu'au schisme de 1054. Recherches historiques et juridiques*, Rome 1954; F.J.Thomson, 'Economy', *JTS* NS 16, 1965, 368-420; Kilian McDonnell, 'Ways of Validating Ministry', *JES* 7, 1970, 209-65; K.Duchatelez, 'De geldigheid der wijdingen in het licht der "ekonomie"', *TvT* 8, 1968, 377-401; id., 'La Notion d'Économie et ses richesses théologiques', *NRT* 92, 1970, 267-93 (268 n.3, bibliography); id., 'L'Économie baptismale dans l'Eglise Orthodoxe', *Istina* 14, 1971, 13-36 (bibliography, 14 n.3).

18. For Cyprian, cf. the study quoted in the next note; Firmilian, *Inter op. Cypr., Ep.* 75,7; cf. the Apostolic Canons (IVth century) which are recognized by Orthodox canon law, c.68.

19. Cf. the general introduction to *Traités antidonatistes de S.Augustin, Oeuvres* 28, DDB 1968, 87-117 (for the Donatist position, inherited from St Cyprian, 48-70).

20. Ecumenical Patriarch Meletius Metaxakis in 1922; Jerusalem and Cyprus in 1923; Alexandria in 1930; all invoking the economy. Cf. *Irénikon*, 1937, 358 n.3; 1940, 50. Holy Synod of Bucharest, 20 March 1936, without invoking the economy, but demanding and waiting for a doctrinal declaration of the Anglican episcopate officially expressing its agreement with Orthodox dogma. Moscow conference of July 1948, cf. A.Wenger, 'L'Église Orthodoxe et les Ordinations Anglicanes'; *NRT* 76, 1954, 44-55.

21. Decision of the Holy Synod of the Church of Greece, with an appeal to the economy, text in *Irénikon* 17, 1940, 99. Mgr Kotsonis, who was Archbishop of Athens, affirms that the economy is applied only to those who want to enter or return to the Orthodox church, and not to churches which remain separated (cf. 164f.).

22. This was also said by Professors Bratsiotis and Balanos, and Archbishop Chrysostom Papadopoulos.

23. Roumanian theologians had already made several studies of the question, see the references in G.A.Galitis, art.cit., 230 n.33 and 235 n.47.

24. Reference and translation in *Irénikon*, 1937, 354, 356, or *Istina*, 1969, 22.

25. In reply to Dr Headlam, Bishop of Gloucester, *Report of the Joint Doctrinal Commission between the Anglican and the Eastern Church*, published in *The Christian East*, Summer 1931. 'It is true that the church has the power to reject the priesthood of schismatics, but it does not have the power to recognize the ordination of churches where the apostolic succession has been broken' (63). And cf. P.Dumont, 'La Délégation Orthodoxe à la Conférence de Lambeth', *Irénikon* 8, 1931, 241-68.

26. K.Duchatelez, *Istina* 1969, 23; P.Dumont, *Irénikon*, 1937, 357.

27. Cf. F.J.Thomson, *JTS* NS 16, 1965, 382.

28. G.Florovsky, 'The Limits of the Church', *CQR* 117, 1933, 17-31. In the same terms: Paul Evdokimov, *L'Orthodoxie*, Neuchâtel-Paris 1959, 343, and Metropolitan Sergius at the Conference of Moscow (of which he became Patriarch in 1943); cf. A.Wenger, art. cit., above, 54. The Roumanian theologian Liviu Stan also accepts that non-Orthodox like Anglicans are 'a part of the pleroma of the church' (cf. *Istina*, 1969, 235 n.47).

Jerome Kotsonis, 'The Validity of Anglican Orders according to the Canon Law of the Orthodox Church', *GOTR* 3, 1957, 182-96; 4, 1958, 44-65, distinguishes between a strict authenticity of sacraments, e.g. that of ministry, which are valid according to *akribia* from the Orthodox point of view, and an authentifiable potentiality which would be valid according to economy, i.e. could be authenticated by its entry into the sphere of grace formed by the Orthodox church. C.J.N.Bailey, 'Validity and Authenticity: The Difference between Western and Orthodox Views on Orders', *St Vladimir's Seminary Quarterly* 8, 1964, 86-92, criticizes this view. He notes (89) that it is the same as that of St Augustine towards the Donatists. Bailey re-establishes what he calls the true Orthodox perspective, the key concept of which is that of authenticity, not validity. There is authenticity when a sacramental act is performed within the limits of the sphere of grace which is the one church, that body which continues unaltered the institution of grace deriving from the apostles of the risen Christ and the gift of the Spirit, by means of the undivided church.

29. *Ep.* 188 (First Canonical Letter), can.1: PG 32, 669.

30. *Actes de la conférence des chefs et des représentants des Églises orthodoxes autocephales réunies à Moscou*, 2 vols, Moscow 1949. Cf. A.Wenger, 'L'Église orthodoxe et les ordinations anglicanes', *NRT* 76, 1954, 44-55.

31. Text of the Acts, II, 250f., quoted by A.Wenger, 53f.

32. Op.cit., 182: 'The economy exists when by necessity or for the greater good of certain people or the entire church, with competence and in certain conditions, a derogation of *akribia* has been allowed, temporarily or in a permanent way, the piety and purity of dogma at the same time remaining unaltered.'

33. Mgr Kotsonis seems to me to maintain a harder line here than the Fathers whose texts I have cited above (he quotes some of them, 160f.).

34. Thus, for example, when the forty-eighth canon of the Sixth Council adds a reason for divorce to what the Orthodox church finds in Matt.5.32 (cf. 126). One could cite other examples. Note that when the question of divorce came up during the fourth period of Vatican II, Fr André Scrima explained the Orthodox practice of the remarriage of the innocent party by the theology of the economy; cf. *Le Monde*, 2 October 1965; A.Wenger, *Vatican II. Chronique de la Quatrième Session*, Paris 1966, 215-17.

35. 'Economie et théologie sacramentaire', *Istina* 17, 1962, 17-20.

36. Syropoulos, *Mémoires sur le concile de Florence*, Paris 1971, 169.

37. Syropoulos, 129.

38. Scholarios, *Orationes in Concilio Florentino habitae*, ed. J.Gill, Rome 1964, 117.15-22.

39. Cf. also Scholarios, 51,4 to 52,2.

40. PO XVII, 460,11-461,2.

41. Cf. PO XVII, 454,19-458, 22.

42. PO XVII, 469, 2-4.

43. PO, 469,35-470,2. For the whole passage, 468,7-470,2.

44. Again Scholarios (quoted n.38), 110, 19-111,8; 116,25-117,5.

45. Cf. PG 160, 168D-170B, cf. PO XVII, 469, 27-31.

46. Cf. Gregory Nazianzus, *Or.36 contra Arianos* 12, PG 36, 230B, 628C.

47. PG 160, 168D.

48. Cf. *De Purgatorio disputationes in Concilio Florentino habitae*, ed. L.Petit and G.Hofmann, Rome 1969, 26, 12-37, cf. 70,15-20. Bessarion also maintains the same view in *Oratio dogmatica de Unione*, ed. E.Candal, Rome 1958, 13, 18-33; cf. 15,21-16,13.

49. Cf. *De purgatorio*, 102,38-103,10.

50. Scholarios, 56, 30f. For the whole passage, 55,26-57,2.

51. *Quae supersunt actorum graecorum concilii Florentini*, ed. Gill, 31, 24-30.

52. *Acta Florentini*, 31, 24-30.

53. Ibid., 374, 117, 5f.: *henoseos, schema loipon kata triton...*

54. Ibid., 116, 344-37. For the whole passage, cf. 116,25-117,5.

55. *Quae supersunt* (n.51), 405, 25 – 406, 3. Cf. in the same context 405, 14-19.

56. Ibid., 407,2-16.

57. Scholarios, 10,33-11,2. For the whole passage, 8,11-11,2; 17, 19-22.

58. PO XVII, 446,38-447,9.

59. Op.cit.(n.36), 414,25-492,22.

60. H.Kotsonis, *Problèmes de l'Économie ecclésiastique*, Gembloux 1971, 94f., distinguishes the two concepts. *Synkatabasis* is broader than economy. It is a general inner inspiration, whereas *oikonomia* is a precise and relatively fixed institution the definition of which can be found in n.32 above. Without pushing things too far, the reader can check in the original that in the references given the concepts are used somewhat in an inverse sense by Syropoulos. For him, *synkatabasis* designates a precise concession, whereas *oikonomia* appears in a very broad sense.

61. Op.cit. 414, 26-31; for the whole passage, 414,25-416,8.

62. Ibid., 444,29-446,15.

63. 446,1. ; also 416, 1f.

64. 446,5-9 and PG 116,667BC. For a complete life of Theodore Graptos, ibid., 653-84.

65. 446, 7-8.

7. A Structure of Duality in Unity?

1. D.Stremooukoff, *Vladimir Soloviev et son oeuvre messianique*, Paris 1935.

2. H.Riesenfeld, 'Accouplements de termes contradictoires dans la NT', in *Alberto Debrunner sexagenario sacrum. Coniectanea Neotestamentica* IX, Uppsala 1944, 1-21. 'Land and sea' is frequently used in the Middle Ages to express a sovereign domination.

3. Cf. Ps. 8.5; 144.3.

4. Cf. Deut.17.6; 19.15; Matt.18.16; II Cor.13.1; I Tim 5.19; Heb.10.28; John 8.16f.; Cf. H. van Vliet, *No Single Testimony. Study on the Adaptation of the Law of Deut. 19: par. into the NT*, Utrecht 1958.

5. Cf. *Tradition and Traditions*, London 1966, 374. Scripture and tradition, understood as the two eyes which have to be open to understand the Christian mystery, are another example of dual unity.

6. J.Jeremias, 'Paarweise Sendung im NT', in *New Testament Essays. Studies in Memory of T.W.Manson*, Manchester 1959, 136-44; there is a material imitation in the mediaeval law of the *socius*.

7. *L'Ecclésiologie du haut Moyen Age*, Paris 1968, 262f.

8. There is nothing relevant for our theme as I conceive it in the bibliography of J.Fischer, *Oriens-Occidens-Europa. Begriff und Gedenke 'Europa' in der späten Antike und im Frühen Mittelalter*, Wiesbaden 1957.

9. The bibliography on the Orthodox positions and the character of Eastern Christianity is enormous, whether in general or on particular chapters. It is impossible to go into detail here. L.Zander, *ER*, April 1963, 478f., recommends P.Sherrard, *The Greek East and the Latin West*, Oxford 1959. The exceptional value of V.Lossky, *The Mystical Theology of the*

Eastern Church, London 1957, has been recognized; there is a popular article by G.Dejaifve, 'Orient et Occident: deux théologies?', *NRT* 82, 1960, 3-19.

10. F.Kattenbusch, *Lehrbuch der vergleichenden Confessionskunde* I, Freiburg 1892; A.Harnack, *Der Geist der morgenländischen Kirche im Unterschied von der abendländischen* (SBAW 1913, reprinted in *Reden und Aufsätze* III, *Aus der Friedens und Kriegsarbeit*, Giessen 1916, 101-40). From the Catholic side see A.Baumstark, 'L'Unité de l'Église selon les conceptions de l'Orient et de l'Occident', *Istina* 1, 1954, 219-25. Because I have no competence, and want to dissociate myself from any possible syncretism, I shall not press the idea of a providential West-East duality to the point of bringing in the spirit and tradition of India. J.A.T.Robinson, *Truth is Two-Eyed*, London 1979, has suggested convergences between Christianity and Hinduism, two approaches to reality which would have to be taken together to arrive at a more total perception. Two-eyed vision should exist in each of these worlds. However, such an attempt is beyond me, and I do not find Robinson's essay very illuminating.

11. *In Philip.*, c.1, Hom. 2,4 (PG 62, 204).

12. Cf. *I Believe in the Holy Spirit*, Vol.3, London 1983, Part Two.

13. Paul VI, *Anno ineunte* of 25 July 1967 on the occasion of the nineteenth centenary of the martyrdom of the apostles Peter and Paul: this is a very important text, carefully elaborated in *Tomos Agapis*, Rome-Istanbul 1971, no.176, 386.

14. Niels Bohr, *Essays. On Atomic Physics and Human Knowledge, 1958-1962*, London 1963. Bohr himself applied his idea of complementarity to the moral and religious domain, in particular in his contribution to *Studia Orientalia Joh.Pedersen...dicata*, Copenhagen 1953, 385-90. L.Morren, 'Complémentarité', in *Synthèses*, Brussels 1947, 340-4; id., 'Un aspect du problème du signe: la complémentarité généralisée', in *Recherches et Débats* 67, 1969, 137-41; C.F.von Weizsäcker, *Komplementarität und Logik*, Naturwissenschaften 1955, 19 and 20; O. Costa de Beauregard, 'Complémentarité et rélativité', *RP* 80, 1956, 385-409; L.von Strauss and Torney, 'Das Komplementaritätsprinzip der Physik in philosophischer Analyse', *ZPF* 10, 1956, 109-29; G.Howe, 'Zu den Äusserungen von Niels Bohr über religiösen Fragen', *KuD* 4, 1958, 20-46; H.H.Schrey, 'Der Begriff der Komplementarität und seine Bedeutung für Erkenntnistheorie und Theologie', *EvTh* 19, 1959, 391-8.

15. L. de Broglie, *La Physique nouvelle et les quanta*, quoted by L.Morren, 341. Cf. L. de Broglie, Dialectica 2, 1948, 326: 'According to Bohr the images of wave and particle are complementary in the sense that although these images are contradictory, they are both necessary for giving an account of all the aspects under which elementary particles can appear to us. In experiments it is one or other of these two aspects which predominates, and which allows these two contradictory images to help us one by one without ever entering into conflict; one gets vaguer as the other gets more precise.'

16. P.Jordan, *Verdrängung und Komplementarität*, Hamburg 1947, according to *RSPT* 1951, 157.

17. Cf. my lecture at the Rencontres internationales de Génève, 5 September 1963; text in *Chrétiens en dialogue*, Unam Sanctam 50, Paris 1964, 1-17.

18. *La Philosophie de saint Bonaventure*, Paris ²1943, 396. Elsewhere, on p.409, E.Gilson quotes this saying of St Bonaventure himself: *Sic ergo ad trahendum jugum Domini junctus est Paulus Petro, Bernardus Benedicto et Franciscus Dominico* (*De SS. Dominico*, Opera, ed. Quaracchi, IX, 595).

19. G.Dejaifve, 'Diversité dogmatique et unité de la révélation', *NRT* 89, 1967, 16-25.

8. What is a Rite?

1. Text cited almost literally by Conrad of Megenberg, *Tractatus contra Wilhelmum Occam*, ch. 7, in H.Scholz, *Unbekannte kirchenpolitische Streitschriften* II, 369f.

2. *Quodlibet*, quoted by M.Grabmann, *Geschichte der scholastischen Methode* II, 545 n.

3. Leo IV (847-55) to Abbot Honoratus, MGH, *Epp.* V, p.864.

4. The *officiorum ritus* vary according to the provinces (J. 11, in *Die Texte des Normannischen Anonymus*, ed. K.Pellens Wiesbaden 1966, 83); *Graecorum episcopi aliis verbis et alio ritu consecrantur* (J.18, p.106). The kings, Solomon, sacrifice according to *ritum visibilem sacramenti, sacrificandi ritum* (J.24, pp.132f.); the king receives the ring *iuxta ritum pontificis* (*De consecr. pont. et reg.*, V, p.158).

5. *Expositio Psalmorum* in Ps. XXXI: *Opera inedita*, ed. D. and O. van den Eynde and A.Rijmersdael, II/1, Rome 1956, p.10.

6. Quoted in the *Collectio Lacensis* II, 446.

7. Cf. G.Müller, 'Um die Einheit der Kirche, zu den Verhandlungen über den Laienkelch', in *Reformata reformanda*, Festschrift H.Jedin, Münster 1965, I, 393-427 (cf. 417-25).

8. I. Hergenröther, 'Die Rechtsverhältnisse der verschiedenen Riten innerhalb der katholischen Kirche', *AKK* 7, 1862, 171.

9. Innocent III, Honorius III, Innocent IV and Nicolas III all make statements in the same terms, quoted in *OC* 32, 1933, 97.

10. Cf. the indexes s.v. *ritus* of *Acta Innocentii III*(1198-1216): *Pontificia Commissio ad redigendum Codicem Iuris Canonici Orientalis Fontes*, Ser. III, Vol.X, Rome 1944.

11. Published by H.Finke, *Konzilienstudien zur Geschichte des 13. Jahrhunderts. Ergänzungen und Berechtungen zu Hefele-Knöpfler 'Consiliengeschichte'*, V and VI, Münster 1891, 117f.

12. Cf. *ST* IIIa q.63 a.3; a. 4.ad e; a.6 ad 1 and 2.

13. *Ritus sacramenti consistit in signis exterioribus*, *IV Sent.* d. 8 q.1 a. sol. 3.

14. Of peoples: John Wyclif, *De civili dominio*, ed. L.Poole, 75; of the church: Marsilius of Padua, *Defensor Pacis*, trans. J.Quillet, who renders it 'the ritual of the church' (384f.); 'the practice of the church' (454).

15. Bull *Laetentur coeli* of 6 July 1439: DS 1303. Cf. G.Hofmann, '*Notae historicae de terminologia theologica Concilii Florentini*', *Greg* 20, 1939,

257-63. Cf. Cajetan, *descendendo ad ritus consuetudinesque ecclesiarum*, *Com. in III*ᵃᵐ q.20 a.12.

16. WA 8, p.413.

17. *Vorlesungen über 1 Mose*, ch.27, WA 43, 503.41ff. A little further on he uses *ceremoniae* in the same sense (pp.521.39 – 522.3).

18. *Ita omnes ecclesiasticas constitutiones, quas pro sanctis et salutaribus recipimus, in duo capita referre licet; alterque enim ad ritus et ceremonias, alterae ad disciplinam et pacem respiciunt* (*Inst.* IV, 10,29).

19. Cf. G.Alberigo, 'L'Oecuménisme au Moyen Age', in *1274: Année charnière. Mutations et continuités*, Paris 1977, 319-39.

20. Cf. V.Peri, *Chiesa Romana e 'rito' greco. G.A.Santoro e la Congregazione dei Greci 1566-1596*, Brescia 1975.

21. Antoine Joubeir, *La Notion Canonique de Rite. Essai Historico-canonique*, Rome ²1961, 15. The references are to Pius IV: constitution *Romanus Pontifex* of 16 February 1564; to Pius V, constitution *Providentia Romani Pontificis* of 20 August 1566; to the Instruction of Clement VIII , *Fontes Codicis Iuris Canonici* I, p.345.

22. Benedict XIV, bull *Etsi pastoralis* 2, no.XIII. *Allatae sunt* 20; Pius IX, decree *Plura sapienter*, 1847. Cf. H.L.Hoffmann, *De Benedicti XIV latinisationibus* in *EJC* 4, 1948, q.54 and as a separate book, Rome 1958. This *praestantia* is in principle abolished today; A. Petrani, '*An adsit ritus praestantior?*', *Apollinaris* 6, 1933, 74-82; Vatican II, Constitution on the Liturgy, no.4, his commentary in *Maison Dieu* 76, 1963/64, 39, and Decree on the Eastern Churches, no.3.

23. *Acta Pii IX* I, vol.3, 407.

24. *AAS* 36, 1944, 137.

25. Cf. I. Schweigl, '*De unitate Ecclesiae orientalis et occidentalis restituenda, documenta S.Sedis ultimi saeculi (1848-1938) illustrata*', in *Periodica de re morali, canonica, liturgica*, 28 June 1939, 209-33; A. Fortescue, *The Uniate Eastern Churches*, London 1923; the decree *Orientalium Ecclesiarum* of Vatican II cites nineteen pontifical documents extending from the eleventh to the nineteenth century no.2.

26. All this is recommended by the scheme prepared for Vatican I, *De rebus orientalibus*, Mansi 53,903f. (Schweigl, 216), and again under Pius XI: Schweigl, 229. Cf. also id., '*De Concilio Vaticano et de quaestione Liturgiae orientalis*', *Greg* 21, 1940, 3-16.

27. Quoted E.Lanne, 'La Conception post-tridentine de la Primauté et l'origine des Églises unies', *Irénikon* 52, 1979, (5-33) 17.

28. No. 29 in his letter of 1053, PL 143, 764; Mansi 19, 653.

29. This is at least what is suggested by G.Florovsky, 'Le Problématisme de l' expérience chrétienne', *Put* 37, supplement, in *Irénikon* 11, 1934, 601f.

30. An example is Innocent IV to his legate in Cyprus in 1253: *Verum quia nonnulli Graecorum jamdudum ad devotionem Sedis Apostolicae redeuntes, et recenter oboediunt, licet et expedit, ut mores ac ritus eorum, quantum cum Deo possumus, tolerantes, ipsos in Ecclesiae Romanae oboedientia praeservemus* (*Magnum Bullarium Romanum*, Lyons 1655, I, 126; quoted O.Rousseau, *Irénikon* 22, 1949, 259 n.1).

31. There is a very detailed commentary on the decree and the history of its redaction: Neophytos Edelby and Ignace Dick, *Les Églises Orientales Catholiques*, Unam Sanctam 76, Paris 1970.

32. Cf. e.g. L.Zander, *Vision and Action*, London 1952, 158f.; *L'Orthodoxie Occidentale*, Paris 1958. I should also mention this fine passage by A.S.Khomiakov: 'What is a rite? The rite is the free poetry of signs and words which the church, an organic unity, makes use of to express either its knowledge of divine truths or its boundless love for its creator and saviour, or the love which unites Christians one to another on earth and in heaven', *L'Eglise latine et le Protestantisme au point de vue de' l'Eglise d'Orient*, Vevey 1872, 206f.

33. I.-H.Dalmais, inaugural course at the Dom Lambert Bauduin Institute in *Union et désunion des chrétiens*, DDB 1961, 11-55. Cf. also E.Lanne, 'Pluralisme et unité: possibilité d'une diversité de typologies dans une même adhésion ecclésiale', *Istina* 16, 1969, 171-90. Basically A. Joubeir takes the same view, as does Dom P.Scherwood in 'Le Sens du rite', *L'Orient Syrien* 2, 1957, 297-314. Finally, the fully documented study by P.E.Herman, '*De "ritu" in Iure canonico*', OC 32, no.89, 1933, 96-158, demonstrates that one cannot keep to a purely liturgical aspect.

9. The Orthodox Church and Roman Catholic Church

1. I would cite the two reports presented to the colloquium *Koinonia* of the *Pro Oriente* foundation in Vienna, April 1974: V.Phidias, 'Anathèmes et schisme. Conséquences ecclésiologiques de la levée des anathèmes', and J.Ratzinger, 'Schisme anathématique. Les conséquences ecclésiologiques de la levée des anathèmes', *Istina* 20, 1975, 75-86 and 87-99 respectively.

2. Letters transmitted in the *Collectio Avelana* (CSEL 35), thus n.161, p.613: *sicut oportet dicere et olim scripsi, utrasque ecclesias tam senioris quam novae Romae unam esse...*' Cf. L.Magi, *La Sede Roma nella Corrispondenza degli Imperatori e Patriarchi Bizantini (VI-VII sec.)*, Rome and Louvain 1972, 46, 52f. The importance attached in this text and many others to the unity of the empire makes one wonder whether we need not take into consideration the Byzantine imperial idea according to which kings are brothers of the *Basileus* and those of inferior category his sons.

3. Anselm of Havelberg, *Dialogi* III, 8 (PL 188, 1219 AB). The sequel refers to the division of the empire, which has resulted in the division of the churches!

4. Quoted, with the Greek text, by M.Jugie, *Theologia dogmatica Christiana Orientalia ab Ecclesia catholica dissid.* IV, Paris 1931, 386f., and cf. 456.

5. *Parole de l'orthodoxie catholique au catholicisme romain*, translated from the Russian by M.Popovitski, Paris 1853; cf. M. Jugie, op.cit., 307f.

6. Quoted by V.Soloviev. Cf. J. Rupp, *Message ecclésial de Soloviev*, Paris 1975, 417, 477.

7. A collection published under the title *L'Union de l'Orient avec Rome*, ed. Pierre Dumont, OC 18, no. 6, 1930, 53.

8. Quoted R.Rouse and S.Neill, *History of the Ecumenical Movement*, London 1958, 672.

9. *Tomos Agapis*, Vatican-Phanar 1958-1970, Rome-Istanbul 1971, 33,82-84. The pope said: 'Entrusting the past to the mercy of God, let us heed the counsel of the apostle: "Forgetting all that has gone before I strive towards that which is ahead, to try to seize it as I am seized by him." We have already been seized by him through the gift of the gospel of salvation, the gift of the same baptism, the same priesthood celebrating the same eucharist, the one sacrifice of the one Lord of the Church.'

10. Letter to Cardinal Bea: *Tomos Agapis* 10, 40f.; *Apostolos Andreas*: cf. *Irénikon* 36, 1963, 541f.; *POC* 13, 1963, 336f.; *POC* 29, 1979, 321.

11. Text in Greek, Latin and French in *Tomos Agapis* no.176, (386-93) 389f.; *DC* 64, 1967, 1385-7.

12. A telegram from Pope Paul VI to Patriarch Athenagoras, 17 October 1969, runs: 'We personally and all the members of the synod are very sensitive to the sentiments expressed by your Holiness and the venerable church of which you are the worthy pastor. We thank you warmly for it and pray to the Spirit of the Lord that this synod may mark a new stage towards the re-establishment of the two sister churches in their full communion...'(*Tomos* no., 269, p.574). One should add the numerous documents in which it is recalled that Peter and Andrew were brothers, cf. pp.103, 378, 584, 590.

13. 'Églises soeurs. Implications ecclésiologiques du *Tomos Agapis*', *Istina* 20, 1975, 47-74.

14. Cf. my *Chrétiens en dialogue*, Paris, 1966, 287f. Note that at the feast of St Andrew 1977, his Holiness Dimitrios I, successor of Patriarch Athenagoras, spoke of the sacraments, baptism and the eucharist, which are common to Roman Catholics and Orthodox: *Episkepsis*, 15 December 1977, 7.

15. Cf. G. Hofmann, '*Notae historicae de terminologia concilii Florentini*', *Greg* 20, 1939, 257-63. Cf. also H.Rees, *The Catholic Church and Corporate Reunion. A Study of the Relations between East and West from the Schism of 1054 to the Council of Florence*, London 1940. It would, however, be more balanced to refer to A.Leidl, *Die Einheit der Kirchen auf dem Spätmittelalterlichen Konzilien von Konstanz bis Florenz*, Paderborn 1966; before Florence each of the two churches believed itself to be the Church, and waited for the return of the other to it.

16. 'For a long time the texts speak as if under the quarrel between Constantinople and Rome there were only one church, a sole church divided between two disunited people', *RSR* 1948, reprinted in *Chrétiens en dialogue*, 109. 'Mutual affinity... If the church is like a body of which East and West are perhaps the two sides', *Neuf cents ans après*, Mélanges L. Beauduin, 1954, 94. 'One must recognize that the conception of the church is basically the same in East and West in that the church is seen as a mystery, a sacramental reality', *L'Ecclésiologie du Haut Moyen Age*, 1968, 323 and cf. 393. To see how the Orthodox Church and the Catholic Church are the same church at the level of sacramentality, read the excellent account by Georges Florovsky, 'Le corps vivant du Christ. Une interprétation ortho-

doxe de l'Église', *La Sainte Église Universelle, Confrontation oecuménique*, Neuchâtel 1948, 9-57. Everything is common to both parties except the pope, but from the Orthodox point of view the pope belongs in the sphere of canon law and not of dogmatics; that is clear at Florence, A.Leidl, op.cit., 215.

17. Thus in a 1952 lecture reprinted in *Chrétiens en dialogue*, 1966, 287, and several times since.

18. Speech to the Roman Curia, 28 June 1980, no.14; allocution to the representatives of other churches, Paris, 31 May 1980. Cf. Secrétariat pour l'unité des chrétiens, Service d'information 44, 1980, 86, 94.

19. L.Bouyer, *L'Église de Dieu, corps du Christ et temple de l'Esprit*, Paris 1970, 629. Qualified approval (with reference to the ecclesiology of C.Journet) in M.V. Leroy, 'Note sur l'unité de l'Église catholique et orthodoxe', *RT* 71, 1971, nos.2-3, 'Un théologien de l'Église, le cardinal Charles Journet', 528-49.

20. A.Stawrowsky, *Essais de Théologie irénique. L'orthodoxie et le catholicisme*, Paris 1966, 168f.: 'The church proclaimed by the Fathers and Vatican II is in its general features the same church as confessed by Orthodoxy. That is enough.'

21. In Anselm of Havelberg, *Dialogi* III, 8 (PL 188, 1219B-1220A); I have quoted and translated the text in my *Ecclésiologie du Haut Moyen Age*, Paris 1968, 384-6.

22. *Reg.* I, 353 (PL 214, 326f.); and cf. my article: ' "Quatre siècles de désunion et d'affrontement", Comment Grecs et Latins se sont appréciés réciproquement au point de vue ecclésiologique', *Istina* 13, 1968, 131-52.

23. Text by M.Jugie, op.cit. (n.4), 386f.

24. Allocution of 25 July 1967, welcoming Paul VI in the cathedral of Phanar, *Tomos* no.73, 378. Cf. the *nea Rome* of canon 28 of Chalcedon.

25. *Tomos* no.275, p.598 (French), 599 (Greek).

26. *Irénikon* 43, 1970, 541: *DC* 67, 1970, 1005. This text has been the object of sympathetic attention from the Anglican side: E.L.Mascall and A.M.Ramsey, quoted in *Irénikon* 44, 1971, 60.

27. Text in *The Conversations at Malines 1921-1925*, ed. Lord Halifax, London 1930, 241-61. Cf. J. de Bivort de la Saudée, *Documents sur le problème de l'union Anglo-romaine (1921-1925)*, Paris 1949, 212, 275f. The history of the report by D.L.Beauduin has been traced, with the help of the archives at Malines and Lambeth, by S.A.Quitslund, ' "United not Absorbed", does it still make sense?', *JES* 8, 1971, 255-85.

28. After a sermon which aroused great interest, 'United not Absorbed', *The Tablet*, 7 March 1970; cf. *Irénikon* 43, 1970, 90.

29. *DC* 1720, 15 May 1977, 457.

30. John Macquarrie, *Christian Unity and Christian Diversity*, London 1975.

31. Cf. *Documents on Anglican/ Roman Catholic Relations*, Washington, US Catholic Conference 1972, 35-41; *Irénikon* 52, 1979, 325.

32. Cf. *DC* 69, no.1621; 3 December 1972, 1061-6.

33. 'Le dialogue entre catholiques et anglicans', *Irénikon* 52, 1979, 323-43.

34. Cf. my '1274-1974. Structures ecclésiales et conciles dans les relations entre Orient et Occident', *RSPT* 59, 1974, 355-90.

35. Cf. ibid., 371.

36. V.Peri, 'Il numero dei concili ecumenici nella tradizione cattolica moderna', *Aevum* 37, 1963, 420-51; *I Concili e le Chiese*, Rome 1965.

37. *Synodum contra eundem sanctissimum Photium definimus omnino damnatam et obrogatam esse, neque synodum omnino appellandam et vocandam esse*, Mansi 17, 490.

38. L.Bouyer, op.cit. (n.19), 678f.

39. AAS 66, 1974, 620. Cf. *DC*, 19 January 1975, 63.

40. AAS, 623.

41. 5 July 1870; Mansi 52, cols. 1113f.

42. *Istina* 20, 1975, 155f.

43. Compare the words of Cardinal Willebrands, above n.25.

10. Diversity of Dogmatics

1. *Unitatis redintegratio*, no.17.

2. Letter of 19 March 1979 to Cardinal Slipyi, no.4: *DC* 76, no.1765, 3 June 1979, 504.

3. Speech at Phanar on the feast of St Andrew, 30 November 1979, *DC* 76, no.1776, 16 December 1979, p.1058.

4. 'Réflexions et perspectives au sujet du rétablissement de la communion sacramentelle', *OC* 15, 1975, 7-25; quoted in *Irénikon* 48, 1975, 219.

5. T. de Regnon, *Études de théologie positive sur la sainte Trinité*, four vols., Paris, I and II, 1892; III and IV, 1898.

6. C. Pesch, *Theologie der Zeitfragen*, Stimmen der Zeit, Ergänzungsheft 82, 1901. *Zwei verschiedene Auffassungen von der allerheiligsten Dreifaltigkeit*.

7. *RHE* 64, 1969, 713-55.

8. Articles in *RTL* and 'Pour un accord oecuménique sur la procession du Saint Esprit et l'addition du Filioque au Symbole', *Irénikon* 15, 1978, 451-69.

9. L.Bouyer, *Le Consolateur. Esprit-Saint et Vie de grâce*, Paris 1980.

10. Y. Congar, *I Believe in the Holy Spirit*, III, *The River of Life flows in the East and in the West*, London 1983.

11. S. Bulgakov, *Le Paraclet*, Paris 1946, 141.

12. Paul Evdokimov, *L'Esprit-Saint dans la Tradition Orthodoxe*, Paris 1969, 76.

13. Cf. Nicole Zeegers Vandervorst, 'La Notion de Foi chez Théophile d'Antioche', in *La Liturgie, Expression de la Foi*, Paris 1978, ed. A.M. Triacca and A.Pistoia, cf. the bibliography in *Ephemerides Liturgicae*, Subsidia 16, Rome 1979, 339-65.

14. *De Trinitate* XII, 55.

15. *De veritate* q. 14 a. 8 ad 5; *ST* II, II, q. 1 a.2 ad 2.

16. C. Andronikof, *Dogme et liturgie*, 13-27 (cf. n.13 above).

17. Sermon given on Sunday 20 January 1980 in Palermo cathedral: *Episkepsis* 224, 1 February 1980, 12.

18. The expression comes from M.Evdokimov, SOEPI, May 1975, 5.

19. However, it should be noted that: 1. an entire school (Duns Scotus, etc.) accepted the Greek idea that the difference of the mode of procession *a Patre* is enough to distinguish the hypostases of the Son and the Spirit. The contrary has never been proved. 2. The principle formulated by St Anselm and taken up by St Thomas, *in Deo omnia sunt unum ubi non obviat relationis oppositio*, does not have the status of a dogma. Cf. *I Believe in the Holy Spirit* III, 81ff., 96ff., 116ff., 204.

20. PL 102, 971f.; MGH. Concilia II/1, 239f.; *I Believe in the Holy Spirit* III, 57.

21. Various studies by Vittorio Peri: 'Il simbolo epigrafico di S.Leone III nelle basiliche Romane dei SS.Pietro e Paolo', *RAC* XLV, 1968, 191-222; 'Leone III et il "Filioque"', Ancora un falso e l'autentico simbolo romano', *RSLR* 6, 1970, 245-74; 'Leone III e il "Filioque" echi del caso nell'agiografia greca', *RSCI* 25, 1971, 3-52; '*Pro amore et cautela Orthodoxae fidei*', *RSLR* 12, 1976, 341-63.

22. The references given by J.Grégoire, art.cit (n.7), 753f. n.1, are as follows: Origen, *Comm. in Ioan.*, I, 2,10 (GCS Origen 4, 45); Gregory Thaumaturgus, *Expos. fidei* (Hahn, 254); Athanasius, ad sensum, *Ep.3 ad Serap.* 5 (PG 26, 633); Basil, *De spiritu Sancto* 18, 47, 49 (PG 32, 152f); Epiphanius, *Panarion*, haer. 73.16; Gregory Nazianzen, *Carmina* I, 3 (PG 37, 632); Gregory of Nyssa, *Quod non sit tres dii* and *Contra Eunom.* 1 (PG 45, 416), John of Damascus, *De fide orthodox.* I, 12 (PG 94, 849). One should also add S.Tarasius, approved by the second council of Nicaea, 787 (Mansi 12, cols.1122, 1154).

23. Syrian epicleses: Renaudot, *Coll.Liturgiarum Orientalium*, Paris 1716, 264, 349, 136. The Fathers: Cyril of Jerusalem, *Catech.* XVI, 24 (PG 33, 352, 353); Epiphanius, *Panarion* II, 52 (PG 42, 281); *Ancoratus* 8 (PG 43, 29); Gregory of Nyssa, *Contra Macedon.*, 10 (PG 45, 1313 b); Didymus, *De Spiritu Sancto* 37 (PG 39, 1065).

24. Cf. Tertullian, *C. Praxean* 25 (PL 2, 190; Kroymann, 280); Marius Victorius, *Adv. Arian.* I, 13 (PL 8, 1047); Hilary, *De Trinitate* VIII, 19 (PL 10, 250); Augustine, *De Trinitate*, II, 3, 5 (PL 42, 847f.); Thomas Aquinas, *C. err. Graec.* II,3; *ST* I q.36 a.2 ad.1.

25. In a treatise intended for the education of the future emperor Michael Ducas, Michael Psellos completed it as follows: 'the Holy Spirit proceeds from the Father and is communicated to us by the Son', PG 122, 688.

26. *De fide orth.* I, 7,8,19 (PG 94, 821, 857).

27. Ps.-Cyril, *De Sacrosancta Trinitate* (PG 77, 1140B).

28. Cf. Athanasius, *First Letter to Serapion*, 14 (PG 26, 565b); Didymus, *De Trinitate* I, 31 (PG 39, 425) and cf. J.Grégoire, art.cit. (n.7), 728f. n.2.

29. *ST* Iª q.36 a.2 ad 4. The expression was taken from a text of the *Martyrium Andreae* (*Epist. presbyterorum et diaconorum Achaiae*), prol. (PG 2, 1217); M.Bonnes, *Acta Apostolorum apocrypha* II, 1, 1898, 2.

30. Ambrose, *Epist.* 13, nos 4-8: PL 16, 952f. Ambrose wanted Maximus the Cynic at Constantinople and Paulinus at Antioch. Bardy-Palanque are severe about Ambrose (Fliche-Martin III, 294). What interests me is the theology of communion expressed by the Bishop of Milan.

31. Sozomen, *HE* 6, 23 (PG 67, 1352). It concerns the faith of Nicaea. But cf. the letter of Damasus *Ea Gratia* to the Eastern bishops in 374 (DS 144f., 147).

32. Cf. *De Spiritu Sancto* II, 5 and 11 (PL 16,783, 800); III, 1 (810); *In Luc.* VIII (15, 1876).

33. *L'Esprit-Saint dans la Tradition Orthodoxe*, Paris 1969, 78.

34. Cf. *I Believe in the Holy Spirit*, III: for Florence, 184-9; for proposals for agreements, 190-9.

35. References ibid., 181f.

36. *ST* Iª q.36 a.2 ad 1; *C.err. Graec.* II, 28.

37. J.Stylianopoulos, 'The Orthodox Position', *Concilium* 128, 1979, *Conflicts about the Holy Spirit*, (23-30) 30.

PART THREE

11. Agreement on 'Fundamental Articles'

1. Apologia of the Augsburg Confession VII.45 (*Bekenntnissschriften*, 245); XV, 49, 52 (306f.); XXIV.6 (350); XXVII, 27 (386).

2. Formula of Concord. *Epitome* X and *Solida declaratio* X: *Die Bekenntnisschriften der evangelisch-lutherischen Kirche*, Göttingen ²1952, 813-16, 1053-6. Still in the seventeenth century, J.Hülsemann, whom I shall mention later, published a *Dissertatio de adiaphoris seu libertate Christiana circa ritus sacros*.

3. WA 10,3, p.14. On the very interesting episode of the intervention of Luther who left the Wartburg in consequence, cf. U. Babenheimer, '*Scandalum et jus divinum*', *ZRG* 59, 1973, 263-342.

4. To illuminate the history of the famous axiom, the French works I used (which contain references to German studies) were: G.Morin, 'Origine de la formule pseudo-augustinienne *In necessariis*', *RHLR* 7, 1902, 147-9; G.Krüger, 'De la maxime *in necessariis*', in *Congrès d'Histoire du Christianisme. Jubilé A. Loisy*, Paris 1928, III, 143-52; P. Jaccard, 'Un mot d'ordre de Luther sur l'unité', in *Cahiers Protestants*, March 1937, 84-101; id., '*In necessariis unitas*', in *Presbyterian Register*, May 1937, 51-4; J.Lecler, 'A propos d'une maxime citée par Jean XXIII: *In necessariis*', *RSR* 49, 1961, 549-60; id., 'Note complémentaire sur la maxime: *In necessariis*', ibid., 1964, 432-8.

5. Quoted by Krüger, 149.

6. Rothenburg am Tauber. Reproduced by Lücke, *Ueber das Alter, den Verfasser, die ursprüngliche Form und den wahren Sinn des kirchlichen Friedensspruches: In necessariis*, Götingen 1850, 87-145.

7. Re-edited by G.Koehler in 1927. Cf. R.Rouse and S.C.Neill, *A History of the Ecumenical Movement 1517-1948*, London 1954, 75f.; J.Lecler, *Histoire de la Tolérance*, I, 351f.

8. Cf. P. Maury, 'L'Unité de l'Église au XVIᵉ siècle et aujourd'hui', *Foi et Vie*, March-April 1959, 65-86.

9. Cf. *Vom Dissensus zum Konsensus. Die Formula Concordiae von 1577*, ed. G.Klapper, Hamburg 1980; B.Lohse, 'Das Konkordienwerk von 1580', in *Kirche und Bekenntnis*, ed. P. Meinhold, Wiesbaden 1980, 94-122.

The Calvinists attacked the Formula of Concord, Rouse and Neill, op.cit., 65.

10. *Institutes* IV, 1,12.

11. *Oeuvres de Calvin* II, *Trois traités*, ed. A.-M.Schmidt, Paris and Geneva 1934, 137f.

12. In *Histoire ecclésiastique des Églises réformées au Royaume de France (1580)*, ed. P.Vesson, Toulouse 1882, 305. But in *Traité des vraies, essentielles et véritables marques de l'Église*, 1572, 62, Theodore gives as fundamental articles the Apostles' Creed, the Decalogue and the Lord's Prayer (R. Voeltzel, *Vraie et fausse Église*, 60 n.151). A dialogue entitled *Le Pacifique*, 1590, between a Reformed and a Catholic runs: The Reformed: 'Both religions recognize that Christ is the foundation and hold the articles of faith contained in the Apostles' Creed, accept the Holy Trinity and the holy sacraments of baptism and the Lord's Supper. It is basically the same religion'; quoted by R.Tavenaux, *Le Catholicisme dans la France classique 1610-1715*, Paris 1980, 19.

13. Cf. Rouse and Neill, *History of the Ecumenical Movement*, 65f.

14. Ibid., 78f.

15. Ibid., 105f. For Ostervald, cf. J.J.von Allmen, *L'Église et ses fonctions d'après Ostervald*, Neuchâtel 1947, 46.

16. Cf. M.E.Nolte, *Georgius Cassander en zijn oecumenisch stresen*, Nijmegen 1951 (review: *RHE* 1952, 278f.); J.Lecler, *Histoire de la tolérance au siècle de la Réforme*, two vols, Paris 1955; R. Rouse and S.C.Neill, *A History of the Ecumenical Movement 1577-1948*, London 1954; F.W.Kantzenbach, *Das Ringen um die Einheit der Kirche im Jahrhundert der Reformation: Vertreter, Quelle und Motive des 'ökumenischen' Gedenkens von Erasmus von Rotterdam bis Georg Calixt*, Stuttgart 1957; R. Schüssler, *Georg Calixt. Theologie und Kirchenpolitik. Eine Studie zur Oekumenizität des Luthertums*, Wiesbaden 1961; P. Meyer, *Georg Calixts Theologische Ethik*, Göttingen 1970; R.J.Verkamp, op.cit., below n.33; for Erasmus, 94ff. It was only after completing this book that I discovered U. Valeske, *Hierarchia veritatum*, Munich 1968 – for Calixtus see 126f.

17. *Ep.* 1334: Allen V, 177f. (Lecler I, 144).

18. 'I have exhorted the theologians to leave out the little questions which serve ostentation more than piety, and to return to the sources of the scriptures and the ancient doctors of the church', *Ep.* 2136 to Louis Ber, 30 March 1529 (Allen VIII, 120).

19. *Opera Omnia* X, col.1663.

20. *De officio pii ac publicae tranquillitatis vere amantis viri*, in *Hoc Religionis dissidio*, Munich 1561. I quote Lecler, op.cit., I, 269.

21. It seems that there is a characteristic Protestant logic here, cf. my *Vraie et fausse réforme dans l'Église*, Paris 1950, 407, 440 (²1969, 348f.,396); R.Voeltzel, *Vraie et fausse Église selon les théologiens protestants français du XVIIᵉ siècle*, Paris 1957, 13. This will still be clear in Jurieu. This idea of a universal church equivalent to the 'communion of saints' in the creed occurs in Bucer: cf. Kantzenbach, op.cit., 127.

22. *De officio*, 25; Lecler I, 270. In the *Inquisitio de Fide* (1524) Erasmus

had suggested the Apostles' Creed as the basis for agreement among the churches.

23. For Wicelius (George Witzel, 1501-73) cf. Lecler, I, 239ff. (above all 241), 266f.; Kantzenbach, op.cit., 176f. Both give an indication of sources and monographs. For Cassander (1513-66) see Lecler I, 266f.; Kantzenbach, 203f., who quotes these significant words: *Catholica traditio tribus notis deprehendatur: Antiquitate, universitate et consensione* (211 n.23).

24. Cf. R.Schüssler, op.cit., 52; U. Valeske, op.cit., 126f.

25. Schüssler, op.cit., 122. The Colloquium consisted of twenty-six Catholics, twenty-four Reformed and fifteen Lutherans. The Socinian representatives had been excluded.

26. Cf. M.Keller-Hüschenmenger, *Das Problem der Fundamentalartikel bei Johannes Hülsemann in seinem theologiegeschichtlichen Zusammenhang*, BFCT 41/2, Gütersloh 1939, 32f.; U. Valeske, op.cit., 123f.

27. 'Whatever does not teach Christ is not apostolic even if Peter and Paul are the teachers. By contrast, whatever preaches Christ is apostolic even if it is Judas, Annas or Herod who do so', *Deutsche Bibel* VII, 385.

28. Faith is single and indivisible: *Com.in Rom.* (WA 56, 246); *De servo arbitrio* (18,604); *Wider Hans Wurst* (WA 51, 516).

29. P. Fraenkel, quoted n.60 below, 317; H.Busch, *Melanchthons Kirchenbegriff*, Bonn Dissertation 1918, 54.

30. *De Ecclesia et Auctoritate Verbi Dei*, 1560; CR, 28, 599f.; Keller-Hüschemenger, op.cit., 53.

31. Keller-Hüschemenger, op.cit., 100-5; reference to his writings, 186.

32. Ibid., 178-84.

33. B.J.Verkamp, *The Indifferent Mean. Adiaphorism in the English Reformation to 1554*, Ohio 1977.

34. Cf. H.Marot, 'Aux Origines de la théologie anglicane. Écriture et Tradition chez Richard Hooker (d.1600)', *Irénikon* 33, 1960, 321-43.

35. Following Marot (342 n.2) and P.Asveld, *Theologia anglicana de doctrinis fundamentalibus*, in *Acta Congressus internationalis de Theologia Concilii Vaticani II, 1966*, Rome 1968, 506-12; cf. Richard Field in his copious *Of the Church*, 1606, who appeals to fundamental articles which he identified with the Apostles' Creed: L.Andrewes, *Responsio ad Apologiam Cardinalis Bellarmini*, 1610; J.Ussher, *Sermon on the Unity of the Church*, 1624, and *Answer to the Challenge made by a Jesuit*, 1639; W.Laud, *Conference with Mr Fisher the Jesuit*, 1639; H.Hammond, *On Fundamentalism*, 1654; W.Chillingworth, *The Religion of Protestants. A Safe Way to Salvation*, 1638; J.Taylor, *Dissuasive from Popery*, 1664; J.Bramhall, *Schism Guarded*, 1658. A.Tanquerey (*DTC* I, cols. 2026f.), speaks of a committee charged by Parliament in 1653 with editing a list of fundamental articles: proposals by R.Baxter and J.Owen. – In his report, about 1635, Dom Leander says that in the Anglican Church there are regular references to the fundamental articles: cf. *Irénikon* 21, 1948, 41; also U.Valeske, op.cit., 137.

36. G.Thils, *Les Notes de l'Église dans l'apologétique catholique depuis la Réforme*, Gembloux 1937, 166f.

37. Studies on Jurieu are numerous. For our concern, in addition to

A.Tanquerey, *DTC* I, 2027f., and G.Thils, op.cit., 169f., cf. R.Strutmann, 'La Perpétuité de la foi dans la controverse Bossuet-Jurieu(1686-91)', *RHE* 37, 1941, 145-89; R.Voeltzel, *Vraie et fausse Église selon les théologiens protestants français du XVII*ᵉ siècle, Paris 1956, above all 54f.

38. *Traité de l'unité de l'Église*, 495.

39. Ibid., 406.

40. *Le vray système*, 212.

41. *Traité de l'unité*, 519.

42. Cf. my account in *Chrétiens désunis*, Paris 1937, 212-25, and T.A.Lacey, *The Unity of the Church as treated by English Theologians*, Church Historical Society XXXV, London 1898. One could clearly cite other references.

43. Tsar Alexander I appealed in the convention of the Holy Alliance, with the aim of uniting all Christians: M.Jugie, *Joseph de Maistre et l'Église Gréco-russe*, Paris 1922, 162f. I quoted earlier the comment by C.Gore, at the Malines Conversations: *Licet, salvo iure communionis, diversum sentire*, and the response by P.Batiffol. F.W.Kantzenbach, 'Das theologische Problem der Fundamentalartikel', *Lutherische Monatsheft* I, December 1962, 542-7, envisaged a superseding of confessional texts by a new interpretation of the whole gospel and called for the composition of an ecumenical catechism. H.Chadwick gave a lecture at Tübingen under the title 'Einigkeit in den fundamentalen Glaubensartikeln', *TQ* 150, 1970, 396-403.

44. Letter of Cardinal Patrizi to the Puseyites, 8 November 1865, republished by the Holy Office on 4 July 1959, AAS 13, 1919, 312-l6; Encyclical *Mortalium animos*, 6 January 1927: AAS 20 (1928); DS 3683. At the same time Fr M. Pribilla expounded the aim of this passage and the authentic aspects one could still accept: *Um kirchliche Einheit. Stockholm-Lausanne-Rom*, Freiburg 1929, 225f. Cf. Pius XII, Encyclical *Orientalis Ecclesiae* of 9 April 1944 for the centenary of St Cyril of Alexandria: AAS 36, 1944, 134.

45. Letter to Leibniz of 30 January 1700; edition of the *Oeuvres de Bossuet* by Lachat, XIII, 146 or *Oeuvres de Leibniz*, ed. Foucher de Careil II, 300.

46. *VI*ᵉ *Avertissement sur les lettres de M.Jurieu*, 66.

47. Cf. Scheeben, *Dogmatik*, no.424 referring to the minimum of dogmas which it is necessary to believe; A.Tanquerey, *DTC* I, col.2029; L. de Grandmaison, *Le Dogme Chrétien*, Paris 1928, 247; M.Pribilla (cf.n.44); A.Rademacher, *Die Wiedervereinigung der christlichen Kirchen*, Bonn 1937, makes a distinction between *Grundlehren* and *peripherische Lehren*; Cardinal Hume, lecture given at Chantilly in April 1978 (*DC* 1745, 610).

48. *La Tradition et les traditions* I. *Essai historique*, Paris 1960.

49. Title of ch. V of *Principiorum fidei doctrinatium Demonstratio*, X, 1572.

50. *Vray système*, 134f.

51. G.Thils, op.cit., 187f. This is the significance of this proposition by Bossuet, *Politique tirée des propres paroles de l'Écriture sainte* VII, art. III, prop. 6 (critical ed. by J.Le Brun, Geneva 1967, 225f.): 'It is not enough

to keep sound doctrine on the foundations of faith; in everything everywhere it is necessary to be united to the true church.' The criticisms by L.Brugère (*De Ecclesia Christi*, new ed., Paris 1878, 236f.) and Tanquerey (cols.2029,33) bear on this question of ecclesiology.

52. J.Guitton, *La philosophie de Newman, Essai sur l'idée de développement*, Paris 1933, 46.

53. Art.cit., above (n.43), 401.

54. Texts and references in F.Gavin, *Some Aspects of Contemporary Greek Orthodox Thought*, Milwaukee and Oxford 1923, 244, 260; in T.Spacil, 74 n.9; 86 n.4; Palmieri in turn quotes Macarius and Philaretos, *Theol.dogm.Orthod.* I, Florence 1911, 21f. For Metropolitan Philaretos cf. also G.Florovsky, in *Irénikon* 27, 1954, 262.

55. Panagiotis N.Trembelas, *Dogmatique de l'Église Orthodoxe Catholique*, Chevetogne and DDB, 1966, I, 31.

56. In *Istina* 24, 1979, 70.

57. Cf. my 'La Primauté des quatre premiers conciles oecuméniques', in *Le Concile et le Conciles*, Paris 1960, 75-109.

58. Cf. my 'Sacramental Worship and Preaching', *Concilium* 3.4, 1968, 27-33. For the centenary of the 'Council of Union' at Lyons in 1274, Paul VI wrote to Cardinal Willebrands, 5 October 1974: *Hoc Lugdunense Concilium, quod sextum recensetur inter generales synodos in Occidentali orbe celebratas* (AAS 66, 1974, 620).

59. P.Polman, *L'Élément historique dans la controverse religieuse du XVIᵉ siècle*, Gembloux 1932, 377f., which quotes above all Wicelius and Cassander, on which cf. also U. Valeske, *Hierarchia veritatum*, 82f.

60. Cf. P.Fraenkel, *Testimoni Patrum. The Function of the Patristic Argument in the Theology of Philip Melanchthon*, Geneva 1961; Polman, op.cit., 34. Melanchthon suggested agreement on the first five centuries as a basis of agreement with the Greeks: E.Benz, *Wittenberg und Byzanz*, 1949.

61. *Opera Calvini* III, 30; cf. *Inst.*IV, 17, 28 (*Opera Calvini* II, 1027).

62. H.Schüssler, *Georg Calixt. Theologie und Kirchenpolitik. Eine Studie zur Oekumenizität des Luthertums*, Wiesbaden 1961, 66f.; details of works, 200 n.1.

63. Ibid., 102f.

64. Cf. *RCE* 2, 1905, 184-7: here one sees that the appeal to this criterion favoured the partisans of 'Catholic' features just as much as those who wanted to prevent their introduction. These proposals were criticized by R.H.Benson, *A City Set on a Hill*.

65. Cf. *Revue Historique de l'Église de France*, 1945, 264.

66. D.Stone, *Outlines of Christian Dogma*, 1900, 313f.; T.W.Allies, *The Church of England cleared from the charge of Schism upon the testimonies of Councils and Fathers of the Six Centuries*, London 1846. This was the time of the Oxford Movement which in fact accepted the criterion of the first six councils: P.Thureau-Dangin, *La Renaissance Catholique en Angleterre* III, Paris ⁴1910, 526.

67. *Of the Church* VI, 51 (in 1606).

68. Jurieu, *Traité de l'unité*, 563; American Presbyterians, cf. *Collectio Lacensis* VII, 1135.

69. From the years 1839-41, G.Florovsky quotes the texts of R.W.Sibthorpe and E.D.Clarke, *Irénikon* 27, 1954, 259. Even A.M.Ramsey, then Archbishop of York, was hesitant in 1956; cf. K.Ware, *Istina* 24, 1979, 24. Cf. the 1906 report of the Royal Commission on Ecclesiastical Discipline, no.10.

70. Cf. *The Holy Ghost and the Church*, London 1924, 274f.; *The Reconstruction of Belief*, 292f.

71. PL 50, 637-78; Vincent of Lerins, *Commonitorium*.

72. A. d'Alès, 'La fortune du *Commonitorium*', *RSR* 26, 1936, 334-56, which deals only with the interpretation of the work: S.Prete, *Il 'Commonitorium' nella letteratura cristiana antica*, Bologna 1962.

73. Thus C.Gore, *Roman Catholic Claims*, fourth ed., 56f.; N.P.Williams, *Northern Catholicism* (which he edited with C.Harris, London 1933, 178, 188); for Newman himself cf. J.Guitton, op.cit., 42-4.

74. The synod of the Old Catholic-Jansenist church at Utrecht began its confession of faith of 14 September 1889 with it; it gave it as a motto to the *Revue internationale des Églises*, which in 1911 became the *Internationale kirchliche Zeitschrift*. And cf. E.Herzog, *Hirtenbriefe*, Neue Folge, Aarau 1901, 72. The Old Catholics have used the Vincentian canon as a weapon against the two dogmas of Vatican I. It is also worth reading J.Speigl, 'Das Traditionsprinzip des Vinzenz von Lerinum. Ein unglückliches Argument gegen die Definition der Unfehlbarkeit des Papstes', in *Hundert Jahre nach dem ersten Vaticanum*, ed. G.Schwaiger, Regensburg 1970, 131-50.

75. Polman, op.cit., 343.

76. A.Spasskij, in a History of the Development of Dogmas at the Time of the Ecumenical Councils, 1908 (published in Russian; there is a summary in *SLT* 5, 1909, 6-13); P.Svetlov, a work analysed by S.Tyszkiewich, *ZKT* 42, 1918, 114-36 (cf. 129); S.Bulgakov, *L'Orthodoxie*, Paris 1932, 42f.

77. H.B.Swete, *The Holy Catholic Church*, London 1915, 241.

78. J.N.Figgis, *The Fellowship of the Mystery*, London 1915, 7, 73 and ch.III.

79. A.Harnack, 'Über sogenannte "Consensus quinque-saecularis" als Grundlage der Wiedervereinigung der Kirchen', *Die Eiche* 13, 1925, 287-99; reprinted in *Aus dem Werkstatt des Vollendeten*, Giessen 1930, 65-83.

80. H.S.D.P. Scott, *General Councils and Anglican Claims*, London 1927; Dom J.Chapman, *The First Eight General Councils and Papal Infallibility*, London 1928. There is a large number of studies on the papacy and the councils, but that by W. de Vries makes them seem flat.

81. *A la découverte de l'espace oecuménique*, Neuchâtel-Paris 1967, 128.

82. Cf. B.D.Dupuy, 'Le Magistère de l'Église service de la parole', in *L'Infaillibilité de l'Église*, Chevetogne 1963, 53-98. Cf. J.Stern, 'Traditions apostoliques et Magistère selon J.H.Newman', *RSPT* 47, 1963, 35-57.

83. A. d'Alès, *Dictionnaire Apologétique de la Foi Catholique*, IV, col.1753.

12. The 'Hierarchy of Truths'

1. Bibliography on the idea of the 'hierarchy of truths' in chronological order of publication:

C.J.Dumont, 'Y a-t-il une hiérarchie de valeur entre les vérités de foi?', leaflet from *Vers l'unité chrétienne*, March 1952, reprinted in *Les Voies de l'Unité Chrétienne*, Unam Sanctam 26, Paris 1954, 157-61

H.Mühlen, 'Die Lehre des Vaticanum II. Über die *Hierarchia Veritatum* und ihre Bedeutung fuʾ den oekumenischen Dialog', *TuG* 57, 1966, 303-35; id., 'Die Bedeutung der Differenz zwischen Zentraldogmen und Randdogmen für den ökumenischen Dialog. Zur Lehre des Zweiten Vatikanischen Konzils von der *hierarchia veritatum*', in *Freiheit in der Begegnung*, Festgabe Otto Karrer, ed. J.-L.Leuba and H.Stirnimann, Frankfurt am Main and Stuttgart 1969, 191-27

W.Dietzfelbinger, 'Die Hierarchie der Wahrheiten', in *Die Autorität der Freiheit*, ed. J.-C.Hampe, II, Munich 1967, 619-25

U. Valeske, *Hierarchia veritatum. Theologiegeschichtliche Hintergründe und mögliche Konsequenzen eines Hinweises im Oekumenischen-dekret des II. Vatikanischen Konzils zum zwischenkirchlichen Gespräch*, Munich 1968 (brief account by A.Klein in *Catholica* 23, 1969, 421-4). Unfortunately I was only able to read this very fully documented work after finishing my own.

G.Tavard, ' "Hierarchia veritatum": A preliminary investigation', *TS* 32, 1971, 278-89

H.Schützeichel, 'Das hierarchische Denken in der Theologie', *Catholica* 25, 1971, 90-111

P. O'Connell, 'Hierarchy of Truths', in *Cardinal Bea Studies II. The Dublin Papers*, Manila 1972, 83-117

Y.Congar, 'On the *hierarchia veritatum*', in *The Heritage of the Early Church, Mélanges G.Florovsky*, Rome 1973, 409-20

J.Weismayer, 'Verkündigung aus der Mitte, ein Beitrag zur Problematik einer Hierarchie der Wahrheiten', in *Sacerdos et Pastor*, Festschrift Fr Loidl, Vienna 1972, 139-57

E.Schlink, 'Die "Hierarchie der Wahrheiten"', in *Tantur Yearbook* II, 1972-73, 27-42

C.Cardona, 'La "Jerarchia de la verdades" segun el Concilio Vaticano II y el orden de la real', in *Los movimentos teologicos secularizantes*, Madrid 1973, 143-63

E.Schlink, 'Die "Hierarchie der Wahrheiten" und die Einigung der Kirchen', *KuD* 21, 1975, 1-12

D.Carroll, ' "Hierarchia veritatum": A Theological and Pastoral Insight of the Second Vatican Council', *ITQ* 44, 1977, 125-33

W.Hryniewicz, 'La Hierarchie des vérités. Implications oecuméniques d'une idée chrétienne', *Irénikon* 51, 1978, 470-91

G.Thils, '*Hierarchia veritatum*, décret sur l'oecuménisme no.11', *RTL* 10, 1979, 208-15 (a review of the main studies)

W.Hryniewicz, 'Hierarchie des verités et Oecuménisme', in *Collectanea Theologica* (Warsaw) 49, 1979, 5-21, in Polish with a French summary.

To this bibliography one could also add numerous publications relating to a short formulation of faith.

2. Thus for O.Cullmann, 'A point which... seems the most important in the whole schema for the future of our dialogue... I consider this passage the most revolutionary to be found in any of the schemas of the present council' ('Comments on the Decree on Ecumenism', *ER* 17, April 1965, 94). U.Valeske: 'In the view of the experts a forward-looking comment at the Council', op.cit. 10. Cf. other references in the articles by Schützeichel, 91, n.15 and Hryniewicz, *Irénikon* 482.

3. *Discours au Concile Vatican II*, ed. Y.Congar, H.Küng and D. O'Hanlon, Paris 1964, 201f.

4. *Modi a Patribus conciliaribus propositi*, 1964, 12 (modus 49 on ch.II): *post 'debent' addatur nova phrasis: 'In comparandis doctrinis, meminerint existere ordinem seu hierarchiam veritatum doctrinae catholicae, cum diversus sit earum nexus cum fundamento fidei christianae.' Maximi momenti enim esse videtur pro dialogo oecumenico, ut tum veritates in quibus christiani conveniunt, tum illae in quibus differunt, potius ponderetur quam numerentur. Quamvis procul dubio omnes veritates revelatae eadem fide divina tenendae sint, momentum et pondus earum differt pro nexu earum cum historia salutis et mysterio Christi.*That all the *dogmas* must be believed equally is affirmed in *Mortalium animos* and in *Mysterium Ecclesiae* of 24 June 1973, *DC* 1973, 556.

5. Para IV, 4b of the document: *DC* 67, no.1571: 4 October 1971, 879. The Declaration of the Congregation for the Doctrine of the Faith, *Mysterium Ecclesiae* of 24 June 1973, para 4, quotes the texts of the decree and of the Secretariat, AAS 65, 1973, 402; *DC* 70, no.1636: 15 July 1973, 667.

6. Cf. A.Mallet, 'Le problème des concepts et du langage dans la théologie et dans la prédication', *Foi et Vie* 57, March-April 1959, 25-37.

7. Preface to the Epistle of James, 1522, Martin Luther, *Vorreden zur Heiligen Schrift*, ed. W.Heinsius, Munich 1934, 106f., and WA *Deutsche Bibel*, VII, 385. Compare a passage from the Preface to the New Testament of 1524, where for the Epistle of James there is the expression a 'strawy epistle'; however, this was suppressed in the complete editions of the Bible from 1534 and partial editions of the New Testament from 1536 (op.cit., 75).

8. Cf. the Sermon of 12 January 1545: WA XLIX, 681. Note, however, that in the Schmalkald Articles of 1537, Luther distinguished three kinds or three levels of articles of faith. First the sovereign articles of the divine majesty, namely the dogmas of Trinity and christology. Then the articles from which nothing must be removed or surrendered, namely the Reformed doctrine of justification with its implications. And finally the articles that are discussed with educated people: sin, law, penitence, gospel, baptism, last supper, absolution, confession, ordination of priests, etc.: official edition of the *Bekenntnisschriften*, 415, 433.

9. *The Faith of the Christian Church*, 1948, 88.

10. *In justificatione impii requiritur actus fidei quantum ad hoc homo credat Deum esse justificatorem hominum per mysterium Christi* (I, II, q.113

a.4 ad 3). Or again: *Principale in doctrina fidei christianae est salus per crucem Christi facta*: *Com. in I Cor.* ch.1 lect.3.

11. Cf. Inge Lönning, '*Kanon im Kanon*'. *Zum dogmatischen Grundlagenproblem des neutestamentlichen Kanons*, Oslo and Munich 1972. For Luther, 72-160.

12. W.Hryniewicz (*Irénikon* 487 n.2) gives the following references: F.Mussner, 'Die Mitte des Evangeliums in neutestamentlicher Sicht', *Catholica* 15, 1961, 271-92; id., 'Evangelium und Mitte des Evangelium', in *Gott in Welt. Festgabe K.Rahner*, Freiburg 1964, I, 492-514; J.Guillet, 'Die Mitte der Botschaft. Jesu Tod und Auferstehung', *Communio* 3, 1973, 225-8; also E.Wolf, 'Die Rechtfertigung als Mitte und Grenze reformatorischer Theologie', *Peregrinatio* II, Munich 1965, 11f.

13. Cf. *Die Kirche im Neuen Testament in ihrer Bedeutung für die Gegenwart*, Berlin 1930, 13. Stephen Neill criticized a reduction of everything to faith (in Christ my saviour) and said: 'Paul's doctrine of the Spirit is far more central and characteristic than his doctrine of justification by faith', quoted I. Lönning, op.cit., 226 n.55.

14. *Symbolics*, XXXVIII. One might also compare the comment of an exegete like A.Oepke: 'In brief, revelation in the NT is the self-offering of the Father of Jesus Christ for fellowship', *apokalupto*, *TDNT* 3, 591.

15. I.Frank, *Der Sinn der Kanonbildung. Eine historische theologische Untersuchung der Zeit bis Irenäus von Lyon*, FTS 90, 1971.

16. Cf. *I Believe in the Holy Spirit*, III, London 1983, 128-33.

17. Cf. J.Ernst, *Die Ketzertaufangelegenheit in der altchristlichen Kirche nach Kyprian*, Mainz 1901; J.Hamer, 'Le baptême et l'Église', *Irénikon* 25, 1952, 142-64, 263-75. For the rest of my account cf. pp.159f. of this book.

18. Cf. L.Charlier, *Essai sur le problème théologique*, Thuillies 1938, 123f.; my article 'Theologie', *DTC* XV, col.381, pp.453-4, written in 1939; *La Foi et la Théologie*, Paris 1962, 23-26. Cf. also R.Gagnebet, *De natura theologiae ejusque methodo secundum S.Thomam* II, Rome 1958, duplicated, 101-52.

19. *Com in Sent.* II d.12 q.1 a.2; III d.14 a. 1 q.sol. et add.2; a. II c.fin, where Thomas speaks of *generales articuli*; q. 2 ad 3; q.disp. a.4 and 2; II^a II^{ae} q. 1a. 6 ad 1; a. 8 sol.; q. 2a 5 and 7; *Com. in Epist. ad Titum*, c. 3 lect.4; *Compendium Theologiae* I, 2 and 185. Note here that J.Gerhard, *Loci theologici*, refers to St Thomas as the basis for his idea of fundamental articles; H.Keller-Hüschemenger, op.cit. 92.

20. *II Sent.* d.12 q. 1 a.2; III d.24 a.1. q.1; II^a II^{ae} q.1 a. 7 and 8. On this question cf. John 17.3; Heb.11.6.

21. Cf. *ST* 1 q 1 a 1. For the cumulative sense of *sacra doctrina* cf. my study in *Église et Tradition*, Le Puy and Lyons 1963, 157-94

22. *Doctrina salutaris cathedra*, *Epist.* 105, 5, 16 (PL 33, 403D).

23. Thus in *IV Sent.* d. 23 q.1 a 1 qa 3 ad 1; d 49 q. 5 A. 5 qa 1; quodl. VII, 14; *ST* I^a II^{ae}, q.106 a.d ad 2; *Com. in 2^a* Epist. ad Tim., ch. 3 lect 3.

24. *Quodl.* I, 14.

25. *Dei verbum*, ch.3, no.11: *Scripturae libri veritatem, quem Deus, nostrae salutis causa, Litteris Sacris consignari voluit'* (my emphasis). The

expression has been carefully chosen to avoid seeming to support a thesis which *materially* limits scriptural inspiration and inerrancy to religious statements or those which talk of salvation.

26. Thus Thomas, *IV Sent.* d.23 q. 1 a.1 q 3 ad 1; *ST* II q.106 a. 4 ad 2; q.108 a.2 sed c.; *Quodl.* VII 14. And cf. my *La Tradition et les traditions*, II *Essai théologique*, Paris 1963, 255-61, and the relevant notes, 346-50.

27. Monographs: G.Hoffmann, *Die Lehre von der fides implicita innerhalb der katholischen Kirche*, three vols., Leipzig 1903, 1906, 1908 (Protestant); R.M.Schultes, *Fides implicita. Geschichte der Lehre von der fides implicita und explicita in der katholischen Theologie*, I. *Von Hugo von St Viktor bis zum Konzil von Trient*, Regensburg 1920.

28. St Thomas offers an interesting explanation: *Minores tenentur explicite credere generales articulos, ut Deum esse trinum et unum, Filium Dei esse incarnatum et mortuum, et resurrexisse, et alia huiusmodi de quibus Ecclesia festa facit*: *De veritate*, q.14 a 11 c.fin. We know that in the Middle Ages the *articuli* were those of the creed.

29. This doctrine occurs with Innocent IV, Schultes 40f.; with Albert, 60f; with Thomas, 76f. The ordinary people keep to the faith of those who are further advanced; Hugh of St Victor, *De sacramentis* I, X, c.3 (PL 176, 332). The *maiores* keep to a more explicit faith *secundum officium suum*: St Thomas, *Sent.* III d.25 q.2 a.1 sol.3.

30. St Thomas, *Sent.* III d. 25. q. 4 ad 3; *De veritate* q. 14 a. 10 ad 11; ST II^a II^ae q 2. a. 6 ad 3 with Cajetan's commentary.

31. K.Rahner, '*Mysterium Ecclesiae*', *Theological Investigations* 17, London 1981, (139-55) 148.

32. Decree on Ecumenism, *Unitatis redintegratio*: 'For men who believe in Christ and have been properly baptized are put in some, though imperfect, communion with the Catholic church. Without doubt, the differences that exist in varying degrees between them and the Catholic Church – whether in doctrine and sometimes in discipline, or concerning the structures of the Church – do indeed create many obstacles, sometimes serious ones, to full ecclesiastical communion. The ecumenical movement is striving to overcome these obstacles. But even in spite of them it remains true that all who have been justified by faith in baptism are incorporated into Christ; they therefore have a right to be called Christians, and with good reason are accepted as brothers by the children of the Catholic Church (no.3).

By the sacrament of Baptism, whenever it is properly conferred in the way the Lord determined and received with the proper dispositions of soul, man becomes truly incorporated into the crucified and glorified Christ and is reborn to a sharing of the divine life, as the Apostle says: 'For you were buried together with him in baptism, and in him also rose again through faith in the working of God who raised him from the dead. Baptism, therefore, constitutes the sacramental bond of unity existing among all who through it are reborn. But baptism of itself, is only a beginning, a point of departure, for it is wholly directed toward a complete profession of faith, a complete incorporation into the system of salvation such as Christ himself willed it to be, and finally, toward a complete integration into eucharistic communion' (no.22).

33. Cf. Bruno Chenu, *La Signification ecclésiologique du Conseil Oecuménique des Églises 1945-1963*, Paris 1973.

13. Tradition and Traditions

1. 'La Bible dans la piété orthodoxe', *Irénikon*, 1950, 177-86. From the Protestant side cf. F.J.Leenhardt, *La Parole et le Buisson de Feu*, Neuchâtel 1962, 19.

2. Text and report of the North American section, *Verbum caro* 17, no.68, 1963, 371-401; of the European section, ed. K.E.Skydsgaard, 403-32; and its conclusions, J.-L.Leuba, 433-42.

3. *Études*, 1963, 104f.

4. Lukas Vischer, *Foi et Constitution 1910-63*, Neuchâtel and Paris 1968, ch.3 (nos.38-76), 'L'Écriture, la Tradition et les traditions', 172-85; cf. also *Foi et Vie* 63, 1964, 18-36.

5. Thomas Aquinas said: *Omnibus articulis fidei inhaeret fides propter unum medium, scilicet propter Veritatem Primam propositam nobis in Scripturis secundum doctrinam Ecclesiae intelligentis sane*, IIᵃ IIᵃᵉ q. 5 a. 3 ad 2. Note that Thomas says *ecclesia*, and not *magisterium* or *papa*.

6. *Verbum caro*, 68, p.389.

14. Theological 'Agreements'

1. This seems to me to be the case with the conversations with the Methodists: two sets of five meetings, between 1966 and 1970, and between 1971 and 1975, each ended with a report: the first series with the Denver Report and the second with the Dublin report. Conversations with the Pentecostals, 1972, report in 1976 (*DC* 1708, 21 November 1976, 983f.). Theological conversations with the Orthodox Church of the USSR: communiqués in *DC* 1509, 1591, 1638, 1691); then Catholics and Orthodox on ministries, 1977(*DC* 1738, 19 March 1978, 262). I would put in the same category the joint documents emerging from dialogues between the Catholic Church and the WCC. They have related to ecumenical dialogue (*DC* 1509, 1968,145f.), common witness and dubious proselytism (*DC* 1575, 970, 1077f), catholicity and apostolicity (*DC* 1582, 1971, 273f.) and the types of relationship between the Roman Catholic Church and the WCC (*DC* 1615, 1972, 759f.).

2. And jointly accepted. Cf. J.Hamer, 'Réflexions sur les dialogues théologiques interconfessionels', *DC* 1634, 17 June 1973, 569-73; Cardinal Willebrands, 'Les Commissions mixtes et leurs premiers résultats', *Osservatore Romano*, 13 December 1973 (*DC* 1646, 20 January 1974, 63f.); B.Sesboüé, 'Quelle est l'autorité des dialogues oecuméniques?', *Unité des Chrétiens* 14, April 1974, 27f.; J.Desseaux, 'Le Point sur les dialogues et "accordś oecuméniques" ', *Unité des Chrétiens* 31, July 1978, 15-20 (I found these pages very useful).

3. Text *DC* 1462, 2 January 1966, 67. Cf. J.Ratzinger, 'Schisme anathématique. Les conséquences ecclésiologiques de la levée des anathèmes', *Istina* 20, 1975, 87-99.

4. Report, *DC* 1668, 19 January 1975, 78f.

5. Cf. M.Villain, *L'Abbé Paul Couturier*, Paris 1957, 142-77; *Introduction à l'Oecuménisme*, Paris 1964, 284-306; *Unité des Chrétiens* 14, 1974, 31f.; the text of the 1956-1970 theses and the 1971-72 'agreements'.

6. The joint theses of 1956-62 can be found not only in *Unité des Chrétiens* but also in *Verbum caro* 70, 1964, 44-53; they were followed by, *Vers une même foi eucharistique? Accord entre catholiques et protestants*, Taizé, 1972; Faith and Order, *The Reconciliation of the Churches: Baptism, Eucharist, Ministry*, Geneva 1974; *Le Ministère épiscopal. Réflexions et propositions sur le ministère de vigilance et d'unité dans l'Église particulière*, 1976; *L'Esprit Saint, l'Église et les Sacraments*, 1979.

7. E.g. those of Cardinal C.Journet, 'L'accord des Dombes sur la doctrine eucharistique', *NeV* 47, 1972, 87f., but above all those of C.Dumont, 'Eucharistie et ministère', *Istina* 18, 1973, 155-207, replied to by J.de Bacchiochi, 'Accords des Dombes et Théologie oecuménique', *Istina* 19, 1974, 160-179-83, which indicates the status of the work and of some texts. I have questions about the use made there of the term sign. In *Unité des Chrétiens* 143, 24, J.-N.Aletti explains that this term implies what is signified in and with what signifies it; in that case it is something very real, but the Thomist thinks only of that which signifies, and in itself the term would seem inadequate.

8. *Reform und Anerkennung kirchlicher Ämter. Ein Memorandum der Arbeitsgemeinschaft ökumenischer Universitätsinstitute*, Munich 1973. Cf. also *DC* 1629, p.340; 1630, p.397; 1632, p.438; all 1973.

9. *Papal Primacy and the Universal Church*, ed. P.C.Empie and T.A. Murphy, Minneapolis 1974; cf. also *St Peter in the New Testament*, ed. R.E.Brown, K.P.Donfried and J.Reumann, Minneapolis and London 1973.

10. *DC* 1755, 7 January 1979, 19-30, followed by an appreciation by Fr Cyprian Vaggagini, from the perspective of Roman Catholic theology and liturgics.

11. Cf. *Irénikon* 41, 1968, 232f.

12. *DC* 1781, 2 March 1980, 223.

13. No.11: 'A special difficulty arises from the fact that it is often difficult for Lutherans to circumscribe the contemporary Lutheran understanding of their faith in a way which commits them. While Catholics can refer to the recent declarations of the *magisterium*, in particular those of Vatican II, the Lutherans can only ever refer back to the sixteenth-century confessions of faith; hence their difficulty in expressing in a way which involves them the pluralism, liberty and vigour of the effective life and witness of faith of the Lutheran churches today.'

14. *Anglican-Lutheran International Conversations. Report of the Conversations 1970-1972 authorized by the Lambeth Conference and the Lutheran World Federation*, no.68.

15. *DC* 1601, 16 January 1972, 88. The article by J.Desseaux cited in n.2 above and that by J. de Bacchiochi quoted n.7 above would be a good commentary on this proposal. Cf. also P.Duprey, 'Réflexion sur le dialogue

entre l'Église catholique et la Communion anglicane', *DC* 1656, 16 June 1974, 586-90.

16. B. de Margerie, *Vers la plénitude de la communion*, Paris 1980; chs. 2 and 3, which are of interest to us, appeared in *Esprit et Vie* 83, 1973, 305-11; 84, 1974, 641-53.

17. *DC* 72, no.1669, 2 February 1975, 126-9.

18. Cf. *Confessions in Dialogue. A Survey of Bilateral Conversations among World Confessional Families, 1962-71*, ed. N.Ehrenstrom and G.Gassmann, Geneva 1972. But the World Council sponsors many multilateral dialogues.

19. The Protestant Church in Germany (Evangelische Kirche in Deutschland, EKD) is a federation of twenty-eight area churches of which thirteen are Lutheran, two Reformed and twelve United; H.Brunotte, *Die Evangelische Kirche in Deutschland*, Hanover 1959; cf. W.L.Boelens, 'Eucharistic Developments in the Evangelical Church', *Concilium* 4,3, April 1967, 48-56.

20. The eight theses are to be found in W.L.Boelens, *Die Arnoldshainer Abendmahlsthesen*, Assen 1964, or in *Una sancta* 15, 1960, 9-11. They are followed, 12-29, by an article by A.E.Buchrucker in which one can see that the three commentators representing the three confessions comment on theses 4 and 5 differently.

21. Text in *Lutherische Monatschrift*, November 1971, 592-4. And cf. M.Lienhard, *Lutherisch-reformierte Kirchengemeinschaft heute. Die Leuenberger Concordieentwurf im Kontext der bisherigen Lutherisch-reformierten Dialoge*, Oekumenische Perspektiven 2, Frankfurt 1972. For the discussions and positions taken cf. 'Wortlaut und Stellungnahmen zur Leuenberger Konkordie reformatorischer Kirchen in Europa', *OeR* 21, 1972, 402-21.

22. J.Vercruysse, 'La Commission ecclésiale des Églises protestantes en Europe. Première réunion des représentants des Églises signataries de la Concorde de Leuenberg, Sigtuna, 10-16 June 1976', *Irénikon* 49, 1976, 435-52.

15. A Catholic 'Recognition' of the Augsburg Confession?

1. Text in *Die Bekenntnisschriften der evangelisch-lutherischen Kirche*, Göttingen [2]1952, 44-137. English translation in John H. Leith (ed.), *Creeds of the Churches*, Atlanta, Ga [3]1982, 63-106.

2. V.Pfnür, 'Anerkennung der *confessio Augustana* durch die katholische Kirche?', *IKZ Communio* 4, 1975, 298-307; 5, 1976, 374-84, 477-9, republished in *Katholische Anerkennung der Augsburgischen Bekenntnisses? Ein Vorstoss zur Einheit zwischen katholischer und lutherischer Kirche*, ed. H.Meyer, H. Schütte and H.-J.Mund, Frankfurt 1977, 60-81. Note that Pfnür's comment followed a suggestion made by a joint working party in Rome in January 1974 and, on 19 June 1974, by the ecumenical commission of the Episcopal Conference of the German Federal Republic.

3. J.Ratzinger, 'Prognosen für die Zukunft des Oekumenismus', *Oeku-*

menisches Forum. Gräzer Hefte für konkrete Oekumene 1, 1977, 31-41, or *Bausteine für die Einheit der Kirche* 17, no.65, 1977, 12f.

4. I have presented the main ones in *RSPT* 62, 1978, 93-95; 63, 1979, 285; 64, 1980, 255-64, 604-11. For the most complete bibliography cf. *Theology Digest* 28/2, summer 1980, 103-19, 120-3.

5. The best approach to this concept is that of Harding Meyer, ' "Anerkennung". Ein ökumenischer Begriff', in *Dialog und Anerkennung*, OeR Beiheft 37, ed. Peter Manns, 1980, 25-41; cf. also W.Kasper,'Was bedeutet das: Katholische Anerkennung der *Confessio Augustana?*', in the volume cited above, n.2, 151-6.

6. This was a theme dear to J.Lortz, as it is to his pupil P.Manns; and cf. J.Koopmans, *Das altkirchliche Dogma in der Reformation*, BEvTh 33, 1955.

7. *De professoribus confessionis Augustanae ad repentendam unitatem catholicam disponendis*, in *Oeuvres complètes de Bossuet*, ed. F.Lachat XVII, Paris 1864, 3-53.

8. H.Jedin, *Katholische Reformation oder Gegenreformation?*, Lucerne 1946, 52-3.

9. Numerous comments. Cf. 'Das Augsburger Bekenntnis im evangelisch-katholischer Gespräch', *TQ* 160, 1980, 82-95, and at the colloquium held in Paris 11-13 February 1980; text *DC* 77, 1784: 20 April 1980, 381-4, and in the minutes of the Colloquium, Le Point theologique 37, Paris 1980, 69-76.

10. 'Katholische Anerkennung des Augsburger Bekenntnisses?', *Confessio Augustana. Hindernis oder Hilfe?*, Regensburg 1979, 241-57.

11. *OeR* 26, 1977/4, 417-25.

12. *Confessione Augustana. Bekenntnis des eines Glaubens. Gemeinsame Untersuchung lutherischer und katholischer Theologen*, ed. H.Meyer and H.Schütte, Paderborn and Frankfurt/Main 1980. Cf. my review in *RSPT* 64, 1980, 260-4. The joint commission between the Roman Catholic Church and the World Lutheran Federation published a declaration dated 23 February 1980, signed by all its members and entitled, *All under a single Christ*.This text has twenty-eight numbered paragraphs, just as the Augsburg Confession has twenty-eight articles. It declares that the Augsburg Confession cannot be isolated from the agreements arrived at after dialogues at various levels between Lutherans and Catholics. It cites the joint commentary that I have just mentioned. It notes with great force the substantial agreement already arrived at. It specifies the points on which agreement is as yet incomplete and which call for clarifications in a future dialogue. It recognizes that the criticism of abuses made in the Augsburg Confession, XXII-XXVIII, has become irrelevant. It ends by looking for a new confession of faith which would be a joint one.

13. Peter Manns has constantly argued for Luther and suspected Melanchthon; cf. my articles mentioned in n.4 above and P.Manns, 'Zum Vorhaben einer "katholischen Anerkennung der *Confessio Augustana*": Oekumene auf Kosten Martin Luthers?', *OeR* 26, 1977, 426-50.

14. There was of course the response of the ecumenical patriarch Jeremiah II: *Wort und Mysterium. Der Briefwechsel über Glauben und Kirche*

1573-1581 zwischen den Tübinger Theologen und dem Patriarchen von Konstantinopel, ed. by the Foreign Department of the EKD, Witten 1958. E.Benz, *Wittenberg und Byzanz*, Marburg 1940; in his articles in *Irénikon* 27, 1956, 165-76 and 391-405, Benz studies the changes produced in the Greek text of the Augsburg Confession to make it accessible to Easterners. At the Paris colloquium of February 1980, Emilianos Timiadis made a severe criticism of the Augsburg Confession: text in *La Confession d'Augsbourg. 450ᵉ Anniversaire. Autour d'un Colloque oecuménique international-ale*, Le point théologique 37, Paris 1980.

15. *DC* 77, 1789, 6 July 1980, 634 (impromptu words). Remember that Paul VI said of his ecumenical activity that it was the most mysterious part of his pontificate.

16. Op.cit. in n.10 above, 256.

16. 'Reconciled Diversity'

1. The idea has been expounded by Harding Meyer, ' "Einheit in versöhnter Verschiedenheit", "Konziliare Gemeinschaft", "Organische Union". Gemeinsamkeit und Differenz gegenwärtig diskutierter Einheitskonzeptionen', *OeR* 1978/3, 337-400. H.Meyer has sent me a very full dossier on the theme, but too late to make use of in these pages, which remain very elementary. The long extract which I have reproduced as an appendix in fact contains all the detailed points in the documents which make up this large and valuable dossier, for which I am most grateful to Harding Meyer.

2. Accra meeting 1974, Beiheft to *OeR* 27, 67.

3. In the study I have made of attempts at union and dialogues carried on down to the present day, I have been struck by the fact that each side jealously preserves its identity, judges the other by comparison with itself and basically is not very open to that part of the truth with which it is confronted. There is little departure from the 'confessional'. That is true, perhaps above all true, of the Orthodox church. As to the Catholic church, without doubt since Vatican II it has done most to be open to these parts of the truth, but it has done too little to submit its attempt at revision to the sovereign criterion of the scriptures.

4. Given the importance of these explanations, I have added them as an appendix to this section. Even at Dar es Salaam there was a declaration that: 'Christian unity is a unity in diversity and not a uniformity. To the degree that the concept of reconciliation in diversity takes account of this element, it comes very close to that of the "conciliar communion" recently developed by the WCC and could not be considered as a competing formula.' Cf. R.Frieling, 'Versöhnte Verschiedenheit und/oder korporative Wiedervereiniguung', *Catholica* 31, 1977, 336-51; there is a stress on 'Versöhnung', on p.347.

5. Y. de Montcheuil, 'La liberté et la diversité dans l'Unité', *L'Église est une. Hommage à Moehler*, Paris 1939, 234-54.

6. Cf. U. Duchrow, 'Eine Oekumene ohne Machtblöcke. Die Einheit der Kirche von Ort suchen und verwirklichen', *LM* IX/6, July 1980, 356-9;

id., *Konflikt um die Oekumene, Christusbekenntnis – in welcher Gestalt der ökumenischen Bewegung?*, Munich 1980.

7. This is how A.Houssiau summarizes his position, 'Images diverses de l'unité de l'Eglise', *RTL* 10, 1979, 131-58. For Moehler's theory of positions which are in confrontation (Gegensätze) or in contradiction (Widersprüche), cf. J.A.Möhler, *L'Unité dans l'Église*, 32, 46; J.R.Geiselmann, *J.A.Möhler, Die Einheit der Kirche und die Wiedervereinigung der Konfessionen*, Paderborn 1940, 47f., and 142-66; also my *Vraie et fausse réforme dans l'Église*, Paris 1950, 238-41.

8. John 17, quoted by Möhler, *Symbolique* 37.

9. There is an account in *TQ* 6, 1824, 642-56. Quoted by B.-D.Dupuy, 'Schisme et primauté chez J.A.Möhler', in *L'Écclésiologie au XIXᵉ siècle*, Unam Sanctam 34, Paris 1960, 197-231.

10. *Gemeinsame Synode der Bistumer in der Bundesrepublik Deutschland*, Freiburg 1976, 780.

PART FOUR

17. Our Present Situation

1. *Living Church*, 1 March 1938, 288 (quoted by C.Lialine, *La méthode irénique*, offprint 74 n.2).

2. *Grande et sainte concile de l'Église Orthodoxe. Commission préparatoire. Étude des thèmes. Première étape. Propositions de la Commission*, Paris 1972.

3. 'Naissance de l'unité ecclésiale', *Lumière et Vie*, 103, June-July 1971, 5-7. Note that this article contains positive and constructive elements.

4. A. Gounelle, 'Pourquoi, après la Confession d'Augsbourg, d'autres confessions de foi dans les Églises de la Réforme?', in *La Confession d'Augsbourg, 450ᵉ* anniversaire, Le point theologique 37, Paris 1980, 93-113. The phrase quoted comes from the discussion, 136f.

5. M.Lienhard, 'Discussion de l'exposé d'A. Gounelle', op.cit., 133.

6. P.Fraenkel, 'Réponse', op.cit., 119f.

7. A.Deissmann, *Una Sancta. Zum Geleit in das ökumenische Jahr 1937*, Gütersloh 1936, 30.

8. J.J.von Allmen, 'Pour une restauration de l'unité chrétienne', *Verbum Caro* IV, no.14, 1950, 49-73, esp. 52.

9. J.J.von Allmen, 'Le Schisme', *BOO* 8, May 1957, 3-16. Wrong for two reasons: 'supposes that God does not yet want unity'; forgets that God works through his servants: 'it is we who are responsible for the unity of the church'.

10. Lesslie Newbigin, *The Household of God*, London 1953, 25f.

11. Cf. Mark 14.58; Acts 7.48; II Cor.5.1.

12. I Cor.15.28. It is impossible not to recall here the great last chapter of Augustine, *De civitate Dei*. Cf. also my *The Mystery of the Temple*, London 1962, 257, 270.

13. *Didache* X, 6.

14. P.Evdokimov, 'Notes préliminaires pour une théologie oecuménique', *Foi et Vie*, September-October 1947, (541-70) 562. One could compare

another Orthodox, L.Zander, *Le Christianisme Social*, September – December 1937 (the great ecumenical conferences in Oxford and Edinburgh), p.294 (with stress on eschatotogical realization; id., *Vision and Action*, London 1952).

15. Op. cit., 25.

16. *In Cant.*, sermo 62.1, PL 183, 1075.

17. *Vraie et fausse réforme dans l'Église*, Paris 1950, 144, 179-81, 333f., 597-603 (^{2}1969, 134. 165f., 301f., 539-44).

18. A. Cardinal Bea, *Pour l'Unité des chrétiens. Problèmes et principes, obstacles et moyens, réalisations et perspectives*, Paris 1963; *Le chemin de l'Unité*, Paris 1969.

19. Thus P.Couturier, *Catholicité*, July 1947, 33; A.Chavasse, 'Ordonnes au Corps mystique', *NRT*, 1948, 690-702; P.Michalon, 'L'Étendue de l'Église', *Irénikon*, 1947, 140-63; L.Richard, ' Une thèse fondamentale de l'oecuménisme: le baptême, incorporation visible à l'Église', *NRT*, 1952, 485-92.

20. O.Cullmann, 'Sind unsere Erwartungen erfüllt?', in *Sind die Erwartungen erfüllt?*, ed. K.Rahner, O.Cullmann, H.Fries, Munich 1966, 39-42.

21. Art.cit above (n.8), 63.

22. Quoted by Evangelos Theodorou, *Istina* 20, 1975, 20f. Paul VI said in his opening speech for the second period of the Council, 29 September 1963: 'This mysterious and visible union can only be arrived at in unity of faith, participation in the same sacraments and the organic harmony of a single ecclesiastical government, though that could be compatible with considerable diversity of linguistic expressions, ritual forms, historical traditions, local prerogatives, spiritual currents, legitimate institutions and favoured activities.'

18. The Unity of Faith

1. Cf. Cardinal Bea, and references in U. Valeske, *Hierarchia Veritatum*, 22f.; also of course Pius XI, *Mortuorum animos*; Pius XII, *Humani generis*.

2. *DC* 1745, 2 July 1978, 510; speech at the European ecumenical meeting at Chantilly, 10-13 April 1978.

3. *ST* II^a, II^{ae} q. 1 a.6 sed c. and *III Sent.* d.25 q.1 a. q. obj. 4. St Thomas attributes this formula to Isidore, as do Albertus Magnus and Bonaventure.

4. Augustine, *De Trinitate* XV, 28, 51.

5. This is what Paul VI did in the case of Shenouda III, the Coptic pope of Alexandria, and then successively with Vasken I (of Armenia) and Yakoub III (Syrian Orthodox). And that is what the Orthodox and non-Chalcedonians did at Geneva in 1970 (*Istina*, 1979, 16).

6. There was a very interesting dialogue on this subject between Orthodox and Anglicans at Moscow in July-August 1976; cf. Kallistos Ware, 'La Conférence de Moscou de 1976', *Istina* 24, 1979, 7-43. For Catholic theology cf. *I Believe in the Holy Spirit*, III, London 1983, 65-7.

7. M.Villain, *Introduction à l'Oecuménisme*, Paris ^{3}1961, 249; ^{4}1964, 297f.

8. G.Dejaifve, 'Diversité dogmatique et unité de la Révélation', in *Acta*

Congressus intern. de Theologia Concilii Vaticani II, Vatican 1968, 712-22, reprinted in *NRT* 89, 1967, 16-25.

9. There are some indications in my *Ecclésiologie du Haut Moyen Age*, Paris 1968, 308-17. In particular there was the role played by the spread of the Roman idea, 'Papa, Petrus ipse', to which the East remained quite alien.

10. *Unitatis redintegratio*, 3, para.14.

11. A. Wenger, 'Vladimir Soloviev et l'Église catholique', *Choisir* 250, Geneva, February 1979, 14-17.

12. Cf. J.Nolte, *Dogma in Geschichte. Versuch einer Kritik des Dogmatismus in der Glaubensdarstellung*, Freiburg 1971 (and my review in *RSPT* 56, 1972, 644-6).

13. Cf. my article 'La "réception" comme realité ecclésiologique', *RSPT* 56, 1972, 369-403.

14. T.Sartory, *Mut zur Katholizität*, Salzburg 1962, 447f.

15. A. de Halleux, 'Palamisme et Scholastique. Exclusivisme dogmatique ou pluriformité théologique', *RTL* 4, 1973, 409-62.

16. Pierre Duprey, *La France Catholique*, 21 January 1972, 11f., n.56.

17. This article only become an object of dispute after its definition by Pius IX: M.Jugie, *DTC* VIII, 964. This shows that the difficulty is connected above all with the intervention of the pope and thus with papal dogma and the unilateral character of the decision. One could make a similar comment on the Assumption.

18. Hamilcar Alivisatos, 'Les Conciles oecuméniques V, VI, VII et VIII', in *Le Concile et les conciles. Contribution à la vie conciliaire de l'Église*, Chevetogne and Paris 1960, 111-23. It is true that the Pope did not intervene in the ordinary life of the Eastern church, but his interventions in crises presuppose something other than a primacy of honour and a position of *primus inter pares*.

19. Evangelos Theodorou, 'Unité et pluralité du témoignage du Christ', *Istina* 20, 1975/1: *Koinonia. Premier colloque ecclésiologique organisé par la Fondation Pro Oriente*, 12-22. The mediocrity of the translation does not betray the idea, which is clear despite such doubtful expression.

20. Damaskinos Papandreou, 'Un dialogo di speranza con la Chiesa ortodossa', *L'Avennire*, 21 January 1979, 5; translated and quoted by G. Dejaifve, 'Hors de l'"impasse" oecuménique', *NRT* 101, 1979, 498-509. It is also worth reading the declaration by Fr Nicolas Afanasieff, *Irénikon* 36, 1963, 470.

21. E.Lanne, 'Églises-soeurs. Implications ecclésiologiques du Tomos Agapis', *Istina* 20, 1975, 47-74.

22. L.Bouyer, 'Réflexions sur le rétablissement possible de la communion entre les Églises orthodoxe et catholique. Perspectives actuelles', ibid., 112-15, above all 114.

23. *Istina*, 144,155,156.

24. References in U. Valeske, *Hierarchia veritatum*, Munich 1968, 185 n.42.

25. H.Mühlen, 'Die Lehre des Vaticanum II über die *hierarchia veritatum* und ihre Bedeutung für den oekumenischen Dialog', *TuG* 56, 1966, 303-35, esp. 326 n.22a.

26. A.Dulles, 'Dogma as an Ecumenical Problem', *TS* 29, 1968, 397-416, esp. 410; 'A Proposal to Lift Anathemas', *Origins* 4, 276, 26 December 1974, 617-21.

27. J.M.R.Tillard, 'L'Expression de l'unité de foi', *Proche-Orient chrétien* 28, 1978, 193-201.

28. In appendix II of *Vers la plénitude de la communion*, Paris 1969. 173-8.

29. Ch. V, 147-72, where he also criticizes the English Jesuit E.J.Yarnold.

30. K.Rahner, 'Membership of the Church according to the Teaching of Pius XII's Encyclical *Mystici Corporis Christi*', *Theological Investigations* 2, London 1963, 1-88; Y.Congar, 'L'Église une, sainte, catholique et apostolique', *Mysterium salutis* 15, Paris 1970, 109-21.

31. Cf. K.Rahner, 'Considerations on the Development of Dogma', *Theological Investigations* 4, London 1974, 3-35. Cf. U.Valeske, *Hierarchia veritatum*, 40f.

32. 'The Task of Theology after the Council', in *Vatican II. An Interfaith Appraisal*, 1966, 396.

33. *Theology Digest*, Winter 1967, 272. I would also like to quote this passage from 'Theologie für Heiden', *Sonntagsblatt* 1966, 25, 15 (Valeske, loc.cit.): 'If the two sides make a resolute effort not to justify by increasingly subtle theological distinctions the confessional differences and separations conditioned by history, sociology, psychology and the grass roots, but to move seriously to a possible common confession which is enough, profound differences remain between the "schools" for a unity of the church in baptism and eucharist and a social unity so far as these are necessary according to the will of Christ. Then if the Catholic church really does not demand anything other than its authentic dogma and its *ius divinum* conveys, then one can – hoping against hope – hope for a unity in the church embracing all those who expressly confess Jesus Christ and relate to him as saviour.'

34. Y. Congar, 'Do the New Problems of our Secular World make Ecumenism Irrelevant?', *Concilium* 4.6, April 1970, 11-21.

35. This is the line taken by J.M.Gonzalez-Ruiz, 'L'Unité de l'Église est-elle possible?', *Lumière et Vie* 103, June/July 1971, 103-16.

36. 'Is Church Union Dogmatically Possible?', *Theological Investigations* 17, London 1981, 197-214.

37. Loc.cit. above n.20.

38. *DC* 1798, 21 December 1980, 1147.

INDEX OF NAMES

228   *Index of Names*

Rupp, J., 201
Ryan, J., 183

Saffrey, H. D., 48
Sagi Bunic, T., 94
Saltet, L., 183
Sanon, A. T., 190
Sartory, T., 171, 223
Saudée, J. de Bivort de la, 203
Scheeben, M. J., 52, 98, 119, 209
Scherwood, P., 201
Schille, G., 185
Schlink, E., 212
Schmid, J., 183
Schmidt, A. -M., 207
Schmitt, F. S., 186
Scholarios, 64, 65, 66, 67, 196, 197
Schrey, M. H., 75, 198
Schultes, R. M., 215
Schulz, H., 199
Schüssler, R., 207, 208, 210
Schütte, H., 146, 218, 219
Schützeichel, H., 212, 213
Schwaiger, G., 211
Schweigl, J., 188, 200
Scott, H. S. D. P., 211
Seidlmayer, M., 187
Sergius, Bishop of Jamburg, 103, 195
Sesboüé, B., 216
Seumois, V., 186
Shenouda III, 137, 222
Sherrard, P., 197
Shorter, A., 190
Sibthorpe, R. W., 211
Simon of Tournai, 78
Simonin, C. R. de, 20
Simonin, H. D., 184
Siricius, 29
Sixtus, Pope, 183
Sixtus III, 187
Skydsgaard, K. E., 216
Slipyi, Cardinal, 204
Socrates, 24, 47, 183
Söderblom, N., 3
Soloviev, V., 70, 170, 201
Sommelath, E., 144
Sozomen, 24, 205
Spacil, T., 194
Spasskij, A., 211
Speigl, J., 211
Spyridion, Metropolitan, 89
Stan, L., 184
Stapleton, 119

Strawrowsky, A., 203
Stemooukoff, D., 197
Stephen, Bishop of Rome, 24f.
Stern, J., 211
Stirnimann, H., 212
Stone, Darwell, 93, 210
Strauss, L. von, 198
Strutmann, R., 209
Stylianoupolis, T., 104, 206
Subilia, V., 182
Svetlov, P., 211
Swete, H. B., 51, 124, 211
Sylvester, Pope, 16
Syropoulos, 64, 68, 69, 196, 197

Tangl, 187
Tanquerey, A., 119, 208, 209, 210
Tarasius, 51, 205
Tatian, 129
Tavard, 130, 212
Tavenaux, R., 207
Taylor, J., 208
Tertullian, 205
Theodore of Beza, 110, 111
Theodore Graptos, 68, 197
Theodore of Mopsuestia, 56
Theodore of Tarsus, 17f.
Theodorou, Evangelos, 51, 172, 192, 222, 223
Theodosius, 102
Theophilus of Antioch, 100
Theophylact, 28
Thérive, A., 181
Theunis, F. J., 182
Thiel, 187
Thils, G., 116, 119, 208, 209, 212
Thirty-Nine Articles, 81, 115, 142
Thomas Aquinas, 28, 40, 56, 75, 80, 100, 102, 104, 128, 131, 132, 169, 184, 190, 205, 214, 215, 216, 222
Thomson, F. J., 57, 58, 59, 194, 195
Three Chapters, 94, 122
Thureau-Dangin, P., 210
Thurian, Max, 123
Tillard, J. M. R., 174, 181, 191, 224
Timiadis, E., 220
Toledo, Fourth Council of, 78
Tonneins, Synod of, 111
Trembelas, N., 52, 60, 120, 210
Trent, Council of, 24, 39, 42, 52, 79, 81, 113, 142, 146, 171, 185
Triacca, A. M., 204
Trocmé, E., 162, 164
Tshibangu, Tshishitu, 37

Turretini, A., 111
Tyndale, W., 115
Tyszkievich, S., 211

Urban IV, 80
Ussher, J., 208

Vaggagini, C., 217
Valéry, Paul, 6
Valeske, U., 130, 207, 208, 209,
210, 212, 213, 214, 222, 223, 224
Vandervorst, N. Z., 204
Vasken, I., 222
Vatican I, 52, 87, 95, 118, 146, 171,
173, 211
Vatican II, 2, 18, 32, 35, 42, 73, 82,
83, 85, 87, 97, 126, 131, 134, 165,
170, 173, 181, 191, 193, 196, 200,
203, 220
Veken, B. J., van der, 183
Vercruysse, J., 218
Verkamp, B. J., 115, 207, 208
Veron, 113
Vesson, P., 207
Victor, Pope, 15, 16, 24
Victor of Aquitaine, 17
Vigilius, Pope, 63
Villain, M., 217, 222, 169
Vincent of Lerins, 113, 123, 124,
211
Vinck, H., 183
Vischer, L., 216
Visser 't Hooft, W. A., 181
Vliet, H. van, 197
Vodopivec, J., 185
Voeltzel, R., 207
Vogel, C., 184, 188
Vratislav II, 187
Vries, W. de, 174, 211

Wace, Dean, 122
Ware, K., 211, 222
Weismayer, J., 212
Weizsäcker, C. F. von, 198
Wenger, A., 195, 196, 223
Werenfels, S., 111
Whitby, Synod of, 17
Wicelius (Witzel), George, 112f.,
208
Widmann, M., 193
Wilfrid, 17
Will, C., 186
Willebrands, J., 3, 88, 91, 92, 95,
137, 155, 204, 210, 216
Williams, N. P., 211
Wolf, E., 184, 214
Wordsworth, C., 117
World Council of Churches, 3, 4,
120, 133, 134, 146, 149, 153, 154,
162, 166, 220
World Lutheran Federation, 5, 139,
140, 145, 149, 219
World Reformed Alliance, 140
Wyclif, J., 199
Wynfrith (Boniface), 18

Yakob III, 222
Yarnold, E. J., 224
Yvo of Chartres, 186

Zacharias, Pope, 31
Zander, L., 197, 201, 222
Zernov, Nicholas, 60
Zinelli, Mgr, 95
Zoa, Archbishop, 36
Zöllner, W., 129
Zwingli, H., 109